# Blood in Zion

How the Jewish Guerrillas drove
the British out of Palestine

*Also from Brassey's*

**DAVID**
*Mutiny at Salerno*
An Injustice Exposed

**PARKER** (ed)
*Winston Churchill*
Studies in Statesmanship

**BAYNES**
*Far From a Donkey*
The Life of General Sir Ivor Maxse

# Blood in Zion

## How the Jewish Guerrillas drove the British out of Palestine

*Dr Saul Zadka*

BRASSEY'S
London • Washington

Copyright © 1995 Brassey's (UK) Ltd

All Rights Reserved. No part of this publication may be reproduced, stored in a retrieval system or transmitted in any form or by any means; electronic, electrostatic, magnetic tape, mechanical, photocopying, recording or otherwise, without permission in writing from the publishers.

First English Edition 1995

UK editorial offices: Brassey's Ltd, 33 John Street, London WC1N 2AT
UK Orders: Marston Book Services, PO Box 269, Abingdon, OX14 4SD
North American Orders: Brassey's Inc, PO Box 960, Herndon, VA 22070.

Saul Zadka has asserted his moral right to be identified as the author of this work.

**Library of Congress Cataloging in Publication Data**
available

**British Library Cataloging in Publication Data**
A catalogue record for this book is available from the British Library

ISBN 1-85753-136-1 Hardcover

Typeset by Solidus (Bristol) Limited
Printed in Great Britain by
Bookcraft (Bath) Limited

To the memory
of my father,
Joseph

# Contents

| | |
|---|---|
| *Preface* | xi |
| *Acknowledgements* | xv |
| *Glossary* | xvi |
| *Map – Palestine 1945* | xix |

**Introduction**   1

**IRGUN INSURGENCY**

1. **Background**   15
   - The Birth of the Irgun   15
   - Strategy   18
   - The Support of the Jewish Community   19
   - Ideology of the Irgun   21
   - The Arab Front   23
   - The Political Campaign   25
   - Characteristics   26
2. **The Revolt**   28
   - The Debate   30
   - The Arab Factor   34
   - The New Commander   36
   - First Activities   37
3. **The Irgun and the Jewish Community**   47
   - The Relationship During the Second World War   47
   - The Relationship During the Revolt   48
   - The 'Saison'   52
   - The United Resistance Front   56
   - Disintegration of the United Front   63
4. **Tactics, Methods and Operations**   65
   - Structure   66
   - Minings, Bombings, Robberies and Confiscations   68
   - Terrorist Methods   70
   - Military Failures   72
   - The Attack on Acre Prison   75
   - The Hanging of the Two Sergeants   78

| | | |
|---|---|---|
| 5. | **The King David Affair** | 89 |
| | *Co-ordination with the Hagana* | 89 |
| | *The British Response* | 90 |
| | *The American Response* | 95 |
| | *Operation Shark* | 95 |
| 6. | **Propaganda and Psychological Warfare** | 100 |
| | *The Propaganda Directed at the British Forces* | 106 |
| | *The Irgun's use of the Courtroom for its Propaganda Campaign* | 108 |
| | *The Irgun's Campaign in America* | 113 |
| | *Conflict with the Jewish Establishment* | 117 |
| | *The Committee for National Liberation* | 120 |
| | *The Rift Between the Committee and the Irgun* | 123 |

## BRITISH COUNTER-INSURGENCY

| | | |
|---|---|---|
| 7. | **The British View** | 131 |
| | *British Reliance on the Jewish Leadership* | 133 |
| | *The Aftermath of the Moyne Assassination* | 136 |
| | *The British Response to the United Armed Campaign* | 137 |
| | *Operation Agatha* | 139 |
| 8. | **British Measures Against Terrorism** | 142 |
| | *The Options: Searches, Immigration Suspension and Collaboration* | 143 |
| | *Exile in Africa* | 146 |
| | *Confronting a Jewish United Front* | 147 |
| | *The Civil–Military Controversy* | 149 |
| | *Hanging, Kidnapping, Flogging and Counter Hanging* | 156 |
| | *Bevingrads and Family Evacuation* | 159 |
| | *Martial Law* | 161 |
| 9. | **Morale and Public Opinion in Britain** | 169 |
| | *The Reaction of Parliament* | 172 |
| | *The Response of the Press* | 178 |

| | |
|---|---|
| **Epilogue** | 184 |
| **Appendices** | 186 |
| **I Proclamation of revolt by the Irgun Zvai Leumi** | 186 |
| **II Some IZL anti-British Operations in Palestine** | 191 |
| **III An Interview with Irgun Commander M. Begin** | 194 |
| **Bibliography** | 197 |
| **Chapter Notes and Sources** | 205 |
| **Index** | 222 |

# Preface

During the 1940s the Irgun Zvai Leumi (IZL) launched an intensive guerrilla campaign against the British Mandate authorities in Palestine. Its members embarked on a struggle unlike any conducted by a Jewish organisation in modern times. They blew up buildings, they sabotaged roads and bridges, they killed and maimed soldiers, they raided military bases, they robbed banks and they attacked strategic targets all over the country and even abroad. By so doing, they endangered the community on whose behalf they claimed to fight and placed themselves against the consensus represented by the official leadership.

But was the Irgun (also referred to as the IZL) instrumental in driving the British forces out of Palestine?

Was it a factor which influenced the decision makers in London reluctantly to withdraw from this part of the Middle East? How effective was the group in military terms? Did it, as it argued, disrupt the country's daily life to the point of exhausting the British will to govern Palestine any longer? How solid was its Jewish backing? Did the community give it enough support? This book will try to answer those questions.

Much has been written about the IZL (the Irgun) campaign, but almost the entire documentary contribution has been made by the Irgunists themselves. Their memories are a mixture of self-glorification, exaggeration, tales of heroism, and inaccuracy. On the other hand, their bitter rivals within the Jewish Community (The Hagana, the Trade Unions and the Jewish Agency) did their utmost throughout the years to tarnish the insurgents' image and play down their role in the struggle. The outcome was a series of claims and counter-claims which clouded the whole issue and turned it into a political-ideological confrontation which continues in Israel to this day. The fact that the paramilitary organisations during the Mandate period are represented now by contemporary political parties has intensified this war of words. Moreover, after 1977, when the right-wing Likud (led by Menachem Begin, the Irgun's commander) came to power for the first time, the debate reached a new height, with the new government trying to claim a monopoly over the historical facts just as the Socialist Left had done at the establishment of the State in 1948.

Even as recently as July 1991, during the inauguration ceremony of the new IZL museum in Tel Aviv, the former Israeli prime minister Yitzhak Shamir (himself a leading figure in the Stern group) said categorically that the Irgun and the Freedom Fighters for Israel (FFI) had brought about the withdrawal of the British forces from the country and the eventual independence of the Jewish state. A few days later, on the 60th anniversary of the Irgun establishment, another former prime minister Menachem Begin broke long silence by hailing the Irgun's armed campaign and dismissing any attempt to compare it with the current Palestinian national struggle as 'blasphemy'. Begin himself, shortly before he died, contributed to the book by agreeing to answer some of the author's questions on the completion of the work. His answers are included in appendix III.

Ironically, the Irgun has become a central talking point even in Palestinian thinking and the PLO has often said that it tried to emulate it in its own struggle against Israel. Some of the Irgun's operations were taught in its military courses and every book on the subject was widely read by Palestinian leaders. In the last decade the PLO used the Jewish struggle against the British as a proof that terrorists can turn into respected statesmen.

Despite the inclination by both Irgun and Hagana supporters to dwell repeatedly on the past, the armed struggle in general and the Irgun's role in particular, have been insufficiently studied and examined in any objective academic work. This book will make an attempt to fill that vacuum and bridge the gap between distorted fact and historic truth. It will, therefore, examine aspects which were neglected by the former insurgents themselves, such as the propaganda campaign in Palestine and America and the way the British reacted to both the military and psychological warfare waged against them by the Irgun.

The book will cover the period from February 1944, the month in which the IZL proclaimed its revolt against the authorities, until the end of 1947, when the British finally declared their intention to withdraw unconditionally from Palestine. It will discuss the interrelations of the British–Hagana–Irgun triangle during those crucial years and observe in depth the efforts made by the Government to combat the terrorist onslaughts against its forces and bring about the demise of the Irgun.

One of the most far-reaching of these measures, the imposition of martial law, will be singled out and discussed in a separate sub-chapter. This British response, designed to eliminate terrorism once and for all through its wholesale measures, has been neglected by all those who have studied the Jewish armed struggle in Palestine. Two of the most important of the insurgents' operations, the Acre Prison break-in and the hanging of two British sergeants, will also be discussed in detail. The reason for selecting these two subjects is their tremendous impact on the ensuing events in Palestine and the fact that, after the British departure, they became a part of the Irgun's mythology, which has distorted the real reasons for the British withdrawal from Palestine.

The armed campaign and the military response to it will be highlighted in another chapter in which the King David operation is examined. This section reviews the bombing of the British headquarters in Jerusalem and the nine immediate punitive measures taken by the British in the aftermath of the outrage. The affair can best illustrate the strategy and tactics adopted by the insurgents and the dilemma which faced the authorities in trying to wipe out terrorism in Palestine.

Surprisingly little of what the British have written about the subject has been found, despite the major role they played in the last years of their rule in Palestine. Although some of the memoirs (notably of the High Commissioner and the Chief Military Commander) made a considerable contribution, first-hand documents are scarce. One of the reasons for the shortage is that many of the British intelligence papers were destroyed during the withdrawal, sometimes on direct orders from London. However, the War Office papers in the Public Record Office offer useful documents with regard to the terrorist activities against the armed forces. The intelligence units of the South Palestine district catalogued many acts of violence and monitored political statements made by leaders of the Arab and the Jewish Communities. The 6th Airborne Division also supplied intelligence reports, many of them concerning measures 'necessary to maintain law and order' in the country. The Foreign Office and the Colonial Office regarded the issue of terrorism mainly as a 'by-product' of the growing political conflict in the country.

Because of its nature as an underground group, the Irgun did not keep orderly archives and its members were careful to put almost nothing in writing. Needless to say, these golden rules of secrecy would have applied to the regular meetings of the High Command, which were not documented until the end of 1943. However, the split within the Irgun (which resulted in the formation of the FFI), the debate of the attachment of the group to the Revisionist Party and the leadership crisis during the Second World War, created domestic frictions which encouraged the senior Irgunists to record some of their highly confidential gatherings. They were convinced that it would have been in the interest of every one of them to leave behind an agreed version of their positions in the light of their disagreements over those key issues. First and foremost was the debate over the armed struggle against the British the timing of which split the leadership. The fear of the insurgents of the campaign's possible failure and their reluctance to take responsibility for it prompted the High Command to start writing minutes from as early as January 1944, three weeks before its self-proclaimed revolt. Transcripts of the minutes from each meeting were hidden inside a milk jar buried in one of the Sharon orange groves where the IZL's headquarters was located. They contained a brief summary of each of the participants' positions, and to avoid disclosure of their real names, included many codenames ('iron' was weapons, 'tourists' were soldiers, 'celebration' was a military operation, 'sickness' was arrest, 'main kitchen' was the CID headquarters and so forth).

In July 1944, the British launched an attack on the site and Irgun members had to destroy all the written material which had been kept there. As a result of the operation only the High Command meetings from July 1944 survived. Unfortunately, in the following November, when the insurgents fell victim to the Hagana's collaboration with the British, their leaders put an end to these meetings and the documentation ceased completely. Despite the fact that they cover a period of half a year only, the transcripts give considerable information on the first year of the Irgun's campaign and the group's difficulties in structuring itself under its new chief commander Menachem Begin. In all, 16 High Command meetings have been recorded, out of which four were held with the district commanders. When it comes to military operations, this author has matched the Irgunists' testimonies with available British documentation to ensure credibility. The same has been done with interviews given to the author by various members of the IZL who were involved in the planning and the execution of many operations and who masterminded the policy of the organisation. This book will set out to measure the disparities between the available source material with the object of shedding new light on the impact of the Irgun Zvai Leumi on the British Mandate and the Irgun's relations with the other contemporary Zionist bodies.

★ ★ ★

Finally, a word about the nature of this book. The story of the Irgun is complex and it is important to see it from both the Jewish and the British sides. Thus my Introduction provides a brief overview of the whole story and is followed by two parts, the first examining various aspects of the Irgun's insurgency and the second considering the British reaction to it, both in Palestine and in London. Each chapter is, in effect, a short essay in itself and some repetition of references to major events in the story was inescapable, for which I ask my readers to bear with me.

# Acknowledgements

I would like to thank the many people who have assisted me in the research and production of this book and express my gratitude to all of them. I wish to extend special thanks to my long-suffering supervisor Dr Wolf Mendl who guided me through the challenging years of writing this Ph.D.

However, this work would not have been possible without the kindness and generosity of Dr Davide Sala and his late wife Dr Irene Sala who tragically died in an air accident in February 1991. I will always appreciate their help to me. A number of Irgun activists, including members of the High Command, such as Yoel Amrami and Shlomo Lev Ami, gave much of their time to make their valuable knowledge available to me. I am also grateful to their Chief Commander, the former prime minister Menachem Begin, who granted me an interview in January 1992, despite his failing health. This manuscript was at the printers when his death was announced. The unofficial historian of the Irgun Zvai Leumi, the late David Niv, made many useful suggestions. In Irgun veteran, Ya'acov Elagar, provided me with many rare photographs.

Staff in the archives where I collected the documents for my work, especially at the PRO in London and the Jabotinsky Institute in Tel Aviv, were most helpful and efficient. To them and to all my friends (including Wendy Levitt, Dr Eli Napchan, Professor Ya'acov Lurch, Victor Levy and David Langsam) I am greatly indebted.

S Z

# Glossary

**Balfour Declaration** – British Statement of sympathy with Zionist aspirations, given by Arthur James Balfour (1848–1930) in November of 1917 when he was British Foreign Secretary. The declaration favoured the establishment in Palestine of a national home for the Jewish people. It has always provoked a hostile Arab reaction and is still a controversial issue in Middle-Eastern politics.

**Begin, Menachem** – (1913–92) – Commander of the Irgun Zvai Leumi and leader of its armed uprising against the British authorities in Palestine. Founder of the Freedom Political Party in 1948 and a member of Parliament until his death. As head of the Likud, became the Prime Minister of Israel in 1977 and led the country to its peace treaty with Egypt.

**Ben Gurion, David** – (1886–1973) – Secretary General of the Trade Union Federation in Palestine between 1921–33 and chairman of the Jewish Agency Executive 1935–48. Prime Minister of Israel between 1948–53 and 1955–63. A strong opponent of Begin and initiated the campaign against the Irgun in the 1940s.

**Exodus** – A Jewish refugee boat with 4515 Holocaust survivors on board which set sail in July 1947 from a French port to Palestine. Blocked by the British Army in the Mediterranean whose soldiers took it over by force and three passengers were killed. The refugees were brought to Haifa port, transferred to other boats and sent back to France, but refused to leave. Finally they were deported to Hamburg where they were forced to disembark.

**Hagana** – A Jewish self-defence military organisation which was founded in Palestine in 1920 following Arab riots in Jerusalem. In the Second World War many of its members joined the British Army, a move which led to the secession of a group that then formed the Irgun. Hagana was very active in illegal immigration and anti-British activities. In 1948 it became the nucleus of the regular army of Israel.

**Husseine, Haj Amin** – Mufti of Jerusalem and Palestinian Arab Nationalist leader. Sentenced by the British to 10 years imprisonment for his roles in 1920 riots. Reprieved in 1921 and appointed Mufti. In 1937 he was dismissed from all duties by the Mandatory authorities. Collaborated with Hitler during the war and supported the Nazi cause.

**Jewish Agency** – Executive body and representative of World Zionist Organisation whose authority and function were first recognised by the British Mandate in Palestine. Between 1929 and 1948 it was the responsible political body negotiating the Zionist position in the country.

**Jewish Brigade** – British Army unit serving during the war. Established in 1944 after previous efforts to form separate Jewish units had been turned down by the British authorities. Served in North Africa and various parts of Europe and disbanded in 1946.

**Kibbutz** – Agricultural community based on collective property, production and consumption. Played a leading role in pre-state Israel and contributed to its military infrastructure.

**Mandate for Palestine** – Mandate given to Great Britain by the League of Nations at San Remo in 1920. Its purpose was to run Palestine in the interests of all the population. Ratified in 1922 and terminated with the establishment of the State of Israel in 1948.

**Meir, Golda** – (1898–1976) – Head of the political department of the Jewish Agency and arrested by the British in 1946. Israel's first ambassador to Moscow in 1948–49, member of the Israeli Parliament and Cabinet, General Secretary of the Labour Party and Prime Minister 1969–74.

**National Committee** – National Council of Jews in Palestine which functioned between 1920–48 as the executive organ of the Jewish Community there. Represented the Community in negotiations with the British authorities. Also responsible for health and education work in the country.

**Palmach** – (Assault Companies) – The striking force the Hagana established in 1941. Organised illegal immigration to Palestine and acted occasionally against the British after the war. Used as spearhead of Hagana against the Irgun during the 'Saison' and fought the Arabs in 1947–48. Integrated into the Israeli Army in November 1948, six months after the country's independence.

**'Saison' (or Hunting Season)** – The period beginning in November 1944 during which the leaders of the organised Yishuv virtually declared open war on the Irgun. The campaign collapsed under the weight of public and religious opposition.

**Shamir, Yitzhak** – Born in 1914 and joined the Stern group in 1940. Arrested by the British a year later and escaped. Reorganised the group, arrested and escaped again. Arrested for the third time and exiled to Africa. After 1948 became one of the members of the 'Mossad' Secret Service and in the 1970s entered Israeli politics. Was a chairman of the Knesset, Foreign Minister and became Prime Minister in 1983.

**Stern Group** – Armed radical underground organisation in Palestine, founded by Abraham Stern in 1941 after breaking away from the Irgun. Fought against the British authorities, even during the war and was responsible for the assassination of Lord Moyne in Cairo. Activities included sabotage and assassinations. Disbanded in 1948 when suspected of killing Count Bernadotte, the UN envoy, in 1948.

**White Papers** – British government statements of policy which were issued in six documents between 1922 and 1939 and played an important part in the history of Mandatory Palestine. Hated, by both Jews and Arabs. Often demonstrated against by the Jews because the sixth paper restricted Jewish immigration and land purchase.

**Yishuv** – The Jewish community in Palestine.

**Yelin Mor, Nathan** – Founding member of the Stern Group. Headed the group after the death of Stern and was elected to the first Knesset in 1948.

**Zionism** – Term which described the ideology advocating the return of the Jewish People to the land of Israel. It was born in Eastern Europe against the background of anti-semitism and anti-Jewish persecutions. Named after a hill in Jerusalem.

**Zionist Congress** – The World Assembly of the Zionist movement, created by Theodor Herzl. The first congress was convened in Basel, Switzerland, in 1897.

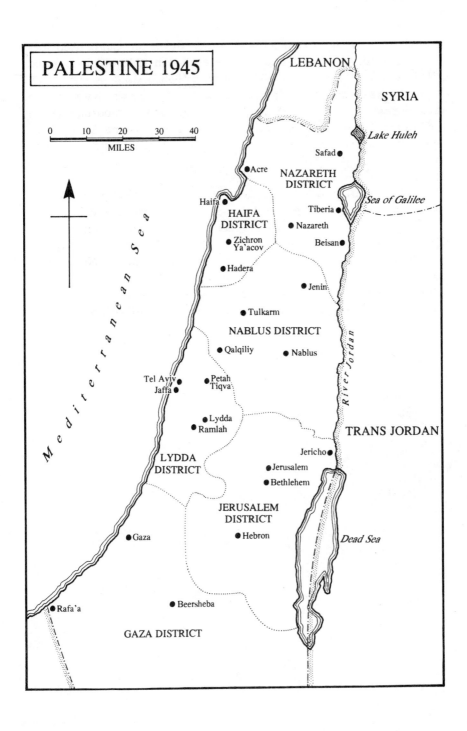

# Introduction

The 'who kicked the British out of Palestine' debate is still continuing in Israel. On occasions, it is being heated up by former insurgents, historians and political parties. The way the question is presented is based on the assumption that one or several factors in the Yishuv brought about the withdrawal of the armed forces from the country. Such a question is misleading. The British evacuation of Palestine was not only prompted by the Jews, whether terrorists or politicians. In fact, looking at the relevant official documents one can conclude that the guerrilla warfare declared upon the British by the Irgun did not trouble the authorities too much during most of the period of the armed struggle and most frequently it was even placed at the bottom of their priorities. The British failed, quite miserably, to combat the growing terrorism against them. Militarily, they proved to be inefficient and their intelligence was inadequate. But politically, they lacked the will to fight and to overcome the insurgents. The army and the police rightly complained that London tied their hands behind their back. The sensitive political circumstances surrounding the issue of Palestine in the international arena did not permit London to give the armed forces a free hand in Palestine.

The Irgun was defeatable. In some periods it was on the verge of disintegration. Perhaps the best proof of its weakness could be found in February 1945, at the peak of the 'Saison', when Begin, himself already chief commander, considered the possibility that he and his men might commit mass suicide which, out of sheer frustration, he regarded as the only way left for them to impress the world. This was disclosed only recently by his close colleague, Eitan Livni, who was in charge of the Irgun's operations.[1]

Begin stunned Livni by complaining 'one morning' about the group's inability to carry out attacks, due to the daily arrests of its members and shortage of weaponry. He suggested therefore that each of the two of them would head 100 people and occupy an area in old Jerusalem in which they would wave the national flag. 'We will die as soldiers to the last of us, so it would not be alleged that the Irgun did not fulfil its mission ...', he said.

Begin argued that it was impossible to know how long the 'Saison' would last and he maintained that the 'damage increases by the day'.[2]

During those days the British neutralised the Irgun easily and, with the help of the Hagana, arrested many of its key members who were sent to exile in Africa. It was the most desperate period in the Irgun's revolt, one year after its proclamation, and reflected the group's inability to cope with the Hagana–British collaboration against it. That collaboration demonstrated the extent to which the authorities, due to the lack of efficient intelligence, were dependent on Jewish co-operation in order to deal with the insurgents.

It could be argued, therefore, that the British could have paralysed the Irgun in 1945 if they had been wise enough to maintain the Hagana's collaboration for a few more weeks. This could have been achieved by rewarding the official leadership politically for its efforts. The reward could have manifested itself in immigration concessions to the Jewish Community. Instead, London, and especially the Foreign Secretary Bevin, who was arrogant and insensitive, disillusioned the Yishuv by conducting a policy which the Jews saw as taking into consideration Arab interests only.[3] The reason for the British attitude was simple. The government played down the importance of the Irgun and did not take it seriously at that stage. In fact, the first armed operations of the Irgun went almost unnoticed and were not regarded as pointing a new direction in Palestine. The British policy-makers, with their rich colonial experience, did not treat it as a deviation from the so-called 'reasonable measure of violence' which they had previously witnessed all over the Empire.[4]

The level of terrorism was containable. Even financially, the damage was not very great. Out of a civilian budget of £23m, the cost of the violence in 1946 was estimated by the Government secretary as only £600,000. The number of casualties during the first two years of the armed struggle was also 'manageable'.

But the Irgun – insignificant in its early period – had misled the authorities, who underestimated it for most of the duration of the revolt. British policy in Palestine pushed the Hagana and Jewish public opinion into the arms of the insurgents and narrowed the ideological gaps between the various factions within the Yishuv. The United Resistance Movement, consisting of the three main military organisations in the country, was the most serious challenge to law and order in Palestine.

But over and above the danger that it posed to the British, the triple co-operation gave a badly needed legitimacy to the Irgun. The community could no longer regard the insurgents as separatists or dissidents, even after the break-down of the movement, and the British failed to understand that. Instead of pursuing their well-tested policy of 'divide and rule' within the Yishuv, and using 'carrot and stick' methods, they antagonised the leadership and isolated the truly moderate figures on whom they had relied for many years.

Despite these political blunders, the British could, militarily, crack down on the insurgents at any given time. Politically, however, the struggle was unwinnable. An 'Iron Fist' policy, which was demanded by the Chief of the Imperial General Staff, was not adopted because of the fear that it would have inflicted heavy civilian losses and radicalised the official leadership even further. Tough measures were also resisted on the grounds that their victims would have been holocaust survivors, thus provoking an outcry outside as well as inside Palestine. Pressure from the American Administration and the Jewish hostile reaction to the British involvement in Palestine played an equally important role in London's hesitation to hit the insurgents hard.

In fact, the British believed throughout that the Irgun's attempt to terrorise the security forces was motivated by domestic considerations. They were partially right in that assessment, since the Irgun and the Hagana represented two rival political factions which sought to dominate the community. But the British let that factor cloud their judgement to the point of failing to realise that, despite the military weakness of the Irgun, the group had managed to exploit the situation to its own political advantage. The IZL became more formidable during 1946, and even more so during 1947, by increasing the number of its members five-fold or more.[5] At that stage, the British lost their grip on security in the country and their rule began to look temporary as it had never seemed before.

Examination of the British documents of the three ministries which were dealing with the Palestine issue shows that the insurgency was seldom brought up for discussion. Arab–Jewish relations, Jewish Agency loyalty, American involvement and the future borders of Palestine were much more topical, creating the impression that the guerrilla warfare waged against them had been pushed to the sidelines. But what disabled the army and police more than anything else was the lack of a coherent policy in Palestine. The security forces were operating in an arena without knowing how long their presence there would last. They were subject to constant changes of Middle East policy by their government and had the thankless task of acting as a buffer between the Jews and Arabs.

Terrorism merely added to the low morale of the armed forces, all of whom hoped to be based in Palestine for as short a time as possible. The inability of London to decide about the future of Palestine until the very last moment created uncertainty in the country and contributed to its instability. Since the general feeling of the 100,000 military personnel was one of being in a temporary situation, the motivation to risk lives and to quell the violence was not a high priority. The quality of the police contributed to the gloomy mood. Most of them were not trained to fight urban terrorism and many of the soldiers had been transferred from Germany after the war. The CID lacked skilled people who knew the country, its citizens and their language, and very often needed Jewish informers to compensate for their shortage of intelligence information.

As a result of these poor circumstances, the British lacked the will to confront the Irgun in a serious way. The martial law imposed in March 1947 was lifted by the authorities after a period of two weeks only. During that time, the British forces took 4.5 million hours to arrest 25 underground members and 50 suspects. That is 200,000 hours for each arrest! These figures speak for themselves. The failure of the last large-scale operation in Palestine before the eventual withdrawal stemmed not only from the Irgun's efficiency and secrecy, but mostly from British military incompetence.

By 1947, it was too late for the government to keep events under control. Lieutenant General Sir Alan Cunningham, the High Commissioner, wrote to the Colonial Secretary, towards the end of the period of martial law, that it would be impossible to put an end to the terrorism simply by military means or by 'other repressive measures'.[6] He feared that the continuation of martial law would push the Hebrew youth into the arms of the insurgents even further. Such an assessment was shared by David Ben Gurion who sent a telegram to Prime Minister Clement Attlee, drawing his attention to the fact that the martial law 'did not influence the terrorists or put an end to their violence. What it did more was to hurt the civilian population and hit the economic infrastructure of the community'.[7]

But, although the Irgunists could not be regarded as a military match for British military might, they indeed won the propaganda war. In some of their military operations, the insurgents excelled themselves by demonstrating skill and imagination. They knew how to exploit both achievements and defeats for their own advantage. The Irgun was in a privileged position which enabled it to score psychological successes even after it had failed badly in various missions, as was the case when some of its members were captured and hanged. When it managed to destroy a substantial number of British aircraft, the psychological victory was dramatic.

Most of the credit for the successful propaganda campaign belonged to the Irgun commander who skilfully linked almost every attack to the Holocaust or the restrictions on the immigration of Jewish refugees to Palestine. Begin was not a military man and the operational side of the Underground was left to other members of the command. Living in hiding, he was not even able to visit his men before they embarked on their missions. His main preoccupation was to accompany each military action or political development with carefully worded pamphlets and broadcasts, which were designed to explain the Irgun's policy and attract the youth in the community.

Surprisingly, despite the Irgun's growing popularity, there was no massive movement to join its ranks. The sympathy was passive and did not manifest itself in a big show of support. Some of its activities won the admiration of certain sections of the community, but hostility towards it within the socialist camp did not lessen, mainly because the Irgun was regarded as a threat to the political hegemony of the Left. In fact, the mainstream of the Yishuv was more hostile to the British than sympathetic to the Irgun.

Herein lies the colossal failure of the Irgun. The organisation could not turn itself into a political force to be reckoned with after the establishment of the state of Israel. The poor showing of its political party, *Herut* ('Freedom'), in the first elections held in 1948, showed that the Irgun was not rooted well enough in the community. Begin, as the leader of the party and the opposition, tried eight times to win power in Israel, but only in 1977, as the head of the Likud, did he succeed in becoming Prime Minister. Until then the country was dominated by the Labour party and its offshoots, while Begin and his colleagues were not even given ministerial posts for many years.

★ ★ ★

Nevertheless, in Israel and to a certain extent in some Arab countries, and certainly within the Palestinian camp, there is a widespread notion that the Irgun and its terrorist campaign prompted the withdrawal of the British forces from Palestine, paving the way for the creation of the Jewish state. In Israel, where the debate about the issue is still frequently repeated, the Irgun's advocates on the right wing have constantly maintained that without the Irgun revolt the British would not have been driven out of Palestine. They used British arguments to validate their claims and argued that the insurgents made Palestine ungovernable for the authorities.

Professor Joseph Nedava, one of the Irgun's historians, claimed that British public opinion was obsessed by the violence and that 90 per cent of the parliamentary debates on Palestine were devoted to the issue of the armed struggle, while only 10 per cent dealt with immigration.[8] This is a typical example of how those who were involved in the revolt overestimated the strength of the Irgun and its impact on the decision-makers in London. Parliamentary records in fact showed that the illegal immigration of Jewish refugees from Europe concerned the British much more than the guerrilla warfare in Palestine.

The plight of the refugees, mostly holocaust survivors, outraged many of the Zionists in Britain and sent shock-waves through America. At times the break-down of law and order in Palestine worried the British politicians, especially after the bombing of the British Headquarters in the King David

Hotel in 1946 and the attack on Goldsmith House, the Officers' Club in Jerusalem, followed by the hanging of two British sergeants, in 1947. Although the mounting toll of British casualties worried many MPs, they still remained more concerned with the cost of maintaining 100,000 soldiers in the country. According to Winston Churchill, Britain had to spend up to £40m in Palestine every year.

Irgun supporters do not miss the opportunity of quoting Churchill since, after becoming the Leader of the Opposition, he became the most outspoken critic of the way the government was handling the crisis in Palestine. Churchill claimed that, if the only way to fight terrorism was by resorting to 'squalid warfare', it was better not to hang on at all costs to tiny Palestine, while abandoning great India and Burma. He was referring not only to the security situation in Palestine, but also, and more fundamentally, to post-war Britain, which was on the verge of financial bankruptcy and suffering a great shortage of coal. In the House of Commons debate on the issue of Palestine on 31 January 1947, Churchill touched on the main difficulty which the armed forces faced in dealing with the insurgents. 'This is a conflict with the terrorists', he said, 'and no country in the world is less fit for a conflict with terrorists than Great Britain. That is not because of her weakness or cowardice; it is because of her restraint and virtues, and the way of life which we have lived so long in this sheltered island.' Churchill emphasised that it was 'impossible for us to imitate the mass extermination methods of the Germans'. He reflected the general mood in the House by saying that the idea of general reprisals against the civilian population would not and could not represent the British name, reputation and principles.[9] During that debate, Churchill called on the House to leave military forces only in the Suez Canal Zone and give up its interest in the strategic aspects of Palestine. But despite expressing outrage in Parliament at the growing terrorism, he lamented the fact that no progress had been made about the political future of Palestine and urged the Government to co-operate with the Americans and to transfer the Mandate to the United Nations.

Churchill exploited Jewish guerrilla action in order to criticise Attlee's policy from the Opposition benches after every major terrorist attack, accusing the government of risking the lives of British soldiers for no good political cause. However, his main concern was the inability of London to carry out the task of policing the opposing ranks of Arabs and Jews, to cope with the problem of illegal immigration, to reduce the financial cost of the British presence and to determine the future of the country.[10]

Oliver Stanley, the Colonial Secretary in Churchill's Cabinet, said in the same debate that the invisible terrorist was an enemy with whom the British soldiers had not dealt in the past. Under such circumstances he could see no future in the Mandate. He also said a month later that wasting the nation's limited financial resources should be stopped. In particular he mentioned the self-imposed security zone in Jerusalem (the 'Bevingrad'), in which the civil servants had become virtual prisoners. The fact that these officials had their families evacuated back to Britain, because of the security risks had contributed to their low morale.[11]

The hanging of the two sergeants (see Chapter 4), as mentioned before, marked a turning-point in the attitude of public opinion towards the continuation of British rule in the country. The hanging united Labour and Conservatives in the demand to return the Mandate to the United Nations. The House of Commons was reminded that since Attlee had taken office, 79 military and 40 policemen had been killed; the figures for the wounded were 180 and 79 respectively. The number of soldiers in Palestine at that time varied between 80,000 and 100,000.[12]

The Irgun's historians are correct in saying that British politicians found the situation quite unbearable after the 'Goldsmith House' explosion and the double hanging. But only then was the general outrage translated into the realisation that the Mandate rule could not be maintained under such circumstances.

However, there were others who argued that, if Britain wanted to consolidate its grip on Palestine, it could have done so by applying harsher methods. First and foremost among the proponents of this line of reasoning (who mainly consisted of high-ranking army officers) was Field-Marshal Lord Montgomery, who demanded far-reaching military measures such as imposing prolonged martial law, the arrests of community leaders, collective punishments (including house demolitions) and instant capital punishment.

Although many in the government agreed that a brutal policy could put an end to terrorism, Montgomery simply ignored the political dimensions of the problem. He did not take into account the American reaction, nor would he have hesitated to put the leadership behind bars. Montgomery was motivated by the belief that the abandonment of Palestine meant the surrender of Britain's prime military base in the Middle East.[13]

The Field Marshal had prejudiced his relationship with Bevin over Palestine, as well as with Arthur Creech-Jones, the Colonial Secretary. In addition, he did not hide his hostility towards the Jews and predicted that they would be destroyed by the Arabs after the British evacuation. 'The Jews have made a great mistake', he wrote, 'and will probably get it in the neck.'[14] The King David explosion outraged Montgomery and he wanted at all costs to cripple the insurgents as much as possible, even if it was before the final retreat.

At a meeting with the members of the United Nations Special Committee on Palestine, on 17 July 1947, Lieutenant General Sir Alan Cunningham, the High Commissioner, supported Montgomery's views, saying that if the armed forces had been allowed to use the fire-power of all their weapons, – terrorist activity would have ceased 'within hours'.[15] However, Cunningham's personal view was opposed to such harsh measures, fearing that they would push the moderate majority into the arms of the extremist minority. He remembered only too well what had happened on 29 June 1946, during the so-called 'Black Saturday', when the bulk of the Yishuv's leadership had been arrested. In fact, Bevin was the one who supported the 'Iron Fist' policy of the Chief of the General Imperial Staff. But the Prime Minister and his Colonial Secretary, in an urgent meeting of the Cabinet in January 1947, ruled it out. Creech-Jones, a known Zionist sympathiser, believed that repressive measures were contrary to democratic values; furthermore, without international support, such a move was doomed to fail. Attlee was also influenced by the Chancellor Hugh Dalton who had been touched by the plight of the Jews during the Holocaust and advocated an immediate evacuation from Palestine and other parts of the Empire in order to avoid a 'financial Dunkirk'.

★ ★ ★

Even today some historians in Israel and former Irgun members insist that the terrorist campaign played a leading role in pushing the British Cabinet into reaching that crucial decision. But the British dilemma was quite different. Attlee had to choose between four undesirable possibilities that were bound to incur Arab wrath. First, partition which would create an uproar in the Muslim world. Second, an Arab independent unitary state which would invite Jewish armed resistance. Third, surrender of the Mandate, which would be interpreted as a retreat from the Arab world altogether, paving the way for a civil war in Palestine with the likelihood of terrible consequences for the Jews. The fourth possibility was to impose a solution on both sides, but this would be actively resisted by the two communities and Britain had insufficient military strength to enforce such a solution.

All these options were ruled out after talks with delegations of intransigent Jews and Arabs at the London Conference of January 1947, during which the Jews, strengthened by American support, refused even to sit with the Arabs at the table, knowing that the gathering would not produce the partition which became the Jewish official policy.

As if to add to the existing difficulties, Montgomery warned that it was essential to have troops in Palestine to defend the Suez Canal, while Lord Tedder, Marshal of the RAF, argued that the British military position in the Middle East depended on the co-operation of the Arab states. Bevin, for his part, emphasised the importance of oil supplies. At the beginning of 1947, the British realised that they could hold out no longer and their retreat became inevitable. On 14 February the Cabinet accepted a recommendation, made jointly by Creech-Jones and a reluctant Bevin, that Britain should submit the Palestine problem to the United Nations.

Thus, failure to secure the agreement of both the Jews and the Arabs, to accept any basis for negotiation between them, contributed more than any other factor to the British decision to refer the problem of Palestine to the judgement of the General Assembly of the United Nations.

This is not to say that the British had finally abandoned their hope to continue their military presence in the country. In fact, despite referring the Mandate to the UN, they did not give up the option of administering the country for the years to come. Only towards the end of 1947, in August and September, did London come finally to the conclusion that it could no longer control the diplomatic and military developments in Palestine.

The Irgun's action in the hanging of the two sergeants in July of that year created a sense of outrage, exacerbated by the mining of the site of the murders, which can only be described as colossal. In Britain the reaction was one of near hysteria. The public did not call for revenge; it demanded evacuation.[16] That response surprised the insurgents themselves who had been afraid of a backlash. However, apart from five Jews who were killed in Tel Aviv on the following day, when some soldiers went on the rampage, the general sense of revulsion was not followed by a spirit of retaliation. The government and the authorities were fully aware that the security situation could deteriorate further and that repressive measures could give rise to more atrocities against the armed forces. The British were faced with two choices: either to break the resistance by force, or to give up the undesirable Mandate, which had given birth to so much hatred, misery and humiliation.[17]

The hanging did not in itself change British assessments of the situation in the country. The ground was already fertile for the evacuation, and the submission of the problem to the UN had been decided upon a few months earlier. A tendency to single out that particular event and make it a main factor in the final decision to retreat is grossly exaggerated. But it could be singled out as the event that psychologically touched public opinion more than any other and made the British people intolerant of those who continued to maintain that British Middle Eastern interests lay in Palestine. 'British soldiers are being killed daily and an enormous amount of money is being wasted without achieving anything which resembles law and order. The tax-payer and the British people do not like it', J Garcia Granados, a member of the United Nations Special Committee on Palestine summed up the situation. 'In this small country nearly 30,000,000 dollars spent for police in one year! More than 2,000,000 dollars a month !'[18] In fact, one-tenth of the armed forces of the entire British Empire occupied a territory the size of Wales. There was one soldier for every 18 inhabitants in the country, one for every city block. The drain on the economy for military upkeep alone amounted to close on £40m per annum towards the end of the Mandate years.[19]

The gloomy reality for the British in Palestine was that, without American support, and with equal hostility towards them from both Arabs and Jews, they found themselves in a no-win situation from which only one solution could emerge. If, during 1946 and the first half of 1947, the Government thought that both communities would have to reach a compromise for which the British presence would be vital, it later became apparent that a civil war in the country was inevitable, since both sides were heading for a confrontation. Such a conclusion overshadowed the opinion of the military establishment.

The British realised, especially after the failure of the London Conference, that they would pay a heavy price for imposing their own solution on the communities. To a certain extent they were willing to impose a solution on the Jews in order to avoid a rift with the Arab and the Muslim World. But the Arab refusal to accept not only partition, but other favourable plans, left the Government with no ally in the country. Holding on to Palestine became a prospect which could have only created hostility towards the British in other parts of the region.

It would be fair to suggest that in July 1947 the decision to quit Palestine was already ripe. Firstly, it was generated by the outcome of the UN Committee which advocated partition, a solution which was not supported by London because of Arab rejection. Secondly, that same month had witnessed the hanging of the two sergeants, which might not have provoked such an outcry had it happened earlier. Thirdly, the arrival of the *Exodus* refugee boat in July 1947, highlighted the plight of the 'illegal' Jewish immigrants. The returning of the boat to Germany, whence many of the Holocaust survivors had arrived, damaged the British. The Zionists exploited its propaganda value to the full and the British seemed to have lost the last battle in psychological warfare. In September 1947 they finally and formally decided to return the Mandate to the United Nations. The terrorist factor contributed to the decision, but was far from the decisive factor. Its main strength was its ability to 'legitimise' itself in the eyes of the Jewish Community without necessarily increasing its military scope.

While in 1946 it was still possible to quell the violence, a year later it was no longer a matter that the British could handle except at a severe political price. When the Irgun killed 17 British officers in March 1947 at the Officers' Club in Jerusalem, the immediate British response was to retaliate against the insurgents in order to inflict the maximum punishment on them. The authorities wasted no time and imposed the longest martial law in the country's history. The failure of that measure to produce the necessary results was a breaking point in their ability to eliminate the terrorist campaign. It was a turning point in British military and political thinking. It was quite clear then that, however harsh the measures that the armed forces might use, any retaliation was doomed to fail without the support of the Jewish leaders. With detention camps in Palestine and Cyprus full of refugees and immigrant boats being sent back to Europe, the leadership was no longer willing to co-operate, let alone collaborate, with the authorities.

It is interesting to note that Bevin, in his speech to Parliament in February 1947 told the House about the Cabinet decision to refer Palestine to the UN without mentioning the Jewish armed struggle. He ignored the Hagana, the Irgun and the Stern group and attributed the failure of his policy to Truman's attitude and his dependence on the Jewish vote in America.[20] Such reference reflected Bevin's well known obsession with the 'Jews of New York' and their influence in the White House, but it may also reinforce the opinion that the British did not regard the insurgency as the most pressing problem of all. Bevin, until the very last minute, believed that, provided Truman did not 'stab him in the back', his forces could have stayed in Palestine and a political solution, accepted by both sides, would have been within reach.

During the last critical years of the Mandate in Palestine, the British complained many times that the Jewish Agency and the Hagana were co-ordinating their activities with the underground groups. This allegation was certainly true during the period of the United Resistance Movement. Except for that period the Irgun had been acting mostly on its own and sometimes with FFI. On many occasions it had been persecuted by its Jewish rivals.

But, retrospectively, the three fighting organisations complemented each other by playing various roles which in the end accelerated the British withdrawal and brought the Yishuv closer to independence. The British needed the support of the Jewish Agency, and its military arm the Hagana, in order to win the support of the majority and avoid a confrontation, which would have led to a blood bath, with all the community. The dissidents themselves needed the moderates, whose support the British were afraid to lose before making harsh decisions to crack down on the Yishuv. Begin himself was the first to acknowledge this by telling his Hagana counterparts that had the Irgun not existed, they would have had to invent it. During one of those meetings, while referring to the three Jewish groups which operated within the Yishuv, he said: 'In fact there is here a division of roles; One organisation advocates individual terrorism, the other conducts sporadic military operations and there is a third organisation which prepares itself to throw its final weight to the decisive war'.[21] The moderates did not accept that assessment, but ironically they saved the community from likely British reprisals at times and indirectly increased the popularity of the insurgents, whose terrorist campaign often went punished. More significantly, the Irgun, which had played its fair share in the struggle to oust the British, did not have the required military strength to confront the Arabs in the inevitable war which started on the day after the final British withdrawal from Palestine on 15 May 1948.

The Irgun, one of the most efficient and sophisticated urban guerrilla groups in modern history, could not by itself set the political agenda in Palestine during the 1940s. But despite the British potential ability to crush the Irgun revolt, the group played the role of catalyst and won the psychological battle in both countries. This role could have brought calamity on the Jewish Community, but in the end it helped it, as a secondary factor, to reach its goal.

★ ★ ★

This brief survey of the events in Palestine that led to the departure of the British and the end of the Mandate, opening the door to the creation of the new State of Israel in 1948, has, I hope, set the scene for the chapters which follow. In these we will consider the nature of the Irgun Zvai Leumi and its campaign and the measures taken by the British to counter it.

# Part One

# IRGUN INSURGENCY

CHAPTER 1

# Background

The body in question, the Irgun Zvai Leumi, was a separatist organisation which did not represent the community on whose behalf it operated. Even its political concepts were motivated by an ideology that sharply contradicted the principles of the Jewish Community in Palestine. Ironically, the Irgun did not come into being for the sake of launching an armed struggle against the British. It was the product of the policy of restraint adopted by the official leadership in response to constant and violent Arab attacks on Jewish civilians.

When a small group of people split from the parent movement, the Hagana, in 1931, the anti-British campaign was not on the agenda at all. On the contrary, the separatists did not even think about such a possibility throughout the 1930s and the beginning of the 1940s, leading up to the last year of the war. In a country where the Arab population enjoyed a clear majority, the British were regarded at that time as an ally, capable of shielding the Jews from the growing threat of the enemy.

The Hagana, established as early as 1920, was the defence organisation of the Yishuv (Hebrew for the Jewish Community) and subordinated to the Jewish Agency and the trade-union federation, which composed the official representative bodies in the country. The defecting group called itself Hagana B or National Hagana to emphasise the alternative path it had selected, but it made no impact in Palestine. Apart from staging a few isolated retaliations against some Arab targets (planting bombs in buses, market places and other urban areas), the new organisation proved ineffective and without a solid enough following within the Community. It is no surprise that most of its founders gradually returned to the parent movement after a few years.

## BIRTH OF THE IRGUN

Only in 1938, after the Arab terrorist campaign intensified further, did the remainder of the 'National Hagana' became the 'Irgun', the National

Military Organisation. For the first time its members expressed the wish to counter Arab attacks by retaliatory measures on a large scale, but they were unable to match their rhetoric with deeds, due to their lack of competence.

When three of the organisation's youngsters took the law into their own hands and prepared an abortive attack on an Arab bus in the Galilee Heights in the summer of 1938, many of the Irgun leaders deplored the action. In the first years of its existence, the organisation did attack Arab centres of civil population but failed to increase its influence beyond the political margins of the country.

At that time, the Irgun was dominated by the leader of the Zionist-Revisionist Party, Vladimir (Ze'ev) Jabotinsky. He was an advocate of the British cause in the Middle East and strongly opposed a Jewish revolt against the Mandate. He, in fact, regarded the Irgun as the military wing of his party and demanded complete discipline.

Shortly before the beginning of the Second World War, some members of the Irgun stated, for the first time, that if the British authorities maintained the policy of restricting Jewish immigration to Palestine, the Jews would have no choice but to take military action against HMG. Moreover, they claimed, co-operation with the Mandate regime was a grave mistake because, in their opinion, the British had no intention of surrendering Palestine to its Jewish population.

The concept was shared by radical members of the IZL's High Command, led by Abraham Stern, who became frustrated with the affiliation to the legalist Revisionist Party and wanted to disassociate himself from it. The British refusal to form a Jewish Brigade within their own army reinforced Stern's argument and he won support among some of the Irgun members.

However, the then Irgun chief commander, David Raziel, disagreed with the militant section of the organisation. Being faithful to Jabotinsky, he accepted the notion that in the event of a war between the Allies and the Germans, the Irgun should do its utmost to assist the British by all its modest means. At stake was not only the future of the European Jews, but also the Community in Palestine which faced a possible invasion of German forces from Northern Africa.

Raziel, and many of his close colleagues, who were in prison for anti-Arab activities, were released soon after the war broke out. They committed themselves fully to co-operate with the security forces, to the extent that they even decided not to participate in an anti-White Paper demonstration organised by the official leadership in February 1940 against the immigration restrictions it introduced. In addition, the IZL had collaborated with British intelligence, thus causing an enormous amount of criticism and disillusion among its more radical members. They denounced Raziel as a commander who knowingly gave up the independence of the Irgun for the sake of British and Revisionist interests.

When more command members were released from prison, Raziel found himself in a minority, facing friends who urged him not to join the British Army. Raziel then resigned, but the Revisionist Party refused to accept his decision. Although he accepted the Party demand to return, the IZL High Command found it difficult to accept him back. In general, the Irgun was in a state of a disarray.

Jabotinsky's sudden death in August 1940 left the Revisionists without a central authority and eased the desire of the extremists to quit the Irgun. About 100 of its members took over some of the IZL's ammunition depots and formed a new group called 'Freedom Fighters of Israel' (FFI), later known as the Stern Group (or the Stern Gang by the British). Those who did not follow Stern, found their way to the British Army, some rejoined the Hagana and others simply left the country.

The bulk of the Irgun, despite the confusion, acted on behalf of the British Army and executed missions in enemy territories. During one of them, in Iraq, Raziel, who was commanding the operation, was killed. While the Irgun engaged itself in the general war effort, the inevitable split within the organisation became a reality. The FFI, a tiny group with no resources or public support, tried in vain to harass the British rule in Palestine while the Irgun was out of action.

Thus the outbreak of the Second World War put an end to the Irgun's anti-Arab campaign which had started to gather pace. The war had radically changed the aims of the organisation. The Irgun, as a fighting unit, was in fact neutralised during the war and its activities were shelved for most of the war years.

In November 1943, when the first horrific reports on the extermination of European Jewry reached Palestine, a new attempt to resist the British was made. Elements from various existing organisations in the Yishuv, formed a group called *Am Lohem* ('Fighting Nation') in a bid to unite the Community against the British. The Government was accused by the group of blocking the way of the Holocaust survivors to safety. Its first mission was to kidnap the High Commissioner of Palestine, John McMichael, but the attempt was unsuccessful. The Irgun headquarters in Jerusalem refused to supply arms to the group and the Hagana gave its members an ultimatum to quit the illegal body. Another, more important reason for the quick demise of the group was the refusal of David Ben Gurion, the leader of the Jewish Agency, to back the initiative. The Yishuv was not yet prepared for a military struggle.

But by the beginning of 1944, the attitude had changed. Its leaders concluded that Britain had betrayed the Jews who joined her army and supported her policy during the war.[1] For the Irgun, the British insistence on complying with the White Paper policy of restricting immigration to Palestine irrespective of the Holocaust, amounted to the completion of the Nazi 'final solution', since the Jewish refugees had nowhere to go.[2]

The Irgun, for the first time, adopted the view that only an independent state and separate army could provide the solution to the suffering of the Jews. Since such a notion was not consistent with the British presence in Palestine, the Yishuv was left with no choice but to rid the country of the British rule. This could be achieved only by armed struggle. The trouble for the Underground was that the ground was not yet ready for such a development. But the Jewish population, despite its traditional support for the British (highlighted by the Balfour declaration of 1917), was more prepared to question the moral validity of the Mandate than ever before. While the official leadership was adamant that all the diplomatic options should be examined, the Irgun was not prepared to wait any longer. Its new commander, Menachem Begin, proclaimed a revolt on the first day of February 1944, even before the war was over. (See Appendix I).

## STRATEGY

The Irgun did not delude itself that its armed rebellion would be powerful enough to remove the British forces from Palestine. The aim was too ambitious and the group was not ready at the time to accomplish such a mission, nor did it hope to achieve independence in four years time.[3] Begin, in the face of an opposition within his own central command, lacked the elementary means and the structural basis for that purpose. That is why in the first part of its guerrilla campaign, the Irgun failed to leave an immediate mark on the Yishuv, due to its inability to conduct military operations on a large scale. The wisdom behind the timing of the proclamation of the revolt was debatable. It came after the Irgun's unsuccessful attempts, by means of persuasion, to turn all the Jewish units which served in the British Army into a Jewish army. It came also when Hitler was still capable of making one more show of strength at the Battle of the Bulge. Moreover, the proclamation, because of the haste in which it was made, increased the suspicion that the IZL was interested, among other objectives, in dominating the Yishuv by using military force.[4] The Irgun had failed to prepare the grassroots for its new policy.

This inferior start by the Irgun imposed a certain strategy on it. Its central command adopted the concept that only strategic targets (as opposed to the assassinations of individuals conducted by the Stern Group), either economic or military, would be subject to its attacks. Only non-stop harassment which would paralyse daily life in Palestine and make it ungovernable, would be fruitful.[5] As a result of this policy, communication lines, civilian and military transport and factories faced the danger of possible assaults. When the Irgun, especially during 1946, was better able to hit vital targets, it began to strike army bases, police headquarters, airfields, intelligence centres and arsenals. Their inability to reach this full terrorist potential, immediately after the proclamation, cast some doubts over their pretensions to play a decisive role in the anti-British resistance.

As has been noted, improvements in its military capacity enabled the Irgun to widen its operational possibilities. Concentration on specific objects and their relative success in hitting them, shaped the guidelines of the insurgents: British authority, based on prestige, was an outcome of a long tradition of colonial practice. Only impressive operations which would undermine this authority, would bring them to the conclusion that an ungovernable country was not worth retaining, in terms of human life, manpower, financial resources and political damage.[6] Therefore the operational campaign had to be linked to world-wide political efforts, by taking the greatest advantage of international public opinion, mainly in the USA, which favoured the Jewish cause after the Second World War. But even when the IZL established itself 'on the highway', it was far from capable of defeating the security forces. The IZL succeeded in making use of anger and frustration caused by the European Holocaust in the Yishuv, which granted it a degree of support without which it could achieve nothing. However, the military power of the insurgents was no match for the British army and police. It consisted mostly of small, effective and publicity-seeking operations which hit British military and civilian targets and disrupted daily life in Palestine.

## THE SUPPORT OF THE JEWISH COMMUNITY

The Second World War found the Jewish population in Palestine united as it had never been before. The Hagana, as well as the Irgun, joined the British Army. The community as a whole, especially after receiving the terrifying news of the European gas chambers, was recruited into the allied military effort. Apart from the Stern members, who were regarded at that time (even by the IZL) as a collection of criminals and lunatics for taking the decision to fight 'British imperialism' during the war, the Yishuv was united behind the British forces. The military potential of the Irgun was, in any case, very small at the time. Thus, while all were concentrating on the European front, the Palestinian question was frozen for at least four years. The proclamation of the revolt put an end to the co-operation between the would-be insurgents and the authorities. Like any other guerrilla group, the Irgun had to win the support of the civilian population. This need was all the greater because of the topographical structure of Palestine which lacked the mountains and forests vital for an underground movement. The Irgun was forced to operate inside the urban population centres as 'part-time insurgents' – behaving during the day like ordinary civilians and going underground as the sun set.[7]

The difficulties of the Irgun in the battle for public support were enormous. Most of the Jewish inhabitants living in Palestine during the 40s were sympathetic to the socialist parties. The guerrillas had to fight against the Hagana, the Histadrut (the influential Trade Union Federation), and the Jewish establishment headed by the British-oriented leaders of the Jewish Agency. They had to fight against the traditional support for the British, against the philosophy of non-retaliation and the belief that only diplomatic measures could solve the conflict.[8]

The IZL, judged by a few anti-British but mainly anti-Arab operations before the war, was regarded by the Yishuv as a militant group which justified its means in order to achieve its final goal. It was identified as the military unit of the Zionist Revisionist Party (ZRP) which was situated on the extreme right of the political arena and its roots in Palestine were weak. The socialist sections of the community were much more powerful than the ZRP and the Irgun, not only as a result of receiving the majority of popular support, but also because of their economic resources and agricultural settlements. This political block treated the IZL as intending to impose their belief on the community and to dominate the street, and later the leadership, by force.[9]

Another difficulty facing the Irgun's bid to win sympathy derived from the general opinion among the population that any kind of violent methods against the government would harm the community and risk the lives of many innocent people. The Jews voiced the fear that such a danger might also have shifted the British balance between Jews and Arabs towards the latter. The former wished to be regarded as responsible, sane, co-operative and capable in due course of being trusted with the running of their own country.[10] One might assume that these odds would have put an end to the Irgun's chances, even before the organisation started its revolt. However, at the same time, the international political reality and the way the British conducted their policy appeared to serve its interests. Denying the sea shores to refugees, making pro-Arab declarations, introducing hostile White Papers, committing some anti-semitic slips of the tongue and what appeared to the Jewish Community to be a policy of violating promises and agreements given to them in the past – all these actions served the interests of the Irgun. The population felt that loyalty to the British crown had not paid off.[11]

The Jewish hostile and emotional reaction to London's policy increased the military potential of the insurgents. The British, in fact, compensated for the disadvantages which the IZL faced. By widening the consensus against them, they gave legitimacy to the Irgun's acts and made the public psychologically prepared for the idea of armed struggle. The Hagana, on the other hand, did not assess the situation properly. It did not consider the possibility of armed resistance even when the community felt betrayed by Britain. Instead, it accused the Irgun of jeopardising the harmony and the peacefulness of the local population. As a result, the Hagana and the Jewish leadership were identified with British policy by some parts of the community, who appeared to be in favour of the insurgents. The security measures taken by the authorities in response to the first few operations of the Irgun escalated the confrontation between the government and the local population. The British precautions were not sufficient to paralyse the Irgun, but effective enough to cause anger in the community.[12]

## THE IDEOLOGY OF THE IRGUN

The IZL inherited some of its ideological principles from the Zionist Revisionist Party (ZRP). The legacy applied mainly to the geographical borders of the future Jewish state. These, according to the ZRP, should have been based on the 1917 Balfour Declaration, which awarded the Jews a national home on both banks of the Jordan river. When the revolt broke out, this promised map was the symbol of the insurgents; hence, their bitter antagonism to the various partition plans which aimed to divide Palestine between Jews and Arabs.

However, the Irgun was not of one mind. Many of the insurgents opposed the Revisionist Party due to its British orientation and its attitude towards applying violent methods. In fact, the party's leader, Vladimir Ze'ev Jabotinsky, remained faithful to the path of co-operation with the British almost until his death in August 1940.[13] Before the revolt, the political conviction of IZL was based on the pro-British doctrine of Jabotinsky, the goal of which was to bring about a change in British anti-Zionist policy.[14] The Irgun, in its early days, contrary to what its leaders said, was not necessarily seeking to drive the British out of Palestine, but only to get rid of the components of British rule – the police, the administration and even the Army. One might argue that the British presence in Palestine was not opposed by the Irgun in the first place. Even after the proclamation of the revolt, when the Irgun was not certain of its capability, it was willing to negotiate with the British, enabling them to stay in Palestine as long as a Jewish state was on its way to independence.

The Revisionist–Irgun links were one of the reasons which brought about the split with the Stern Group. The latter held the opinion that the armed struggle had only one aim – defeating British imperialism. In their view, all means for achieving this aim were justified, including forming an alliance with the Italian fascists or the Soviet Communists.

But only part of the Irgun was under the influence of the Revisionist Party. In the wake of the revolt, the links between the two were in fact broken and disputes over this issue continued to exist. In 1946 many Jewish youngsters joined the Underground and the gap between them and the European-born party was sharply increased. Despite the differences with the parent movement, the fact that the IZL had an ideological identification placed it on the right in the political confrontation with the powerful socialist camp. This conflict was fully expressed during the 'Saison' in which the socialist-oriented Hagana collaborated with the British during six months of hunting down which paralysed the Irgun.[15]

The Stern Group, which was more militant in its support of violence and terrorism, managed to escape the campaign. Furthermore, their leaders were offered rescue and shelter in some of the kibbutzim in order to avoid their capture. This was contrary to general opinion in the Jewish Agency, which, after finding out that the Sterns had tried to establish contact with the Axis Powers, declared that they must be torn out by the roots. But after the Irgun's revolt (and despite the Stern's assassination of Lord Moyne) the FFI was not hunted down. This double attitude of the Jewish–Palestinian leadership needs to be explained.

Hagana historians argue that the leadership suspected that the Irgun was not only interested in fighting the British, but also in dominating the community, even by terrorist methods.[16] The Hagana regarded the Sterns as a small guerrilla group, modelled on the Irish pattern of resistance, which could not jeopardise its hegemony.

The Irgun, on the other hand, especially after increasing its popularity, inspired more fear. But what the Hagana did not admit was the fact that the 'Saison' merely reflected the ideological confrontation between right and left. It was not just a disagreement over the anti-British strategy adopted by the Irgun and rejected by the rest. Rather, it was a conflict about the dominance of the Yishuv. It was part of the ideological fight for the sympathy of the population before and after the establishment of the Jewish State. It was also a clash between two different political notions which almost reached the brink of a civil war.

The Irgun's mode of operations was influenced by other guerrilla movements operating outside Palestine. Begin himself was an admirer of Garibaldi and Mazzini, the heroes of Italian unification. The Irgun had connections with the French anti-Nazi resistance movement, the Maquis. It included in its educational programme some lessons about the Irish rebellion (and the Easter Uprising), the Italian Risorgimento, the Boer War in Africa and the Greek rebellion. In its many publications in Palestine and beyond, the Irgun used to compare itself to other anti-imperialist resistance movements all over the world and referred to itself as the nucleus of the future Jewish Army.

## THE ARAB FRONT

The political controversy over the territorial question of Palestine was not the only one to reflect the differences between the Irgun and the rest of the community.

Its leadership had difficulties in fully expressing its attitude towards the Arab population. At the end of the 1930s and the beginning of the 1940s the insurgents retaliated against the Arab civilian population in Haifa, Jaffa, Jerusalem and Nablus, causing the deaths of many innocent people, as reprisals against similar attacks on the Jews themselves. These activities caused protests inside the Revisionist Party and especially within the Yishuv's moderate leadership.[17]

The conventional opinion, expressed by both Right and Left, which maintained that the Irgun held a traditional anti-Arab position, both hawkish and uncompromising, was not entirely accurate. In fact the IZL's attitude towards the Arab question was not consistent at all. The insurgents emphasised in their appeals to the Arabs that they regarded them as neighbours. In their revolt proclamation they even pledged to grant full equality to the Arab population whom, they promised, would have full emancipation in the new Jewish state. Simultaneously, by expressing support for a Jewish majority, they opposed the implementation of any partition plan in Palestine.

In the proclamation itself Begin denounced the Arabs who 'awaited the coming of Rommel, the redeemer, while their leader, the Mufti, dispatched orders from Berlin'. By branding the other Arabs in Iraq, Syria and Egypt as 'Hitler's agents', Begin emphasised what he had seen as British betrayal, by stating that the Jews had 'stood the test' and remained loyal to London during the crucial period of 1940–1. (See Appendix I.)

Before the Second World War the Irgun was engaged in a ruthless bombing campaign against the Arabs. After the war the group called on them to co-operate in order to drive the British out of Palestine with a view to settling the dispute between them by peaceful means. 'Britain is our common enemy', Irgun pamphlets repeatedly told the Arabs. From the tactical point of view, the Irgun leaders wanted to fight one front only and ironically, the Stern group exerted some pressure on them not to adopt an anti-Arab line. Both organisations, therefore, urged the Arabs, on several occasions, to preserve law and order and these attempts, created the impression, at least within the FFI, that a Jewish–Arab understanding was possible even in the long run.[18] Indeed, as a gesture of goodwill, Irgun members broke into British textile warehouses and distributed huge quantities of captured goods among poor Arabs.[19]

But the Irgun leaders underestimated the Arabs and their strength. They were, most of all, interested in settling the conflict with the British. They did not believe that the Arabs would give up their national aspirations, so the policy of conciliation was mainly tactical. They wanted to avoid a second front. 'We show that we are in a conflict with the British only ...', Begin wrote.[20] He and his aides played down the Arab factor. They regarded the Arabs as an element of almost no weight whatsoever, a weak community which was incited by the authorities. They were convinced that Arab strength had been artificially blown up by the British. Only the latter and the Jews, Begin believed, would make the final decision about the future of the country. This opinion was the outcome of the Irgun's concept that if 'the British were removed from the country, the Jews could easily overcome the resistance of the Arabs ...'.[21] This conclusion contradicted the IZL's belief that the Jews would reach an agreement with the Arabs over the dominance of Palestine. So the Irgun's appeals to the Arabs were tactical and calculated.

Although they underestimated them, the IZL did not want another enemy in the arena. Therefore, since 1941 and until the 1947 partition plan was publicised, the Irgun managed, except in a few cases, to maintain the policy of not attacking the Arabs. This decision prevented the British from continuing to apply the policy of 'divide and rule' which characterised their pre-war politics in Palestine.

In 1947, when London's decision to pull out its soldiers was announced, the Arabs imposed on the Jews, Irgun and Hagana alike, the necessity of opening a second front, after remaining relatively passive for five years. The IZL then had to fight both the Arabs and British, attacking the latter and protecting the civilian population from the former. However, not being ready for such a development, the community was exposed to some Arab operations which caused many casualties. The crucial decision of the United Nations to divide Palestine in November 1947 found the Irgun in a process of reorganisation. It contributed to its failure to predict the inevitable outcome and prompted a further, more radical, outburst of violence in Palestine.[22] The public security of the Yishuv was tragically abandoned for a few weeks. In Jerusalem, while the guerrillas' attention was focused on the anti-British struggle, the whole Jewish commercial district was destroyed by Arab nationalists. The fact that the Jewish civilian rear had been exposed to massive Arab assaults was critical, especially later, when the 1948 Israeli–Arab war took place in Palestine.

## THE POLITICAL CAMPAIGN

As if to compensate for its military shortcomings, the Irgun, throughout its violent campaign, was engaged in aggressive verbal warfare against its enemies. Accompanying each of its terrorist operations with ideological and political rhetoric was one of the Irgun's most effective weapons. It served the insurgents to publicise their activities and to make a favourable impression on the Jewish youth. From the outset of the revolt the Irgun structured its propaganda unit, gave it prominence and appointed the head of the unit as a member of the High Command. The vocal psychological campaign was directed towards Jews and British alike. The Hagana and the Jewish Agency were a constant target for its attacks and their leaders were accused of collaborating with the government.

The psychological offensive against the British had a double aim: to influence public opinion on one hand and to lower the morale of the soldiers in Palestine on the other. To achieve that objective, the Irgun chose to concentrate on two subjects – the plight of European Jewry during the war and the immigration restrictions imposed on the refugees who wanted to reach the safety of Palestine's shores. The British counter-insurgency measures were also exploited to the full by the IZL. Exiles, curfews, hangings, mass arrests, flogging and martial law were all used to portray the insurgents as freedoms fighters, resisting a repressive regime. During that campaign victims became martyrs, trials turned into political showpieces and government policy proved to be a propaganda asset for the IZL in Europe and particularly in the USA.

The Irgun wanted to extend its activities overseas, but its relative failure to hit British targets abroad was overshadowed by its success in conducting an effective and efficient propaganda war in Europe and particularly in the USA. The Irgun owed this success to its contacts in Europe and to Peter Bergson who established and headed the reputable American committees (for saving the Jewish People and for the Jewish Army) and the League for a Free Palestine (ALFP). Through these bodies, the Irgun recruited American politicians, actors, businessmen, authors, artists and other prominent people to its cause. The committees were similar to those formed in the European countries after the Nazi occupation. Bergson's groups were more sophisticated and applied the most advanced propaganda methods. They were aggressive, impudent and popular. They were so highly active that they even angered the established Zionist leadership and embarrassed the American president.[23]

The campaign of the IZL made the maximum use of the international situation created after the war. Bearing in mind that the propaganda activities started after most of the Jews were murdered and before the 'Final Solution' was imposed on Hungarian Jewry, we can understand how great was the impact of the campaign. In America, the League stressed the Christian commitment to the 'Bible People'. In France, the insurgents compared themselves to the French underground and took advantage of the situation in Algeria when related to the Arab conflict. Thus, while it could have been easily beaten on the battlefield, the Irgun clearly won the propaganda war against the authorities who were finally forced to leave Palestine in disgrace.

## CHARACTERISTICS

The Irgun Zvai Leumi represented a new form of guerrilla organisation – a cross between a large terrorist group and a small army. The latter reflected the desires of Irgun's leaders, who aimed at embarking on large-scale military operations in order to impress Britons, Jews and international public opinion. Some of their missions indeed lived up to such expectations, but most of them had failed. The more successful ones were the least spectacular, ambitious and complicated. At the same time the group usually refrained from individual assassinations and kidnappings and, unlike the Stern Group, made strong efforts to refute the allegations of its terrorist nature. Following its strategy of undermining the government authority and disrupting the daily routine of its army, the IZL made its strongest impact through 'hit and run' activities of which buildings, rather than soldiers, were its target. In doing so, the Irgun's campaign of violence could have inflicted misery upon the Jewish community. To walk such a tightrope requires skill and efficient propaganda machinery on which Menachem Begin, the chief commander, put a special emphasis.

The Irgun's rank and file consisted mainly of Jewish youngsters, many oriental origin, who were not attracted to the secular socialist parties from which the Hagana recruited its members. They were 'part-time' insurgents, leading a secret life from parents, friends and children. Except for a few full-time people, nearly everybody lived above ground, often in their own homes, under their own names, fearing informers and waiting for a midnight knock on the door.[24] Before engaging in military activities they would undergo military training and take part in indoctrination seminars in small groups. 'They are not gentlemen, they are the most dangerous thugs in existence', said Lord Casey, British Minister for the Middle East.[25] 'The Irgunists mostly wore summer khaki drill and carried tommy-guns. They looked much more sinister ...', wrote Edwin Samuel, the son of the first High Commissioner in Palestine. 'Being kidnapped by them or the Stern Gang was always a possibility ...'.[26] The insurgents themselves, however, chose to define themselves as 'a fighting family', a dedicated band of brothers with intimate loyalty, who had gambled on the future of the Yishuv by proclaiming their revolt at the beginning of 1944.

CHAPTER 2

# The Revolt

The military power of the Irgun in early 1944 consisted of less than 600 men and women of whom only 200 were combat fighters, 40 guns, 200kg. of explosives, 150 hand grenades, 60 pistols, four sub-machine guns, and eight pounds sterling.[1] Yet, on the first of February, the newly-appointed commander, Menachem Begin, issued the proclamation of the organisation's armed revolt against the British Mandate authorities in Palestine.

The Irgun had no previous military experience on a large scale, nor had it demonstrated any capability for hitting military targets in its early days. Many of its members had served as soldiers in the British army between 1940–44 as part of its policy to fight the Nazis alongside His Majesty's forces.[2] Despite this, at that time they were not militarily capable of conducting a guerrilla campaign in the country. The radical shift from co-operation to confrontation even surprised many Irgun supporters. Some of them were in favour of delaying the armed struggle as long as the war was in progress and others argued that they were not yet prepared for prolonged warfare.

During the Second World War the Irgun reached its lowest point and its leaders voiced the fear that without drastically changing its course, the group would face extinction. The caretaker commander, Ya'akov Meridor (Viniarsky), founded an organisation during the war that he himself described as 'a relatively small group with a few hundred starving people with no money or alternative means'.[3] At the end of 1942, when the British rejected the idea of sending IZL's members to operate behind enemy lines, Meridor came to the conclusion that the Irgun should rid itself of the commitment to the British in order to rebuild the organisation as a fighting force. This would enable his men to strike against the government should British policy remain as it was in the pre-war period.[4] Meridor was right in his assessment. Years of inactivity had eroded the Irgun's membership. The stores of arms and explosives had been severely depleted and the weapons arsenal had been reduced to almost nothing.

By 1945 the Irgun still possessed no printing press, no radio station, no other communications equipment and no technological resources.[5] So, while participating in the British war effort the Irgun tried to prepare itself during that transitional period for what was lying ahead, by quietly recovering arms on a small scale, collecting funds, starting training courses and recruiting new members. Menachem Begin, a soldier in the Polish Army, and unknown to most of the Irgun members in Palestine, was appointed as chief commander in December 1943. He soon detected a growing unrest within the rank and file of the group which had been manifested in an unauthorised attack launched by some members on a British transport company. The accumulated frustration amongst the guerrillas who were eager to act was coupled with the Jewish hostility towards Britain for not allowing Jewish refugees to immigrate to Palestine. The sympathetic attitude of the Irgun towards the British turned into hostility and antagonism even before the war was over.[6]

Against this background Begin assumed command of the organisation. A month later he wrote a political manifesto which he thought would explain to the Jewish community and the world at large, the Irgun's commitment to paramilitary activity. He drafted the proclamation early in 1943 while he was still a soldier in the Polish army.[7] He himself recalled: 'The manifesto was due to appear not in January 1944, but in the first half of 1943. It was drafted when I was still a private – I was never more than that – in a foreign army. Because of indirect circumstances, inside and outside the Irgun, our zero hour was delayed'. The proclamation, aimed at the 'Jewish Nation in Zion'[8], was divided into two parts. The first consisted of the facts created by the war as the Irgun saw them; the second concluded that no option was left for the organisation except a military one. The document accused the Government of rejecting all proposals to establish 'a Jewish fighting force to engage the German armies in direct combat'. It emphasised the fact that the Jews in Palestine had agreed to a truce and that the community offered its assistance to the Allies. That resulted in the recruitment of over 25,000 volunteers in the British Army in the hope that Britain would establish a Jewish brigade. The proclamation went on to indicate that Arabs in Iraq, Syria, Egypt and Palestine supported the Nazi regime and awaited the arrival of General Rommel in Palestine, while their spiritual leader, the Mufti of Jerusalem, received orders from Berlin. Article 7 of the document described the slaughter of the European Jews[9] and, turning to the British, the Irgun accused the government of ignoring appeals to rescue the Jews on the dubious grounds that it would interfere with the achievement of victory. Furthermore, His Majesty's Government was considered to be solely responsible for preventing Jewish immigration to Palestine, thus indirectly contributing to the Holocaust. This, the IZL claimed, was 'despite Jewish loyalty and Arab treachery ...'. Begin concluded that 'there can no longer be an armistice between the Jewish nation and its youth and the British administration in the Land of Israel which has been delivering our brethren to Hitler'. His major demand to the British was: 'immediate transfer of power to a provisional Jewish government'. Addressing himself to the youth whose support he wished to win, the new commander called on the community to raise the banner of a citizen's war. His other demands were: To refuse paying taxes to the 'oppressive regime'. To demonstrate day and night against the authorities. To defy any order issued by the British. To be prepared for strikes in all public and private enterprises. To boycott schools and devote all time and energy to the war.

## THE DEBATE

The proclamation, whose slogan was 'Freedom or Death', was a political manifesto and not an ideological document. It was the first call to specify the demand for an independent Jewish sovereign state in Palestine[10] as a final objective. It was reminiscent in tone and context of the words of one of Begin's heroes, Guiseppe Garibaldi, when the latter summoned his famous 'One Thousand' forces to battle against Italy's foreign oppressors with the cry 'Roma o Morte' in 1859.[11] But although Begin was adamant that the armed struggle was inevitable, he did not rule out future co-operation between the Irgun and the British. This was conditional upon the removal of the government's objection to the idea of a Jewish independent state. Nathan Yelin Mor, one of the Stern group commanders, was critical of the statement and emphasised what in his opinion was the key sentence of it, when the Irgun accused London that the 'cease-fire declared at the beginning of the war was breached by the British regime ...'. Yelin Mor, who regarded the revolt proclamation as justification for his own group's militant argument, wrote that Begin's claim contradicted the truth and helped him to understand the Irgun's 'mistake' of holding fire during the war.[12] In his view the IZL had unilaterally declared a cease-fire in which the British played no part. The Government itself did not breach any agreement since it had never promised that in exchange for loyalty it would make concessions to the Irgun after the war. The Sterns were right in making the point which reflected that the Irgun support of the British had partially derived from weakness.

But the debate within the militant section of the Yishuv was important since the proclamation proved that behind the rhetoric, the Irgun was still interested in the continuation of the British presence in Palestine under certain conditions. The FFI found it remarkable, for example, that the British were referred to by Begin as the 'White Paper government' to suggest that the possible removal of the White Paper policy would 'rehabilitate' the British in the eyes of the Irgun. But there was also a reference to the 'British regime' which was blamed for the 'shameful betrayal of the Jewish nation', thus losing the moral basis for its continued presence 'in the Land of Israel'. Mor himself concluded, by the way the declaration was formulated, that the IZL was not interested in breaking its ties with the authorities. Indeed, the Irgun, while calling for the immediate transfer of power to a provisional Jewish government, proposed a mutual 'assistance pact' with Great Britain. That point was acknowledged afterwards by the High Command member, Shlomo Lev Ami, who argued that 'there was no need to point out that the (future) Hebrew Government would offer an alliance with Britain'.[13] Indeed the political basis of the Irgun's anti-British revolt during 1944-5 did not go beyond the limits of the Jabotinsky's 'doctrine of pressure'. They were still trying, but then by force of arms, to coerce Britain into supporting a Jewish state. But, despite its militant tone, the Irgun refrained from calling for the withdrawal of the British forces from the country.

Though never explicitly stated, it could be suggested that the IZL, at this time, was not seeking to drive the British forces out of Palestine, but rather to get rid of those components of British rule, closely identified with neo-colonial status, notably the police and the administration. Therefore, this proclamation could be seen as a compromise between the realistic and the idealistic viewpoints, represented by the Revisionist-conservative approach, in contrast to the position of Begin, who was determined to intensify the struggle. As indicated above, the Irgun's military power could not match the rhetoric of the declaration of the revolt. The announcement itself hints at why Begin decided on 1 February 1944 as the appropriate moment for the revolt.

Once the request to establish a Jewish army unit within the British forces was refused, the Irgun reached the conclusion that armed struggle provided the only available means of retaining the little support it had within the community. The British rejection strengthened the position of the Stern Group, who claimed that their initial policy of continuous harassment of the British, regardless of the Second World War, was justified. The Irgun leadership was forced to confront the possibility that the few members who remained faithful would eventually depart and join the Stern Group. The revolt announced by Begin was aimed at these members and, therefore, derived from purely internal difficulties. The Irgun's call upon the community to wage war against the authorities was primarily to maintain its influence. It was not capable of organising nation-wide resistance, nor could it use the diplomatic means which were being applied by the Jewish Agency. On the other hand, it condemned the use of individual terrorism adopted by the Stern.

The main reason for this move was the need to disassociate itself from the more radical group whose position was regarded by the Yishuv as one of fanaticism and blind militancy. But another, no less important reason was the wish to retain the possibility of future negotiations with the British. Unlike the Stern, the Irgun wanted to leave its political option open, while holding the view that, in any case, the Stern's terrorist campaign was counter-productive and could only harm the community. Strategically, therefore, the only alternative left for the Irgun was to hit and harass the civilian infrastructure of the Mandate.

Disrupting the daily life of the administration, attacking the immigration apparatus and carefully selecting its military targets, later became the hallmarks of the Irgun. Explaining why it did not wait until the war was over, the Irgun said that by the time of the declaration, the victory of the Allies over the Germans was assured. More than that, the Jews were not granted any status in the post-war peace conferences.[14] It also claimed that the danger of the German forces invading Palestine from the south had been removed.[15] Eli Tavin, one of the Command members, wrote that the 'news about the extermination of millions of Jews while the British refused to allow the survivors to enter Palestine, and the already obvious victory of the Allies, influenced the decision to start the revolt'.[16] In addition, Begin based his policy on the perceived inability of the British to maintain their influence in the Middle East. He also regarded America as the country which would have 'the largest and the most influential Jewish community' after the war.[17] He believed that Western public opinion, including that of Britain itself, would be 'dismayed at the prospect of British boys being killed or wounded fighting against Jews after the Nazi Holocaust'.

Ya'acov Meridor, Begin's predecessor, admitted that the proclamation was a political act without much military background. 'When we published it on the walls of the cities and the villages, the British could not believe their eyes. They even regarded it with a certain contempt and with many doubts.'[18] Begin claimed that the declaration of the revolt electrified the IZL members: 'Its men were more than ready for the action they had awaited so long.'[19] On the other hand he admitted that the reactions outside the Irgun were disappointing, since 'I had laboured so hard in drafting the proclamation'. In fact, many people in the High Command had little confidence in their ability to turn words into action. 'They looked upon it as a bluff, and expressed the fear that it would undermine their prestige', and were determined not to fail at the early stages of the period under the new command without sufficient means to ensure military action.

Doubts had arisen within the Irgun's High Command, however, about the decision to publish the manifesto. Some had argued that the public should be informed of the nature of the rebellion and its objectives in advance.[20] 'Domestically,' as Shlomo Lev Ami indicated, 'it was preferable to attack first and to declare (war) afterwards.'[21] Levi suggested that the best way would be to make such preparations as necessary in advance of the proclamation and to commence action afterwards.

A strong advocate of the 'attack first' approach was Eliyahu Lankin, one of the key men in the command. 'When Begin brought up the idea to publish a manifesto about opening war against the foreign regime in Palestine, we voted against it because we thought that this would not be treated seriously. It was better to start acting and then publish the reasons. Not the opposite, to precede words by action'.[22] The controversy was acknowledged by Begin. 'Many friends and others did not treat our proclamation seriously. None of them believed that there would be any follow-up, or any follow-up to the follow-up. I heard a typical complimentary comment: 'Begin is a public speaker, and now that he's gone underground and can't make speeches, he's begun to write them on the walls.'[23] Begin managed to convince the Command that by committing such a political act, the IZL would start with small-scale actions and then expand its scope in due course. He defended the announcement with much resolution. He said that a 'declaration will prepare the ground, the atmosphere and public opinion for the activities we intended to carry out'.[24]

Even so, few of the High Command supported his move wholeheartedly. Lankin, despite his misgivings, represented the opinion of those who sided with Begin. He held the view that the struggle should have taken place even before February 1944, when the attempt to organise the 'fighting Nation' was made. Lankin stressed: 'When we came to terms with the total destruction of the Jewish people in Europe and we saw that the British were not willing to halt their anti-Zionist policy, but were in fact escalating it, we saw no point in waiting for the final outcome of the war.'[25] Begin himself, being aware of his subordinate's opinion, recorded in his memoirs that before the proclamation, the Command considered long and earnestly whether it was desirable to start at once with action rather than with explanations. 'Some of my colleagues felt that both external and internal reasons dictated that we start with a military attack and not with a political declaration ... They do not respect words unless those are backed by action.'[26]

Lankin and the Irgun were convinced that unconditional Jewish co-operation with the British would not alter the British attitude towards the fate of Jews in Europe or the issue of immigration to Palestine. Furthermore, such co-operation, he claimed, would convince world opinion that the relationship between the government and the Yishuv was totally harmonious. The IZL maintained that the British themselves did not wait for the final conclusion of the war, in the sense that they 'continued to oppress the Zionist Community of Palestine'. Lankin summarised: 'Begin was the first to declare a revolt against the British regime as a foreign ruler who illegally controlled the Land of Israel which belonged to the Hebrew people. It was the first time that the IZL set itself one and only one goal: to fight against what we called the government of oppression and to establish an independent Jewish state.'[27]

Yelin Mor, himself a bitter rival of the Irgun, being one of the FFI commanders, agreed that 'the proclamation was important' because it indicated that IZL had abandoned its old way. But he considered that the term 'revolt' showed unfounded arrogance and contradicted the facts.[28] 'When they published it our men were already buried in the cemetery of Tel Aviv. Hundreds were arrested and many others were walking armed in the streets. It would have been better to call it an acknowledgement of guilt and a desire to repent.'

Under a new High Command, the Irgun recognised the fact that the British were still involved in their war against the Germans, despite the Jewish Agency's claim that 'Begin ignored the Anti Nazi struggle'.[29] Therefore, the insurgents made it clear that they would not strike against any military targets which could have assisted the government's war effort. They kept announcing that they declined to attack such targets, not because they 'felt pity for the English' but because 'we do not wish to damage their military strength.'[30] Samuel Katz, the command member in charge of propaganda, said: 'As long as Britain fights Hitler, the attacks will be executed only against its civilian administration, not against its army.'[31] This statement was made by the Irgun in order to strengthen their public image, but at the same time it reflected the underground's limited options due to its military weakness. The Irgun was aware of the possibility of being considered by public opinion as a potential saboteur of the war effort. It also had to combat the notion that it would have been feasible to fight the British without jeopardising the security of the Yishuv.[32]

Begin, mindful of such prospects, placed a great deal of importance on the political aspect of the struggle. 'Political explanations, clear and persistent, would have to accompany the military operations', he wrote.[33] Thus was born and published the 'revolt' proclamation.

## THE ARAB FACTOR

In his revolt proclamation Begin portrayed the Arabs in Iraq, Syria, Egypt and Palestine as Hitler's allies, as opposed to the Jews who 'remained loyal to the British'. However, by conducting guerrilla warfare against the British only, the IZL excluded the Arabs from its targets. The Arab community was marginalised and almost caused no concern.[34] The Arabs were ignored not only because the Irgun was not strong enough to fight two enemies, but also because it genuinely believed that at some point it could win Arab sympathy for the struggle. This assumption proved to be naive and ill-founded. This hope was clearly expressed by the Irgun pamphlets to the Arabs, telling them that under Jewish rule they would enjoy equality, freedom and prosperity. Indeed, when a Jewish driver was murdered by Arabs in Haifa, Begin, in spite of the pressure against him from his colleagues, refused to retaliate, claiming that 'the authorities would be content to see such tension because they could then claim to be acting as peace keepers'.[35] He maintained that the authorities wanted to shift the Jews into a conflict with the Arabs. 'We should not be dragged into this provocation', he added.[36]

Begin did not regard the Arabs as an independent factor in Palestine and always thought of them as an instrument used by the British against the Jewish community.[37] He also put forward the bizarre idea of the 1936 Arab rebellion as having been invented deliberately by Britain in order to provide an excuse for limiting Jewish immigration.[38]

By avoiding conflicts with the Arabs, Begin claimed that he was 'securing the flank' of the Yishuv. He explained the point to the Irgun district commanders by telling them that the anti-British armed campaign prevented the Arabs from attacking the community. He based his assessments on admissions made by Zionist officials, the widespread feelings of the masses and intelligence reports from Arab circles themselves. 'They have been struck by fear from the Hebrew weapon and would not dare turning it against them', he told his subordinates. 'We proved to them that we are not dealing in a war between Jews and Arabs but between Jews and the regime ...'.[39] Begin's assessment of the Arab issue was not shared by the Hagana, his main Jewish adversary. In a meeting with one of the latter's leaders, Moshe Sneh, in October 1944 he was told that although the operations could have deterred the Arabs, they could also prompt the Arabs to revolt.[40] Begin, in return, criticised the Zionist leadership and accused it of committing 'a fatal mistake in the last 25 years' by adopting the line that the quarrel in Palestine was between the Jews and the Arabs while the British were the decisive judges. 'It is a lie', he told Sneh, 'a lie that the English imposed on us. We resist it, we say it to the Arabs ... and we prove it in deeds, not only by words, by showing that the conflict is between us and the English. The Arabs are not our enemies.'[41] Barely two weeks later, the Hagana accused the Irgun of plotting to annihilate vast sections of the Arab community in Palestine during the Second World War. Yisrael Galili, one of its leaders, branded the Irgun as 'fascist' and told a group of Palmach commanders that in the past some of the IZL representatives had forwarded a plan to liquidate ten per cent of the Arab population while the battle of El Alamein was being fought.[42] However, there is no means of confirming that such a plan had ever been devised by the Irgun. Galili's remarks, therefore, should be seen as part of the venomous war of words which engulfed the Yishuv during that period. Regardless of the Irgun–Hagana rift the Arabs had already shown signs of division, military weakness and heavy reliance on the British in 1944.

The first Irgun operations had emphasised this state of affairs. Begin concluded: 'The first aim was achieved in the early stages of the revolt: we succeeded in nullifying the local Arab factor.'[43]

## THE NEW COMMANDER

But besides the argument on the Irgun's chances of conducting an effective rebellion, Menachem Begin, the new commander, had to overcome two difficulties. The first was the resistance of the Revisionist Party to the plan of fighting the British. The leadership of the party expressed such strong opposition to the move that the High Command had to hide its first activities from the rank and file.[44] Above all, the IZL wished to disassociate itself once and for all from the invariable restrictions imposed on them by the Revisionists who wanted to preserve their legitimate status. Begin himself was heavily influenced by Jabotinsky (the leader and founder of the party) although he had died four years before the 'revolt' and he recognised the need to pass on his message to the whole community. He therefore decided to free the Irgun from its political affiliation and to emphasise its independence. The second obstacle was Begin himself. His appointment to lead the underground movement caused resistance among the veteran Irgun members. He was unknown to most of them, he had not previously been an IZL man, he lacked military experience and was ignorant of guerrilla warfare. His reputation came as the person who had headed Betar (the youth movement founded in 1924 by Jabotinsky) in Poland until the outbreak of the war. The argument against him was that it was inconceivable that a stranger could win the faith of the top commanders.

They wanted somebody who had grown up in Palestine. But, as Meridor, the driving force behind Begin's appointment, pointed out, Begin was the 'natural choice'. This reflected one of the Irgun's weaknesses – the inability to find the most suitable man for the task within its ranks. While the traditional Irgun members had considerable talent, Begin emerged as the only individual in the movement with both leadership qualities and a consistent set of policies for organising hostilities against the British. He, therefore, reinforced the view that revolt was the right option, and thereby helped to save the Irgun from stagnation. This is not to say that the organisation did not have capable people at its disposal. On the contrary,

But it was desperate to absorb somebody who, in addition to his leadership qualities, could be the man to guide the Irgun into a new path which might save it from stagnation. Being an outsider proved in the end to work in Begin's favour since he provided a refreshing perspective and original ideas and was determined to embark on an armed campaign, while averting a possible power struggle at the top of the organisation.

Begin's choice was also made possible due to pressure put on the Irgun in Palestine by its activists abroad, notably in America, where the Irgun was launching an aggressive propaganda campaign. Begin reached Palestine in April 1942. Before that, as we have already noted, he had served as a soldier in the Polish army headed by General Anders. He spent a year in a Soviet prison, charged with Zionist activities, and was released after the Russian–Polish agreement on the establishment of a Polish army in the Soviet Union. Although he did not belong to the IZL, his militant views with regard to the continuation of the British mandate, were well known while he was still in Poland. He was kept informed about the situation in Palestine, and knew about the plans of 'Fighting Nation' to kidnap the High Commissioner. He was regarded by the Revisionists as an activist who shared the opinions of Avraham Stern. After his arrival in Palestine his extreme anti-British opinions had an increasing impact on the IZL leadership. After his release from the Polish Army, Meridor nominated him his successor as Irgun commander. Those who favoured his candidacy also knew of him as the main challenger to Jabotinsky, the Revisionist leader who opposed the idea of an armed struggle. But as Meridor indicated, 'both the moderates and the activists in the Irgun believed that a new man would change matters in their favour. Eventually, he disappointed those who hoped that he would preserve the integrity of the Revisionist Party...'[45] The author Arthur Koestler, one of the Irgun's most enthusiastic supporters at that time, described him as 'an exceptionally gifted organiser and propagandist who succeeded in resurrecting the Irgun within a few months.'[46]

## FIRST ACTIVITIES

Aware of the progress of the war, the American intervention and the defeat of General Rommel in North Africa, Begin had to act swiftly in order to make clear that in going underground, the IZL was about to adopt a new policy. Expectations pinned on him were high. He was facing growing impatience among the Irgun members who, feeling frustrated with 'incompetence' and the policy of 'self restraint', wanted to take the law into their own hands by acting against the government. In one case, on 11 January 1945, some of the Irgun members launched an attack on the British transport company of 'Still Brothers' without the permission of the High Command. The small-scale defection to the ranks of the Sterns worried Begin a great deal. It is therefore not surprising that he planned the first operations against the British administration a short time after taking command.

Begin restructured the IZL into an organisation that fitted with his concept of modern underground warfare. The country was divided into districts, each under the responsibility of a senior officer. The men were distributed into assault units, propaganda, recruitment teams and others. He then proposed a series of spectacular underground operations which were designed to humiliate the authorities and force them to resort to repressive measures, which would antagonise the Yishuv, thereby strengthening the IZL.

However, his immediate task was to save the Irgun from total disintegration. The public was informed about the 'revolt' by pamphlets, posters and illegal broadcasts. The Irgun insisted that at the time of the proclamation it had almost 1000 members at its disposal. This may not have been the case, since many of them were still serving in the British Army and others deserted out of protest. Begin had 600 Irgunists, but with his weapons he could not arm more than 200 men. The 600 might have included sympathisers in the Revisionist Party, though in January 1944 the Irgun had broken all formal connections with its leadership. In fact, the Irgun never had more than a few dozen members on full-time service, as will be explained in a later chapter. At times it had less than 20 small units and never more than 30 or 40. These were the hard core of the IZL strength. They were assisted by part-time members who took part in ad hoc activities.[47] But, because of the small size of the urban areas in which action took place, they did not need many more activists. Meridor explained: 'It was enough to start with small operations and continue with big ones to convince everybody of our serious intentions.'[48]

On 12 February 1944, the IZL simultaneously attacked the immigration offices of Jerusalem, Jaffa and Haifa and inflicted heavy damage to the buildings. The message of the insurgents was clear: to hit civilian institutions which were held responsible for the 'White Paper' policy. Begin said afterwards: ' We decided that we would not tolerate an office which kept Jews out of Palestine at the time when our brothers were being dragged to death in Europe ...'.[49] On 26 February, a similar triple attack took place against the income tax authorities, 'the main instrument to exploit the Hebrew workers and civilians by the government of betrayal'.[50] This was consistent with one of Begin's warnings in his proclamation: 'We shall not pay taxes to a government that did such things', referring to the blockade of the seashore for Jewish refugees. By using such slogans, the IZL addressed itself not only to the Jewish workers but also to the left wing of the community in order to win the widest support amongst its opponents.

On 23 March, the Irgunists launched another attack in the three main cities, against the headquarters of the Central Intelligence Department (CID). The attack coincided with more news about the horrific scale of the destruction of European Jewry. The Irgun made an immediate link between the struggle in Palestine and the mass extermination. In a pamphlet published soon after the first attack to cause British casualties, the IZL declared: 'We are the brothers of the destroyed Jews in Munich, Berlin, Paris, Bucharest and Budapest. We came to the Land of Israel not to save ourselves, but to save our tortured brothers. We will not give up and with our bodies we will break open the locked gates ...'[51]

Although the IZL made attempts to avoid casualties, the 'National Committee', the official representative of the Jewish establishment, reacted bitterly, perhaps more so than the British. It denounced the insurgents as a 'gang of lunatics who do not refrain from the most disgraceful crimes'.[52] Chaim Weizmann, the President of the World Zionist Congress, expressed shock and anger. The message from the Hagana was similar and was not without a display of contempt: 'They have 'commanders', they have 'pistols', even bombs and they 'make operations'. Then they bill posters with noisy announcements on the walls which tell us about heroism of units and daring clashes ... They have a war with HMG ... but in that war innocent blood is spilt ... not only of policemen, but also of Arabs and Jews. They do not have either national responsibility and political logic, or a simple moral sense'.[53] The operations were condemned by all moderate sections of the Jewish Community.

The 1944 revolt undermined the political plan of the Jewish Agency which reacted forcefully against IZL tactics. The Hagana (under the guidance of Ben Gurion, chairman of the political department of the Jewish Agency) was used later as an internal security force in the struggle against terrorism. Neither of its rivals could compete with the Hagana in military terms, but the 'dissidents' (the nickname given to IZL and FFI by the Jewish Agency) challenged the authority of the Yishuv leaders and by their very existence undermined the status of the leadership as the sole representatives of Palestine Jewry. They also raised the idea that the Irgun would take over the community by force and blackmail, although they expressed the hope that 'nothing could harm our relations with the authorities'.[54] The Stern Group regarded the IZL revolt as a 'war' which was aimed at domestic consumption. Yelin Mor welcomed the first attack on the immigration authorities, but expressed 'concern' about the manner adopted by the insurgents to warn the British. As Koestler wrote: 'The Irgun continued to give warning before each operation so that, as far as can be ascertained from press reports, the number of British police killed did not exceed two.'[55]

But Yelin Mor was not impressed by those precautions. 'We regarded it as a nicety incompatible with a struggle against a foreign regime.... They looked at it as a demonstration, not as a war...'[56] Later he wrote in *Hahazit* (the Front), the organ of the FFI: 'It might be that HMG is interested in those harmless activities which enabled the Jewish youth to unload its anger ...'. He called the revolt: 'Opportunism disguised as heroism ...'.[57]

Such attacks did indeed reflect a compromise between Begin, the activist, and the other members of the High Command. The latter were worried about the impact the first acts could have had on the Yishuv. Begin, to appease his colleagues, and to distinguish the IZL from the Sterns, adopted a strategy designed to minimise British casualties.

The most surprising reaction was that of the British themselves. They played down the importance of the attacks and dismissed them as transitory. This was reflected by the Commonwealth Minister who, speaking in Parliament, distinguished between the Stern and the IZL, saying that the latter preferred to attack 'inanimate holes' and not soldiers and policemen.[58] He also said that those who saw the revolt proclamation posted on the walls, greeted it with boredom or indifference. Constable T Wilkin, one of the most effective CID men in Palestine (later assassinated by the Stern Group), told his superiors that 'there is nothing to worry about'.[59] The attacks on the empty British offices at night proved that in the short term Wilkin was right. The attack on the CID Headquarters was ambitious 'so much so that anyone hearing about it in advance would burst out laughing at the sheer impudence of the thought'.[60] The CID bombing resulted in some British and Irgun casualties caused by the insurgents' mistakes. 'Bombs in empty government offices were one thing, but dead policemen and shoot-outs were quite another, a rebellion did exist', wrote one of the IZL officers. The general immediate reaction was that the Irgun (as well as the Stern) just carried out a few symbolic strikes for political purposes.[61] Meridor admitted that 'at the beginning, the operations were modest and pretentious. People sneered at us and said: "Look, they declare a revolt, but they bomb a window of the income tax building on a Sunday." But these were the beginnings of serious action.'[62]

To sum up, the British committed their first error of judgement in not taking the threat behind the first harmless operations seriously. This attitude frustrated the IZL even more. The Irgunists, delighted by what they regarded as 'a successful start', were determined to demonstrate their skills and terrorist methods on a far larger scale. The High Command, at that time, had no long-term strategy, and only the first few operations had been planned. In the words of Meridor 'we knew that the following step would be to strike against soldiers and police bases. But we could not foresee the developments; how many would be arrested, how many would get killed. What we knew was that the British would be unable to cope with it, especially when American pressure would come.'

However, despite the outcry of the legitimate Jewish leadership, the insurgents started to win some support in other sections of the community. The insurgents, accompanying their acts with a similarly aggressive propaganda campaign, made a strong impression on the youth. In a few months they almost doubled their membership and increased it to over 800 men.[63] Some of them joined the Underground from circles outside the Revisionists and many of them were of oriental origin. This was described by the British as a most dangerous development because of 'the increase in numbers of young Jewish men and women being infected with the gangster virus. They are providing recruits for the terrorist organisation.'[64] The comment was mainly related to the Stern Group after their abortive attempt to assassinate the High Commissioner of Palestine on 8 August 1944.

This concern was not shared by the decision makers in London who dismissed these acts as sheer 'gangsterism'. In fact, one cannot blame the British for being indifferent. During 1944 there were only a few significant acts against the authorities. After the combined attacks on the immigration offices, the income tax and the CID Headquarters during February and March, the IZL ceased to operate until May of the same year. On 17 May 1944, the Irgunists invaded the government broadcasting station in Ramallah to mark the anniversary of the 'White Paper'. Two months later they launched another attack on the intelligence centre in Jerusalem. On 14 July the Land Registry Office in Jerusalem was gutted and two Arab constables were killed. On 18 July, the High Commissioner MacMichael reported to London: 'Available information indicates that the security position may have deteriorated and the outlook is not encouraging.'[65] On 29 September four police stations were attacked and some arms were seized. After that attack the Irgun issued the following statement: '... In all these attacks the principle of face-to-face engagement has been followed. We have taken all precautions in order not to hit the civilian population, whether Jewish or alien ... therefore, we will demand *de facto* and *de jure* the recognition of our rights as an underground army. For this recognition we will fight by all the means at our disposal.[66]

From the time the revolt was proclaimed in February 1944 until the beginning of the following year, the Irgun carried out eight major attacks against the governmental civilian infrastructure. The Irgunists (as well as the Sterns) recognised the undoubted fact that it was impossible for them to win a military victory over the British forces. What they set out to do was to provoke controversy in London and throughout the world generally and to force the British to commit an increasing degree of their resources to the campaign.[67] However, these operations failed to produce the required impact and achieve their goals. The major difficulty which the Irgun faced at this time was the small size of its fighting force. In 1944 an ultra-secret combat division was formed and produced problems within the ranks. In reality, during that year, the Irgun had only two combat units, that of the front-line fighters (called *Hak*) and another one composed of members assigned to other duties, who seldom engaged in military operations.[68] The weakness of the IZL was reflected in a meeting of the Command which took place in Tel Aviv on 6 August 1944, five months after the rebellion had started. During the meeting Begin was confronted with head-on criticism as to the way the Irgun was organised and the members trained. Officers complained about the lack of communication between the various units, administrative inefficiency, shortage of means of propaganda and, above all, the small number of its members.[69]

On 17 August 1945, a week after the Stern Group failed to assassinate the High Commissioner MacMichael, four of the IZL top commanders met to discuss their plans for the future. Begin admitted that 'no real progress had been made', and that it was time to decide whether to confront the British directly or not. He urged his friends to escalate the campaign. But, as was the case before the proclamation of the revolt, the other three members (Levy, Lankin and Livni) felt that the moment was not appropriate for a new wave of action since 'our men are not qualified for such a serious clash' and that 'we do not know if they would be able to cope with the challenge without pre-training'.[70] But Begin was eager to demonstrate the Irgun's strength by making a demonstrative operation to maximise public impact. He brought up the idea of taking over the Wailing Wall, where restrictions were imposed by the Government on Jewish prayers including the prohibition to blow the traditional Shofar on Yom Kippur (the Day of Atonement). Begin suggested that the insurgents should declare in advance their intentions of keeping British forces away from the Wailing Wall area so that those who wished to pray would be able to conduct their service without outside interference. The main object of such a show of strength on Yom Kippur was to win respect, support and popularity among the Jewish community.

Again, Begin's colleagues were sceptical and cautious. One of them expressed the view that giving such a warning to the authorities would render the whole action unsuccessful and the general impression would be of another failure on the Irgun's part. Besides, he claimed, the guerrillas were not yet prepared for this sort of action and it would be better to devote efforts and energy to recruiting new people and raising money. 'Many of the commanders have been arrested, many others have left and not come back yet, and we are in urgent need of replacements for them.' Begin was also told that the Irgun should declare a cease-fire in order to give a chance to the new Labour Government which had just taken over in London.

Begin's critics regarded the political development in Britain as a golden opportunity which provided the Irgun with a transition period during which it would be able to regroup itself.[71] As expected, Begin, afraid that his revolt would lose momentum, disagreed with the views expressed by his subordinates and vehemently insisted on executing the mission at the Wailing Wall. He believed that a warning would force the Government to come to terms with the underground. He totally rejected the idea of declaring a truce, mainly on the grounds that no relief could be expected for the Jews in Palestine as a result of the elections in Britain. 'The oppression is at its peak and no break would be justified', he told the Command members. The latter, although agreed 'in principle', appeared to cast many doubts on Begin's judgement, but the powerful commander, as on previous occasions, exercised his power and the mission went ahead.

On 27 September 1944 posters plastered all over Jerusalem announced that anyone who interfered with the service at the Wall would be treated as a criminal and punished. The British kept away from the scene, and they did not react, as had been feared, with any drastic action.[72] The IZL's mission was a complete success, in spite of the Jewish Agency's denunciations. The success was all the greater since the High Command did not have any intention of opening fire on anyone in the midst of the Jewish crowd on its holiest day of the year.

However, the IZL simultaneously carried out a series of attacks on four police fortresses to coincide with the Day of Atonement. The British were not prepared for operations elsewhere than Jerusalem, and more important, if they had interfered by banning the blowing of the Shofar, such an action would have been regarded by the Irgun as a retaliation. At night the British kept away from the wall and the Irgun attacked the Tegart forts. The attacks took place in Haifa, Bet Dagan, Karta and Qalqiliya. The British reacted with surprise to the deterioration of the situation in Palestine. The Cabinet pointed out that 'the attack on the High Commissioner is serious enough, but 150 men in four simultaneous assaults ...', was too much.[73] Begin had won the day and his struggle within the Command. Psychologically, it was a disaster for the British and a significant victory for the Irgun. In Jerusalem, the British were plainly driven into a humiliating withdrawal. Yom Kippur proved that the British could be challenged successfully. More important, the security forces, for whatever reasons, did not seek revenge.[74] All the doubts within the IZL and the professed fears of the Jewish Agency had proven groundless.

This mission showed that in spite of the confusion and the disarray, the Irgun was still capable of saving face by taking effective action. After all, 'most of them were professionally qualified and many had advanced technical expertise in engineering, weaponry and explosives. This underground army certainly had skills comparable to the best European partisan organisations of the Second World War; it was well within their capability to build lengthy underground tunnels, dislocate rail systems, mine roads and engage in infiltration and espionage.'[75]

The Wailing Wall incident made the Zionist establishment worried about the possible outcome of these operations in the Yishuv. The Jewish Agency feared Irgun influence on the Hagana after it was found that many members in its ranks had tried to give vent to their feelings through acts similar to those of the Irgunists, even though they disagreed with their overall ideology. The British administration was less concerned, yet the military authorities admitted that the terrorist campaign was increasing, 'culminating in the unsuccessful attempt to assassinate the King's representative, large scale attacks on police stations, and the brutal murder of a police officer on the streets of Jerusalem ...'[76] The killing referred to the assassination by the FFI on 29 September 1944 of Constable Wilkin, who had been on the terrorists' list for a long time. Following this incident, Colonel Catling, one of the key administrators, commented that it showed that the British did not take the terrorist threat seriously enough in 1944. In fact, the British expressed more shock and dismay at the Stern's operations which advocated terrorism against individuals, than those of the IZL, which aimed at hitting government targets.

The British attitude towards the insurgents was much hardened after the killing of Lord Moyne. He was the British minister for the Middle East who resided in Cairo and was assassinated by two of the Stern Group on 6 November 1944. The assassins were hanged after a short trial and the Irgun vehemently condemned the action. The FFI had proved that its terrorist campaign could bring about enormous publicity to the insurgents, despite the fact that some of its actions were counter-productive. But the Government did not make the distinction for a long time between the final aim of the two groups and their methods of attacks. Their aims, according to a military intelligence report, were jointly based upon 'the inherent desire of the majority of the Jews to see maximalist aims achieved. That is to say, a Jewish State covering Palestine and ultimately Trans-Jordan'.[77] The outcome of the Wailing Wall operation made Begin jubilant, but even before that, in his briefing to his colleagues on 23 July 1944, he expressed satisfaction at 'six months of war which created a strong echo and prompted the media world-wide to write about us'.[78] But even the public prestige that the Irgun won did not save Begin from criticism within his own headquarters. It has been spelled out by Lankin, who at the end of September complained that despite the growing sympathy that the group had acquired in Jerusalem on Yom Kippur, and the attacks on the four police stations, the Irgun was a paralysed organisation which suffered many structural deficiencies. In his opinion the Irgun's over-emphasis on military efforts made it neglect its infrastructure.[79] Begin, in his reply, summed up his motives for starting the violent campaign against the Mandate. He told the commanders that the Irgun was faced with two alternatives: either to start establishing itself within the Jewish community as an organisation in time of financial and leadership crisis, or to begin a rebellion without taking into account the domestic conditions. He said: 'We have chosen the golden path: we have started the war while our structural reorganisation is not yet completed. If we look back, we would conclude that we have no reason to regret it.'[80]

At that meeting, he therefore, embraced all the suggestions put to him by his subordinates about the required organisational arrangements, but ruled out the possibility of ceasing hostilities without political reasons . In fact, at another meeting with his district commanders two weeks later, he was proud to use quotations from the British press as an indicator of the deep concern with which the authorities viewed the situation in Palestine. *The Times* warned of anarchy, the *New Statesman* called for an 'immediate solution' and *The Economist*, admitted that Jewish terrorism had begun to bear fruits. Begin was also certain that the declaration made by the American War Minister to allow unlimited Jewish immigration to Palestine was as a direct result of the Irgun's activities.[81] At the beginning of his campaign, Begin trusted the Irgun's ability to win the support of the majority of the Jewish youth in the country. But the Irgunists did not delude themselves over their capability to deploy a vast resistance organisation.

They managed though to achieve it for six months in 1945, when they agreed with the Hagana and FFI on joint operations and close military co-ordination among them. But they badly needed the support or at least the tolerance of the Yishuv. The Irgun hoped that by responding to its activities, the British would react strongly, even brutally, and thus aggravate the Jewish community to the point of making it more willing to back the guerrillas. Paradoxically, the Irgun's inability to win over the majority of the community to its policy, made its existence possible. The assessment was shared by the Hagana and the Jewish Agency that without their controlling power and the responsible role they played the British would not hesitate to destroy the Yishuv. This was partially the case since HMG had other obligations deriving from the new situation facing the Empire after the war. But it is fair to say that the Agency's dominance of the Yishuv protected the community from serious harm. The British strategy was to isolate the insurgents from the rest of the population, with the help of the Jewish establishment. However, even some of the Yishuv's moderate leaders were willing to use force against the anti-Zionist policy of the British. These developments created the background against which the British-Yishuv-Irgun triangle faced its most crucial and violent years in Palestine.

CHAPTER 3

# The Irgun and the Jewish Community

The political views of the Irgun, its ideology and activities in Palestine, could not be viewed in isolation from other forces in the Jewish Community. Since its birth, at the beginning of the 1930s, until its dismantling in 1948, the evolution of the organisation was closely connected with the attitude of the official recognised leadership of the Yishuv – the National Committee, the Jewish Agency, the Trade Union Federation and their military arm, the Hagana.

## THE RELATIONSHIP DURING THE SECOND WORLD WAR

Co-operation, but mostly confrontation, characterised the relationship between the two sides during the years of the Irgun's armed revolt against the British authorities. Hence, it is most important to examine the complex relationship between the separatists and the majority of the Yishuv, since it was also a conflict between two different ideological concepts which tried to win the hearts and the minds of the Jewish Community in Palestine.

The Irgun's decision to side with the British during the war cost it dearly. The radical group, led by Avraham Stern, a member of the High Command, broke away and formed the 'Freedom Fighters for Israel' (FFI). The split also reflected the debate within the organisation with respect to the domination of the Revisionist Party. While the commander, David Raziel, supported the continuing attachment to the party, the Sternists argued that the military body should remain independent and reserve the right to go its own way. The Irgun was also outraged by the decision of the Sterns to harass the British even during the war. While continuing to retaliate against Arabs, IZL members were careful to refrain from shooting British policemen and soldiers.[1] The Jewish leadership, which began defying the British by intensifying illegal immigration efforts, faced a moral dilemma when Britain declared war against Germany. Ben Gurion, head of the Jewish Agency, explained the Yishuv's position by spelling out his famous phrase: 'We would fight Hitler with Britain as if there is no White Paper[2], and we will fight the White Paper as if there is no war.' His attention was mainly focused on the number of Jewish immigrants allowed to enter – 50,000 people until 31 March 1944. But the extent of the dilemma was even graver when it was learned that even during the first ten months of the war, the British Navy continued to stop illegal immigrants off the Palestine shore, either sending them back to the sea or imprisoning them in special detention camps.

The British also insisted that the Hagana should hand in all its weapons and they were adamant that no purchases of Arab land should be allowed in any part of the country. When the authorities and the Hagana were on the verge of confronting each other on the issue of disarmament, Italy joined the war on 10 June 1940 and the Government abandoned its plans. The British wanted to avoid a situation in which they would have to deploy numerous forces in Palestine in the event of possible Jewish riots. They also feared hostile reaction in the United States.

Accordingly, the British released many of the Hagana members who had been arrested for organising illegal immigration, military training and reprisals against the Arabs. Yet, Jewish immigrants from war-torn Europe continued to be stopped and sent back, thus creating a series of human tragedies which later shaped the Yishuv's resistance to the continuing British Mandate. At that time, while Rommel's forces were advancing in North Africa towards Palestine, many of the Hagana units joined the British Army, while the Irgun put its intelligence service at the disposal of the authorities. When the danger was over, in summer 1942, both camps started to prepare for the struggle to come.

## THE RELATIONSHIP DURING THE REVOLT

The Irgun had, in fact, ceased to exist as an important and independent body since the start of the War. Because it was passive and hesitant, the Irgun lost many of its members to the Stern Group and to the Hagana. Its reluctant co-operation with the British, deprived them of the reason for their separate existence. Without money, arms or sufficient manpower they resorted to bank robberies, which caused uproar and dismay in the Yishuv.

When the IZL's High Command realised the horrific extent of the Holocaust in Europe and after its request to establish intelligence units within the army was rejected, it disassociated itself from the British. On 27 May 1943, the Command informed its members about the resumption of the war, because of the White Paper policy. However, the Irgun's move was confined to rhetoric.

Only after the Irgun started in its campaign against the Mandate, did the organised Yishuv become increasingly concerned about its implications. The military activities of the dissidents (including the Sterns), were regarded as posing a double threat: they could provoke the Government to take repressive measures and they could endanger the hegemony of the Socialist camp within the Jewish Community. Whatever the Jewish Agency could have done to reduce the threat, it risked the possibility of encountering resistance. Its leaders assumed that extradition would have caused civil war and isolation would win the insurgents some sympathy, but they ruled out co-operation with them.[3]

The only way to avoid a total confrontation was to influence the dissidents. Since the Revisionist Party was no longer in control of the organisation, the Jewish Agency and the Hagana held secret meetings with Begin, the first of which took place on 8 October 1944. The man who met him was Moshe Sneh, the second most important figure in the Yishuv's leadership after Ben Gurion. Begin drew a line between the British Administration in Palestine and the British Government in London. His struggle, he told Sneh, was not against the British nation but against the oppressive regime in Palestine. 'England is not our enemy', he told him. Sneh, during this fascinating encounter, accused Begin of conducting a terrorist campaign without any knowledge of the political consequences. He argued that the recent waves of attacks against Government institutions jeopardised the future of immigration and insisted that even reprisals against Arabs could be counterproductive. 'You also make the English get used to crushing Jewish resistance' ..., he said.[4] He also warned him that the Irgun's eventual attempt to win support and control in the Yishuv would lead to an inevitable clash with the mainstream of the Community. Begin explained the Irgun strategy behind its 'revolt'. He said that simultaneous attacks on the three CID centres in the country, for example, were powerful enough to shake British prestige, and made the necessary impression on the Arabs.

Begin was convinced that if such activities persisted, the British would be forced to negotiate with the insurgents. He added that armed struggle would enhance Jewish importance in America, which had an increasing interest in the Middle East.[5] He also made another interesting point. Attacking the British would demonstrate to everybody, in particular the Arabs, that the Jews had a quarrel with the British. 'The Arabs are not our enemies', he told Sneh. That would signal to the Arabs that Jews were merely interested in ridding themselves of the 'foreign' regime and desired peace with them. Begin also said that the Irgun's campaign had built up national aspirations and a fighting spirit amongst the young and prepared them for the struggle to come.

He admitted that the Irgun operations did not take account of political considerations, but, surprisingly, put it down to the fact that the organisation did not want to be a political power in the Yishuv. 'The Irgun has no political aspiration', he told Sneh, and, to his amusement, he added that 'after the death of Jabotinsky (in summer 1940) the Irgun concluded that the only man who could lead the political war of Zionism is Ben Gurion'.[6] At the end of that conversation, the Hagana representative demanded obedience to the central authority, or at least a temporary halt in the campaign. Begin rejected both ideas and warned that the Irgun would not sit idle if the Hagana and the Agency took up arms against it. 'The conclusion', wrote Sneh in his report, 'is that they want to impose their way on everybody'.

Three weeks later, on 31 October 1944, another meeting took place between the Jewish Agency and the Irgun. Representing the former were Eliyahu Golomb, commander of the Hagana, and again Sneh. Begin and Lankin, a member of the Central Command represented the IZL. Golomb, who opened the discussion, assured the opposite side that the Hagana would never allow anybody to disarm them. However, calling for 'national discipline', he argued that terrorism could do immense harm to the Jewish Community. He said that most of the British failed to make a distinction between Hagana and the 'dissidents' and believed that the Jews divided the roles between moderates and radicals in order to achieve their final goals. Golomb, a pragmatist, did not express his entire objection to violent means, but he criticised the timing. 'You have restored a spirit of pride in the youth' he told Begin, 'but the damage is far greater ...'.[7]

He accused the Irgun of imposing its terrorist methods on the Yishuv. He said that its 'blackmail threats' created fear in the community because 'people are submitted to intimidation of all kinds'. He pointed out that the Irgun had caused the war against Hitler to be forgotten, simply because the organisation did not differentiate between the Germans and the British. 'We depend on the English and only with their help would we be able to fulfil our aims', he declared. He demanded that all forms of terrorism be stopped immediately.

Golomb's summing up was not without a challenging tone. He expressed reluctance to engage in civil war, but did not hesitate to warn that the Hagana would not refrain from threatening the Irgun since 'we would have to take all steps in order to stop your activities ... this might bring you destruction ... we would have to stop you, whatever the cost might be'. Golomb's words reflected recognition of the potential strength of the Irgun which, despite the slow start of its revolt, had captured the imagination of much of the Jewish youth. Sneh, who joined the conversation, reminded Begin that he and his colleagues represented the majority of the Yishuv. He urged him to accept the discipline of the Jewish Agency although he approved the Irgun's separate entity.[8]

However, Begin did not bow to the pressure. He refused to be bullied. 'You threatened me with destruction' he told them. Talking about the extermination of the Jews in Europe, he catalogued British actions against refugees who wanted to reach Palestine's shores. Britain, he said, ignored minimal Jewish interests. The Yishuv, on the other hand, had been restrained and obedient, but to no avail. He expressed amazement that the Jewish Agency, even at that stage, was willing to give the British another chance to prove their sympathy to the Jewish cause. Begin told them that the Irgun campaign had hit the headlines in many countries and that the British press demanded a solution to the Palestine problem. In short, he surprised his listeners. 'You could exploit our operations to increase your pressure on the Government, certainly while expressing reservations about them', he said. 'We think that your duty would have been to invent us, had we not existed ...'. Begin and Lankin refused at the end of the five hour meeting to accept the Jewish Agency's control, and rejected suggestions that the Irgun should declare a temporary cease-fire. Begin himself summed up the meeting in a document which he wrote after it ended.

In particular, he recorded two points : first was Golomb's conviction that the Labour Party would win the general election in Britain and would make a radical shift in its attitude towards Palestine. The second point which struck Begin occurred when the four men were about to depart. Begin and Lankin told their counterparts from the Hagana that there was no justification for the Hagana to 'enter' between the Irgun and the British. But Golomb said: 'We will enter ...', hinting that he would not be deterred by the prospect of a war against the dissidents.[9] These contacts revealed that despite the growing hostility between the two camps and the fact that the Irgun 'went underground', lines of communication were open. It also exposed Begin as a pragmatic leader who did not delude himself that the Irgun alone would be able to overcome the British.

Begin criticised the Hagana for not being able to take practical advantage of the fact that a militant element in the Yishuv had resorted to armed struggle in order to accelerate the process of Jewish independence. He repeated his wish to see Ben Gurion as the leader of the struggle. Without playing down the importance of immigration and settlements, he regarded the 'revolt' as an attempt to fill a long neglected vacuum which could have complemented the other tasks that the Hagana was fulfilling. However, Begin did not realise that, while previously the Hagana had tried to destroy the insurgents independently, now it would do so in close collaboration with British intelligence ...

## THE SAISON

The blatant political irresponsibility of Begin's response to their approach, finally drove the leaders of the organised Yishuv to declare what amounted to open war on the Irgun. Beginning in November 1944, this ruthless campaign, verging on civil war and involving kidnapping, deportation, imprisonment and assassination, came to be known as the *Saison* (or Hunting Season). It was a most difficult time for the Irgun, while the authorities enjoyed the Hagana's full co-operation. However, for the terrorists it was a short-lived defeat. During that period, the campaign quickly back-fired. The public at large viewed it with dismay, the spiritual leaders ruled that the campaign was against Jewish religious law and despite its early success, the *Saison* was doomed to fail. The Irgun became the underdogs and the British, for their part, failed to live up to the Jews' political expectations of them. Ironically, the catalyst to the *Saison* was not necessarily the Irgun's refusal to lay down their arms. It was the assassination of Lord Moyne.

Within the Jewish Agency there were two parties – the Zionist Religious Party and the right-of-centre 'General Zionists' – who were strongly opposed to any collaboration with the British. Ben Gurion, who wanted to avoid a split, reached a compromise with them by which the Hagana would gather information about the dissidents but refrain from handing them over to the government. Now the assassination changed everything. Fear of British collective punishments and the escalation of the terrorist campaign made the Agency determined to root out the insurgents. That task was taken on by the Hagana's best combat unit – the Palmach.

In a special session of the Trade Union Federation, the Histadrut, which was closely connected to the Agency and in fact controlled the Hagana, Ben Gurion outlined the new policy of the Yishuv against what they coined as the 'separatists'. These included four points:

1. To expel any supporter of 'those gangs' from their places of employment or from the school where they study.
2. To deprive them of any shelter or hiding places.
3. To resist their threats and intimidation.
4. To inform the authorities about their whereabouts.[10]

The trade union conference approved the measure, while one of its sections, the 'United Labour', called for the complete destruction of the 'Fascists'.[11] At the same time it refused to collaborate with the British for reasons of prestige and propaganda.

However, the *Saison*, which started in November 1944 and ended in

March 1945, had implemented Ben Gurion's four points. Some of the Irgun's High Command members were abducted and handed over to the British[12] and others were captured and even killed.[13] The results for the dissidents were devastating. Most of the Irgun operational capability was destroyed and many of its members were isolated by friends and neighbours.

The Zionist organisations in the Yishuv were under constant pressure to increase the scale of the collaboration. One of the leaders who advocated such a policy was Dr Chaim Weizmann, head of the Zionist Congress, the main international body of the movement, who wrote to the War Cabinet on 18 December 1944, indicating that the co-operation with the authorities in stamping out terrorism was 'proceeding satisfactorily'. He informed them in this top-secret letter that 500 names of suspects had already been supplied to the police, as a result of which over 250 had been arrested.

Weizmann, who then spent most of his time in London, believed that despite the natural difficulty in penetrating any secret organisation, a 'severe blow has been dealt to them' and that 'there is every determination to pursue the campaign until decisive results are achieved'. Weizmann condemned the Irgun without mentioning its name and assured the War Cabinet that the Yishuv had taken all the necessary measures to curb Jewish violence so that 'nothing will happen which could aggravate the situation'.[14]

Four days after sending the letter, Weizmann made his first visit to Palestine for seven years. His arrival was kept a close secret by a handful of Zionist-socialist leaders, fearing that an attempt might be made on his life by the IZL or Stern group. Weizmann was clearly shaken by Moyne's murder even four weeks after it happened.

On his arrival he used expressions like 'I was never so depressed in my life when the news came to London', or 'My heart told me that the assassination was a Jewish act ...'. To the Jewish Agency Executive he said that he was ashamed to 'look at Stanley's face', referring to the Colonial Secretary, and added that 'only a short time ago I had been demanding concessions in regard to the (Jewish) Brigade and immigration ...'. He then warned that if 'this cancer in our body is not uprooted once and for all, I shall be unable to show my face again in London'.[15]

The 'Saison' was based either on passing information to British agents or abducting Irgun members for investigation and imprisonment or by handing them over to the authorities.[16]

Lankin, who was one of the first to be kidnapped in Autumn 1944 (and subsequently deported to Africa) said that there was another form of collaboration. Hagana informers used to accompany British agents and identify the terrorists for them in the streets, the bus queues and other public places. He admitted that the Hagana had struck the Irgun very hard, by putting many of its members and commanders out of action, by discovering arms caches, printing presses, archives and meeting places. The 'Saison', in fact, paralysed the Irgun, not least because more than half of its leaders were arrested and the rest were in hiding.

Amichai Paglin, who was in charge of the Irgun's military operations, reinforced that assessment by claiming that the Hagana had confiscated 'big quantities of arms'. He also claimed that the Hagana had bungled some of the Irgun's operations 'at the last moment' by giving British intelligence vital information. He added that lack of financial resources had handicapped the Irgun's ability to function to the point of 'not renting overnight rooms for its members'. Many of them had no food to eat for some days. However, Paglin stressed that, despite the blows, the Irgun was still capable of launching attacks on the British, although not on a large scale. He said that, ironically enough, the 'Saison' had had its own positive results since the disappearance of many members made way for fresh youngsters to take their place.[17]

Meridor believed that informing was the hardest measure taken by the Hagana and the Jewish Agency against the dissidents. The informers were acting as 'detectives' and followed the Irgunists on foot and by car. 'Others intimidated their victims by breaking into their houses, taking them away during the night and in front of their families, and subjecting them to interrogations and torture'.[18] The collaboration was made simple by appointing Hagana liaison officers who were in regular touch, almost on a daily basis, with regional British police officers. Sometimes, the 'middle men' were Jewish policemen, working for the CID. Sometimes, British 'striking forces' accompanied Hagana or Palmach people in order to identify suspects and arrest them.

However, the longer the 'Saison' lasted, the more irritated the Yishuv became. The extradition policy did a lot of harm to the Hagana's prestige and with no British 'rewards' in sight, the Jewish Community became increasingly tired of the 'hunting' campaign. What helped most to end the collaboration with the British was the Irgun's policy of non-retaliation. This was Begin's most commendable move during the entire struggle of his organisation for national freedom. He was, of course, motivated by the Irgun's weakness, but he called for restraint and refused to be provoked. Begin also knew that in the case of a civil war, the Irgun would be eliminated while the main benefactors would be the British. He had to impose his will on his colleagues in the High Command. The majority resisted the non-retaliation policy, but had to bow in the end to the will of their commander.

More puzzling was the Hagana's decision to direct all its hostility towards the Irgun and not the Stern group, which was more militant and was responsible for the assassination of Lord Moyne. Yelin Mor, one of the three Stern commanders (after the killing of Stern himself on 12 February 1942), tried to explain the Hagana's policy in his memoirs. He claimed the Hagana feared violent resistance by the Sterns, while the Irgun had declared that it would not retaliate.[19] Yisrael Eldad, his colleague at the troika (the other was Yitzhak Shamir), who was at that time under arrest, wrote that the Irgunists themselves testified to him in prison that the Irgun's policy of restraint did not deter the Hagana.[20]

However, the truth of the matter was that the FFI had negotiated a deal with the Hagana in which it committed itself to stop its terrorist campaign against the British. For the Stern Group it was an exercise in winning time, which enabled the Hagana to concentrate its efforts on the Irgun. Yelin Mor himself denied the allegation, but noted that negotiation did take place. Meridor, who had been the caretaker commander of the Irgun until Begin took over and then became his deputy, confirmed the report. He said that there was an agreement between the two organisations, although not necessarily a written one. He expressed the view that the Stern group 'with its manoeuvring ability and its ambition to adapt itself to the most convenient war situation, found itself unable to act at that time. The group was thinking about the future'.[21]

The Hagana had another reason to ignore the Sterns during the *Saison*. The FFI was too small an organisation and did not pose any threat to the hegemony of the Hagana or the Jewish Agency in the community, certainly not to the extent of the Irgun. It was much easier for the Hagana to come to terms with the Stern Group, in a form of unwritten agreement, simply because the latter did not represent the extreme of the ideological spectrum of the Yishuv. The Irgun, strongly identified with the Revisionists and regarded as the military arm of the 'National Camp', was more of a danger to the Socialists' aim of preserving their political domination within the Yishuv.[22] Lankin said that the Hagana regarded the Irgun as a 'competing body behind which stood a political party'. He added that, therefore, the Irgun posed a danger to the Hagana's grip on the community. The FFI, on the other hand, was a small isolated group without political backing and it could have been ignored.[23] Eventually, although the Irgun had been crippled as a military organisation, the *Saison* had to be stopped. The non-socialist parties in the Jewish Agency could not take responsibility for what they feared might develop into a civil war. The special task force, consisting of Hagana and Palmach members, was reluctant to carry on with their arrests and kidnapping, and a growing number of youths started to sympathise with the Irgun and to support its militancy. The British, for their part, enjoyed a valuable period of relaxation, during which terrorism against them almost ceased, and did not give away much in return. They did not ease the restrictions on immigration and were not willing to modify any of the other White Paper articles. When the Second World War finally drew to its close and the scale of the Jewish tragedy became more tangible in Palestine, the leadership of the Yishuv embarked on a totally different policy – co-operation, but with the underground movements.

## THE UNITED RESISTANCE FRONT

The end of 1945 and the first half of 1946 witnessed not only an increase in guerrilla activities against the authorities, but also a united anti-British front comprised of the Hagana, the IZL and the Stern Group. The most important factor which contributed to the co-operation of the three organisations was the unfulfilled hopes which the Jewish Community pinned on the victory of the Labour Party at the British elections of 26 July 1945. The Irgun had ceased its activities during the late stages of the election campaign as part of the general anticipation within the Yishuv of a possible Socialist victory.

However, the departure of the Labour Party from what was regarded by the Yishuv as its initial commitment to the Zionist cause, as well as anti-Jewish remarks made by the new Foreign Secretary, Ernest Bevin, paved the way in October 1945 for the establishment of the National Resistance Movement, based on a joint High Command co-ordinating the anti-Government activities.

Ironically enough, the Hagana was the driving force behind that move. It was more disappointed than the other two groups by the policy of Attlee and Bevin on the question of the Jewish National Home and the restriction on immigration. Bevin's speech in Parliament on 13 November 1945 did more than any other single factor to prompt the establishment of the Resistance Movement. On the one hand, he invited the United States to participate in the Committee which was to seek a solution to the problem of the Jewish refugees in Europe. On the other, he voiced the opinion that the European Jews should not desert their countries of birth. He even called for them to re-establish themselves in Europe and argued that 'with all their brilliant talents and ability in production and science', they would be amongst the best contributors to the reconstruction of Europe.[24] Bevin criticised the Balfour Declaration and regarded it as one-sided and short-sighted in its failure to see the interests of the other community. He also indicated that the affairs of the Arabs in Palestine could not be disassociated from those of the large Muslim minority in India. While making a distinction between Jews and Zionists, Bevin remarked that 'if the Jews, with their sufferings, would push themselves to the head of the queue, anti-semitism would be the inevitable result'.[25] The speech was a blow to the leadership of the Jewish community in Palestine.

In hastily-organised debates of the Jewish Agency, the National Committee and the Workers Party (Mapay), the general mood was of defiance. Only struggle was discussed. While joint co-operation with the dissidents was not as yet considered, a general strike had been declared and outrage had been expressed by the public. In Tel Aviv, during a mass demonstration of 80,000 protesters, Government buildings were set on fire and other offices attacked. Six people were killed and many dozens wounded after the British Army opened fire on the crowd. This spontaneous violent reaction continued all week and the authorities had to impose a five-day curfew on the town. Four days later, at the Jewish Agency meeting, the violent clashes were praised by Sneh.[26] After the 'betrayal' of the British Labour Party, any show of restraint was regarded as weakness. The socialist camp in Palestine had suffered a humiliation.

The Irgun immediately seized the opportunity and reiterated its call for an armed struggle against the British. It issued a statement in which it argued that Bevin would have liked to condemn the remaining European Jews to stay where they were, while turning the Yishuv into a minority under an Anglo-Arab rule.[27] The group hoped that the crowd which faced the British forces in Tel Aviv would be organised and 'militarised', so as to launch an armed independence war against 'British tyranny'.[28] But the various official institutions of the Yishuv were plunged into endless debates which exposed their divisions and confusion in regard to the outstretched hand of the Irgun. The activists within the Jewish Agency and Mapay insisted that the refusal of London to abolish the White Paper and to maintain its policy on Jewish immigration, left only one option – to fight. The moderates expressed the fear that any armed rebellion would lead to ruthless suppression by the Government and the disarming of the Yishuv. At the end of the day, the radicals had the upper hand. 'The Jews cannot defeat the Empire, but they can harass it', they said and that was the opinion which prevailed.[29]

It was the first time that the Yishuv leadership had been prepared to take up arms. The Jewish Agency set up a committee of three to supervise the activities of the resistance and the first few activities were very carefully selected by its members. The policy was not to target British personnel but to attack installations used by the army to block illegal immigrants. That is why the first two operations were the bombing of two off-shore police stations.[30] These ensured British retaliation in the form of searches and curfews and led to violent clashes and Jewish casualties which set both sides on course for a prolonged war.

As already indicated, contacts between the Hagana and Irgun had started in 1944. At that time, it was part of the Yishuv's attempts to make the dissidents lay down their arms. There were contacts of other kinds between the Hagana and the Stern Group which, from the beginning of 1945, discussed the possibility of a merger between them.[31] Simultaneously, similar negotiations were conducted between the Irgun and the Sterns, at the end of which a limited co-operation was decided upon. The two organisations set up a 'political council' and co-ordinated planning and operations, but the differences between them could not easily be bridged. The Irgun insisted that the Stern Group should abandon individual terrorism as part of the struggle, but the latter refused. They also rejected the Irgun's dominance in commanding terrorist activities. Ironically, while the two separatist groups failed to reach a serious level of collaboration, the time was ripe for negotiation between them and the Hagana.

The Zionist leadership, apart from the growing frustration at British policy, had its own reason for a reconciliation with the Irgun. It was eager to wipe out the scar that the 'Saison' had left on the Yishuv and it hoped to control the activities of the dissidents by joint planning and co-ordination. Ben Gurion, who advocated such co-operation more than anyone else within the leadership, despite being the champion of the 'Saison', was also concerned at the growing popularity that the Irgun was winning within the Community, especially with its youth. In August 1945, at a Zionist conference in London, Ben Gurion told Sneh that co-operation with the dissidents could be achieved if they committed themselves to obeying the Hagana. The Irgun, which supported a united armed struggle against the British from the start, regarded the changing mood within the Yishuv leadership as a political victory. Its commander Begin, and his Stern counterpart, Yelin Mor, rightly held the view that their association with the Hagana would give them legitimacy and respectability after years of denunciation and isolation. They were eager to present themselves to the community as part of the Zionist mainstream and not as adventuristic fringe groups.[32]

At the beginning of October 1945, the first meeting of the representatives of the three organisations took place. Sneh and Galili, for the Hagana, recommended complete unity. They offered the other two organisations the possibility of joining forces with the Hagana while maintaining some autonomy during the transition period. According to Begin, the Hagana's explanation for such an offer was that however much it wanted to fight the British, there was no justification for the existence of separate organisations.[33] The Stern representative tended to accept the offer, but the Irgun was adamant in rejecting it. Begin's reason was simple: he was not reassured that the Hagana, which had fought the Irgun only a few months earlier, would not change its strategy again. This negative response forced the Hagana to reconsider its offer and revise its approach. The framework, upon which the Resistance Movement was to operate, was based on separate guerrilla activities, excluding confiscation of arms and money.

After some prolonged discussions, the three organisations outlined their plan which included four major points:

1.  Hagana, Irgun and FFI would form the 'Hebrew Resistance Movement' to fight the British.
2.  The Irgun and the FFI would not execute any military plan without the approval of the joint command.
3.  After such approval, the guerrilla experts of the three organisations would work out the details for each operation.
4.  None of the three organisations would be required to have joint approval for conducting confiscation activities.

From its first day, the 'marriage' between the fighting units of the Yishuv was not an easy one. In fact, throughout its existence, the Resistance movement was on the verge of collapse. It was shaky not because of mutual suspicions but for political reasons. From the start, there were other prominent figures, mostly in the Hagana, who strongly opposed the partnership. This opposition was reinforced when the Irgun ran its own actions to seize arms and money, just before the negotiations had started.

These operations brought about a confrontation between the British and the Hagana. Some of the cash robberies which the Irgun conducted at the time raised bitterness in the Yishuv because the victims were Jews.[34] The Palmach, the combat unit of the Hagana, vigorously tried to resist the unification. It expressed complete mistrust of the dissidents and predicted that they would soon violate the agreement. It also feared for its own place in the anti-British campaign but stressed that it was strong enough to handle the armed struggle without outside assistance.

However, reports that the new Labour Government had decided to persist with the White Paper policy of restricting immigration removed all the reservations. While the Jewish Community as a whole braced itself for an inevitable confrontation with the authorities, the Palmach embarked on its first operations within the framework of the Resistance Movement. Quite naturally, the operations were associated with the immigration about which Hagana felt most strongly. Between the nights of 9–10 October 1945, a unit of the Palmach invaded the detention camp of Atlit in the north of the country, where many of the Jewish illegal immigrants were held. Two hundred refugees were released in a bloodless operation which marked the beginning of the armed struggle for the Hagana. The deed was praised by the leadership and described by the Socialist United Kibbutz Movement as a turning point in the war of the Yishuv to 'remove the shame of the existence of concentration camps in the land of Israel...'.[35] The Atlit action inevitably brought about a confrontation between the Jewish Agency and the British High Commissioner, but it also strengthened the former's position within the community. As for the Hagana, the operation was an opportunity to demonstrate its determination to the Jewish youth. It was satisfied that the show of force would stop the feared tendency of Jewish youngsters to join the dissidents as a result of its previous inactivity.

The Atlit invasion, which only involved skirmishes with some British policemen, took place towards the end of the negotiation between the three organisations. During that period, the Irgun continued its usual activities, thus causing anger within the Hagana, whose leaders complained that Irgun actions were not co-ordinated and constituted a violation of the imminent agreement. The FFI also complained that it was kept in the dark. One of the operations, the 'confiscation' of arms at the military camp of Rehovot, came as a surprise to the Irgun itself. Begin did not order the operation which was carried out by a few local members.[36] However, the action gave more ammunition to those in the Hagana who thought that the Irgunists, as separatists, lacked discipline and self-control. In fact, many leaders in the Jewish Agency and the Hagana expressed reservations about the agreement with the dissidents right through to the end of the negotiations. But Sneh, the greatest advocate of the joint action, tried to convince his colleagues that a united resistance would control them and prevent a situation in which terrorism would dominate the community and shatter its hopes for freedom and immigration. In order to avoid such a situation, he said, the Yishuv should be ready for a direct physical confrontation with the authorities.

Sneh was referring to Article 7 in the agreement which committed its signatories to the armed struggle against the British. But while these debates continued, the time for action had arrived. The most dramatic events, which sealed the unofficial agreement for establishing the United Resistance Movement, came on 1 November 1945. On that day Hagana members sabotaged all the governmental railways at 200 points, while the Irgun and Stern planned similar activities. These attacks constituted the first stage of a long series of successful operations against the Government which caused some concern in London.

The British, for their part, regarded the new movement as a domestic phenomenon, rather than as a formidable combined organisation. Their intelligence, in a despatch to London, noted that the main object of the movement was to 'unify all resistance groups of IZL and the Stern Gang into the more moderate Hagana'.[37] During April 1946, a poster issued by the movement pointed out that a deep gulf separated the White Paper

Government from the 'Jewish people in Zion'. The message was: 'An anti-Jewish front of Nazis, Socialists and Democrats has been formed against us: let us reply with the formation of a united Jewish fighting front.'[38] The poster emphasised that the Yishuv must rise above 'narrow-minded party spirit' and ideological differences and finished with the demand that the IZL and the Stern Group should put themselves and their weapons at the disposal of the Resistance Movement.

It is true, as the British Army claimed, that the idea of a united movement was formulated by the Hagana, possibly by the more extreme elements of that organisation. However, the British tended to play down its importance and failed to regard it as a dangerous development for them by treating the United Resistance as a movement designed for internal consumption. Ironically, in some quarters, this turning point was unofficially welcomed by the British who hoped that from then on 'the terrorists would operate under the discipline of the Hagana', in order to wean the insurgents from their terrorist methods.

The Hagana was certainly successful in convincing the splinter groups at one stage that all operations should be temporarily stopped in order to win the support of the members of the Anglo-American Committee who visited Palestine, seeking a solution to the problem. However, after a prolonged period of calm, which reigned in Palestine from 25 April, all three of the Jewish illegal armed organisations decided to act. On 16 June 1946, the Hagana carried out its most destructive and probably most extensive operation to date, with an attack on road and railway bridges all around Palestine's frontiers.[39] On the following night, the Stern Group attacked the Haifa Railway Workshop, suffering many casualties, and members of the Irgun kidnapped six British officers.

The Irgun, on the other hand, did not attempt to sabotage or murder, but took hostages for their two members who had been condemned to death by the Military Court. They captured five officers in Tel Aviv and one in Jerusalem because of their participation in an arms confiscation operation and released them only after the British lifted the death sentences. The intelligence units in Palestine were not surprised by the outburst. The first half of 1946 was characterised by Jewish frustration based on the belief that the recommendation of the Anglo-American Committee would either be disregarded by HMG or not be as favourable as they hoped.

The extremists maintained all along that the British, by restricting Jewish immigration from Europe, were set to placate the Arabs and punish the Hagana for its involvement in the Resistance Movement. With the background of mounting tension, a number of events accumulated which were sufficient to plunge the Yishuv into a full-scale confrontation with the authorities. They were:

1. The famous speech of Foreign Secretary Bevin in Bournemouth in which he denounced Jewish National aspirations in Palestine and spoke sharply against increasing the Jewish immigration quota.
2. The passing of the death sentence on two members of the Irgun, who took part in an attack on a British military base.
3. The alleged discovery of British military plans for the liquidation of the Hagana.
4. The escape from France of the Palestinian pro-Nazi leader Haj Amin, the Grand Mufti of Jerusalem, in what was believed by many Jews to be British collusion with the Arabs.[40]

From then on, the Jewish armed struggle against the British, did not stop until the latter's withdrawal from Palestine. The Resistance Movement did not last long, but it provided the Irgun with the confidence it needed to justify its actions. The three organisations carried out operations on 17 June 1946, and each operation was typical of the attitude and methods of its perpetrators. The abduction of the military personnel in Tel Aviv and Jerusalem on 18 June 1946 outraged the British Government and threatened the existence of the United Resistance. The Cabinet in London had been convened for a special session and Ben Gurion had been summoned by the Colonial Secretary. The Jewish Agency called for the immediate release of the officers and warned that the co-operation within the community was at stake. A meeting of the Joint Command was called at the initiative of the Hagana, and one of its leaders, Yisrael Galili, cast doubt on the continuation of the Resistance Movement. However, whilst both sides confronted each other on that issue, the British commuted the death sentences and the Irgun released the hostages.[41]

The armed forces were not prepared for such large-scale military activity against them, but the intelligence units predicted that the Irgun might attempt to take further hostages if more of their members were sentenced to death.[42] The British concluded that the Hagana, by its own involvement in the campaign of violence, wanted to signal its growing resentment towards their immigration policy. Their assumption was that the group's future policy would be shaped by the decisions which would be taken in London and Washington with regard to that question. As for the other two groups, the British view was that they would not necessarily wait for the outcome of the diplomatic efforts to solve the crisis by political means. The government, therefore, held the view that the Irgun would try to perpetuate the tension in the country and even to intensify the struggle by kidnapping and attacking telegraph and broadcasting stations, while assassinations were expected to be carried out by the FFI.

## THE DISINTEGRATION OF THE UNITED FRONT

The explosion on 22 July 1946, in which the Irgun destroyed part of the British Headquarters at the King David Hotel in Jerusalem (see Chapter 5), had induced the disintegration of the Resistance Movement. But it did not completely cut off relations between the Irgun and the Hagana. One reason for that was the decision by the British authorities to expel illegal Jewish immigrants to detention camps in Cyprus. The new measures, taken in August 1946, caused anger within the Yishuv and slightly diminished the terrible impact of the King David devastation, which had been greeted with dismay by the Jews.

Another factor was the Hagana's determination to continue influencing the insurgents' policy by still maintaining direct links with them and monitoring their action. On two occasions, at least, the Hagana used its political power to dissuade the dissidents from two intended military operations, by using its right of veto in the Joint Command. Yet, its leaders could not convince the IZL and FFI to postpone the military struggle until the start of the Zionist Congress in Basel in December 1946, which was set to discuss the future of the British Mandate.[43] Begin himself admitted that 'the relations between us have never been closer than during the aftermath of the attack on King David Hotel and the reasons were understandable'. He emphasised that for many more days the Irgun and the Hagana continued to outline 'agreed war plans'.[44]

However, the first cracks in the Jewish United Front were in evidence as early as August. Ironically, ideological differences, rather than operational matters, brought about the downfall of the Resistance Movement. The process started when it became apparent that the Zionist leadership had expressed an interest not only in considering a halt to the armed struggle, but in showing willingness to discuss the possibility of the establishment of a Jewish state on only a part of Palestine. This prompted Begin to send a letter to Galili, of the Hagana High Command, in which he claimed that such a political direction left the Irgun free to pursue its own policy without committing itself any more to the Joint Command. The broadcasting station of the Irgun echoed Begin's verbal assault by strongly blaming the leadership for condemning the King David operation. However, the leadership stopped its condemnation after British soldiers shot dead three Jewish civilians who demonstrated in Haifa against the immigration restrictions. The IZL accused it of selfishness and cowardliness and warned that it had been left with no choice but to pursue the armed struggle in its own way.[45]

The Irgun maintained that once the Zionist establishment expressed willingness to discuss the partition of the Land of Israel, it had automatically undermined the moral base upon which it was based. By so doing, the leaders had betrayed their homeland and their commitment to the continuation of the Hebrew Resistance Movement. Facing the choices of 'defeatism' or war, the Irgun declared that it would choose the latter.[46]

The Irgun, which also accused the Hagana of ignoring British searches for weapons and further expulsions of immigrants, finally made up its mind on 8 September 1946 in a broadcast which indicated the end to the joint armed struggle.[47] While remaining faithful to the policy of the Jewish Agency, the Irgun and the FFI yet again dissented from the Jewish consensus.

The IZL, despite the King David setback, was reluctant to quit the united front, but tried to exploit its disintegration by gaining popularity amongst the youth in the Community. Its stand against British treatment of Jewish immigrants won it support which enabled it to maintain its separate existence. Moreover, the Irgun wanted to distance itself from any political concessions and thought that by not being part of the Joint Command any longer, it would have a freer hand to conduct its military operations against the authorities.

CHAPTER 4

# Tactics, Methods and Operations

The IZL was an urban terrorist group, carefully structured and secretly divided into sections and cells. Its strongest advantage was the ability of its members to be part-time insurgents while simultaneously remaining part of the community. Despite having relatively large numbers of supporters (5000 at its peak), just a few dozens of members acted as front-line fighters and participated in most of the attacks on the British military targets in Palestine.[1]

'The visible Underground' was the name that the insurgents liked to describe the nature of their organisation. 'They look like ordinary people ... rubbing shoulders with each other', said one of the senior police officers of the insurgents.[2] He noted that their main advantage was the ability to carry out a terrorist attack and to disappear into the crowd immediately after. Eitan Livni, who was in charge of the Irgun's operations until his arrest in April 1946, outlined the four 'pillars' on which the organisation's tactics were based. The surprise factor was the first. The duration and the withdrawal of the operation came second. Then the emphasis was on intelligence information gathering and military methods.[3]

The insurgents tried their best not to repeat the same method of operation and not to attack the same target twice. Keeping the operation short, limiting its duration to between 10 to 20 minutes was of great importance to the group, which could not cope with British military reinforcements rushing to the scene of the attack. Preparing ways of retreat proved, during the course of the revolt, to be one of the most difficult components of many missions. The Irgun, in many cases, chose the most unlikely routes of withdrawal and did not always succeed in avoiding British incoming troops. Prior to the execution of every mission, the insurgents conducted a surveillance of the targets and used Jewish policemen and government officials as their main source of information. Secrecy was paramount before any act and the participants knew about each operation only minutes before it started. The High Command maintained that the first condition for the success of any plan was the ability to penetrate military installations. To achieve that end, it had to devise imaginative ways of catching the British by surprise.

The Irgun wanted to increase its goals, as well as undermine the safety of the security forces. 'Underlining the Jewish fury, winning sympathy in the community and strengthening the spirit of the youth', were the declared principles, according to one of the Irgun's command members.[4] Indeed, the Irgun hoped to strengthen its political grip on the community through its military campaign. However, the IZL was facing many difficulties in pursuing its military campaign due to inexperience, lack of professionalism and shortage of weapons. Its shortcomings were most apparent in medium and large scale operations, which in many cases resulted in many casualties. A few examples, discussed later, show that, despite its image as one of the most efficient post-war underground groups, the Irgun committed many blunders, some of them costly, which nearly brought about its downfall.

## STRUCTURE

The Irgun was divided into four main units. The combat unit, responsible for operations, the 'Revolutionary Propaganda Unit', in charge of the psychological warfare mounted on the Yishuv, the 'Revolutionary Army', acting as a reserve force for the combat unit and the special assault unit, which was designed to attack Arabs but was dismantled on 17 August 1944. In charge of all these, was the High Command, consisting of 14 senior members who were responsible for 'portfolios' such as propaganda, intelligence, recruitment, training, fund raising, medical services, communications, arms procurement, activities abroad, production, operations and other military matters. Each of them was accountable to the Commander-in-Chief and had direct control of the sub-units which were subordinated to him. The Quartermaster was in charge of equipment, weapon maintenance, home industry and transport. The head of the intelligence unit was responsible for internal security, collecting information in the Arab sector, in the rural areas and from the British army and police. The propaganda unit produced a newspaper (*Freedom*), magazines and leaflets and managed the illegal broadcasting station ('Voice of Fighting Zion'). The planning department, which took charge of the guerrilla activities, was more complex and divided into districts and smaller units. In the early part of 1944 there were nine districts in Palestine.

The intelligence unit was one of the biggest and most effective within the Irgun's hierarchy. It was divided into five departments which dealt with all aspects of the insurgency. The security unit was in charge of collecting information about the British apparatus in Palestine: the police, the Army,

CID, military intelligence, government ministries and censorship. The information sources were normally Jewish officials and policemen who assisted the guerrillas out of loyalty. They supplied the Irgunists with birth certificates, identity cards and other documents, and informed them about the army movements in the Middle East. Another department dealt with the Arab community and it used Arab informers who passed information about arms sales, co-operation with the British and plans to attack Jewish settlements. The third department was responsible for maintaining contacts with the press, both local and foreign. It also obtained details about journalistic material whose publication had been banned by the military censorship. The fourth department spied on other sections of the Jewish community; Hagana, Jewish Agency, the socialist parties, the Kibbutzim and youth movements. The existence of such a body demonstrated its isolation within the Yishuv and the fragility of any temporary alliance or co-operation with other elements of the community. Another department, in collaboration with the information services of the IZL, had the task of translating many of the Irgun's publications into various languages[5] for the consumption of European Jews as well as underground movements within many countries occupied by the Nazis. The information service operated the illicit printing plants and in conjunction with the propaganda unit took charge of the radio station.

The Irgun also had a 'medical service' composed of doctors and nurses who were put on alert during military operations in which they treated those who were wounded in action. In time of emergency they admitted the wounded into backdoors of hospitals where they were working. But more important was the financial arm which was assigned to ensure that the Irgun had enough money to maintain its armed struggle. Funds were obtained by various means: raiding banks, blackmailing, threatening affluent Jews, raising funds at home and abroad and robbing British institutions. The Irgun defined these activities as 'money confiscation', activities which reached their peak when £35,000 were stolen on 12 January 1946 from a British train. But despite the scale of this theft, which increased the Irgun's fortune considerably, the organisation suffered a constant shortage of financial sources, which condemned many of its members and their families to poverty and destitution.

The way the Irgun structured itself ensured secrecy. The junior members were accountable to the commanders of the small units who were subordinated to the deputy district commander. He took his orders from his superior who was accountable to the members of the High Command, all of whom followed the instructions of Begin who met them regularly. The Irgun prided itself on the claim that only a handful of insurgents knew each other and that even the senior members did not know about operations, except a short time before their execution. Indeed it was very difficult for members of the Hagana or Jewish informers working for the British intelligence to penetrate the Irgun ranks.[6] But it was relatively easy for Hagana members to disclose the whereabouts of Irgun suspects during the 'Saison'.

In any case, frequent personal frictions forced the Irgun to review its structure on several occasions and make minor changes. At times the various activities lacked co-ordination, but its pyramidal framework stood the test of the revolt. In late 1947, the Irgun started to make radical reforms in its structure. Facing the likelihood of a comprehensive war against the Arabs after the British withdrawal, the group made far-reaching changes. Instead of small units designed to engage in terror, bigger battalions were established in preparation for large-scale battles. What gave the Irgun a signal for such reorganisation was the decision of the UN Committee to recommend the partition of Palestine. On 29 August 1947 the Irgun divided the country into six districts as part of its reforms. In the following year, on the eve of the British withdrawal, the IZL was heavily involved in ejecting the Arab armed forces from the town of Jaffa and was a major force in the Jewish attempt to take over the Old City of Jerusalem throughout 1948.

## MININGS, BOMBINGS, ROBBERIES AND CONFISCATIONS

A random list of terrorist activities which took place in September 1946 illustrates the nature of the Irgun as an underground movement, committed to overthrowing the 'foreign rulers' of the country.

On the ninth of that month the insurgents launched an attack on the railway network. The following day a similar attack took place against British communication systems in other parts of Palestine. On the 13th the Irgun launched an armed attack on a bank in order to confiscate funds.[7] Seven days later the railway station in Haifa came under fire. Three days after that, the IZL men laid ambush to an oil train. In between, mining and explosions became a matter of routine.

These terrorist activities and others, less significant in scale, characterised the nature of the Irgun as an underground group committed to the destruction of the British military infrastructure in Palestine. Unlike the Stern Group, the Irgun was not, usually, engaged in individual assassinations.[8] It thus reflected the view that it wanted to rid the country, not necessarily of the British civilian presence, but of its military apparatus. A selected list of events in the second half of 1946 illustrates the nature of these activities. An oil pipe-line between the Haifa refinery and the port was blown up on 8 September 1946. Ten telephone exchanges, telegraph lines and other communication centres were cut off, disrupting the contacts between the Middle East Central Command and Palestine (13 September 1946). Seven main railways were sabotaged (11 September 1946). The intelligence building in Tel Aviv was attacked, killing three Britons. The attack on the Haifa train station came a week later, as did a few more assaults on other transport installations across the country. A typical simple operation, which cost life and prompted massive British reaction, was on 8 October 1946, when a mine was placed on the Jerusalem–Jaffa road, killing two soldiers and injuring three. The Army responded with a curfew and the arrest of 1000 suspects and laid siege to nearby villages, disrupting the lives of many Jews and causing huge traffic problems.

While a very powerful bomb destroyed a major part of the British Embassy in Rome, in a well publicised terrorist attack on European soil (30 October 1946), the Irgun continued its campaign of sabotage in Palestine. The mining of roads and railways became so widespread that the authorities decided to stop train movement during the night. The insurgents maintained that these acts of sabotage damaged the British transport network which was used for transferring military equipment and manpower from one point to another. The peak of that activity was reached between 17 and 19 November when the minings were countless. During that period most of the railways were hit to the extent that their Arab workers could not cope with the danger and quit their jobs in protest against not being provided with sufficient protection. They were replaced by the Army which took over the railway system that, according to the Colonial Secretary Creech-Jones, cost the Mandate £300 a day. By November 1946, 12 battalions of British troops were tied down to guarding the railway network. This severely restricted the Army's capacity to mount any large-scale military operations.[9] The Stern group added more of its own, but it went further than mining, shooting those who rushed to the scene to inspect and repair the damage.

Stealing weapons and money constituted a major part of the Irgun's efforts. A typical operation was carried out in the military base of Rosh Ha'ayin (22 November 1945). Twenty insurgents disguised themselves as Arab workmen led by an 'officer' who let them through with his Scottish accent. Seventy sub-machine guns, 2 mortars, 5 machine guns and many hand-grenades were taken.

The attack on the train on 12 January 1946, noted above, was the most lucrative ever carried out by the Irgun. Its members derailed the Haifa–Qantara train with a mine. Two groups then fired on it and captured the guards. They stole £35,000 – money intended for the salaries of the employees of the British administration. In Jaffa, four days earlier, £6000 worth of gold had been stolen from the Arab stock exchange. In the town of Netanya, six Irgunists, disguised as soldiers, drove a truck into an ammunition cellar on 13 April 1946, overpowered the guard and took with them a small quantity of weapons. On 20 May 1946 the Irgun launched a daring attack in the Arab town of Nablus, stealing £7000 from its local Barclay's Bank. These activities took place during the period of the United Resistance Movement in which the insurgents enjoyed the support of the Hagana in their anti-British rebellion. No less successful was the joint triple attack on three military airports in which many aircraft were destroyed on the night of 25 February 1946. In Kfar Sirkin the insurgents crawled towards the base, cut off the perimeter fence and placed explosives under the wings of stationary aircraft, blowing up eight of them. As that operation was being carried out by the Sterns, the Irgun simultaneously attacked two other airports. In Lydda, 11 aircraft were destroyed and in Castanea 12 'Halifax' were set ablaze, while cross-fire claimed the life of one insurgent. In total, 83 underground members took part in the three operations which became a central part of the Irgun mythology. As a result, many RAF aircraft supporting the 6th Airborne Division were transferred to Egypt to avoid further losses.[10] In July 1947 two other major operations were conducted by the IZL. In Tel Aviv an attempt to 'confiscate' weapons was made by using two columns to penetrate the military base, disarming the guards, one of whom was killed. Similar operations took place in Jaffa and Haifa, involving a total of 200 participants in the three attacks. The British imposed curfews and made many arrests, but could not lay their hands on any of the terrorists.

## TERRORIST METHODS

Disrupting the life of the British soldiers serving in Palestine was the basic goal of the IZL. Making their life a misery by attacking them and subsequently confining them to barracks, served that purpose. The soldiers, after the intensification of the terrorist attacks, moved in pairs to avoid kidnapping. Jewish cafés and cinemas were placed out of bounds and difficult living conditions were imposed on the Army.[11] Hitting transport facilities constituted a major part of the Irgun tactics during the entire revolt. One of the means of achieving this was road mining. From October 1946, the insurgents were able to manufacture electronic mines which could be detonated from a distance. Thereafter mining played a central role in the IZL's activities. It was easy to operate and carried few risks to the insurgents.[12] One of the Irgun's most devastating self-made devices was the 'barrel' which caused many casualties among Britons and Arabs alike. The giant barrel was filled with half a ton of explosives, which was rolled down from a lorry onto the target. Such a terrorist attack took place on Haifa police station in October 1947. Thirteen policemen were killed and 28 injured in what the Irgun itself regarded as a retaliation for the turning back of the refugee boat 'Exodus' to Germany. A similar attack was carried out by the insurgents in the Arab town of Nablus.

However, the Irgun's activities were a curious mixture of 'hit and run' tactics and guerrilla operations similar to those of an organised army. Its poor financial resources and lack of effective weaponry forced the organisation to resort to basic terrorist acts of sabotage. On the other hand, its political ambitions and the need to prove itself as a worthy military force induced its commander to demonstrate its ability to mastermind complicated missions. On such a scale were attacks on the Ramat Gan military base and a grandiose attempt to rescue fellow insurgents from Acre citadel. These two operations ended in failure and exposed the Irgun to a big weakness which its leaders had failed to recognise. The Acre break-in brought about the release of a few dozen prisoners but the human cost of the action was very heavy. The other operation also involved casualties and highlighted the 'adventuristic' tendencies of the Irgun, since many of its anti-British raids did not achieve their goals. These daring attacks on British installations, in which many fighters were involved, were carried out for political goals. Such a one was the attack on the King David Hotel which ended in disaster. The common denominator of that type of activity was to hit British prestige in and out of Palestine and to impress the Jewish community by achieving a double aim – to score more points in the would-be political contest with the official leadership and to attract more youngsters to the popular organisation. In some ways the Irgun and the British conducted a 'gentlemen's war' in which unwritten rules of behaviour were obeyed. This mutual understanding was based on the assumption that both sides would refrain from inflicting unnecessary casualties on each other. That was partially the reason for the Irgun's distaste of the Stern's policy of assassinations.

These rules were not always observed and during military operations dozens of soldiers and policemen were killed, mainly in shooting incidents. This was best illustrated when, in response to death sentences passed on Irgun members captured during a raid on a military camp, the insurgents retaliated by kidnapping army personnel on 18 June 1946. Five British officers were then held as hostages and faced the threat of retaliatory execution. As a result of this counter-measure the authorities commuted the sentences and the IZL released the officers on 3 July 1946. Later, when the concession was interpreted in London and Palestine as British weakness in the face of terrorist blackmail, the authorities adopted a much harsher attitude. During 1947 the confrontation between the two sides entered a new bloody phase, marked by mutual hatred and dominated by hangings and counter-hangings. However, at the start of the revolt, the Irgun's main preoccupation was to hit transport and communication facilities across Palestine. The 2 April 1946 highlighted the campaign: on that day train stations, water towers, telephone lines, bridges and roads were sabotaged.

The Irgun prided itself on inventing a special home-made mine which was attached to the rail and was activated by the weight of the train. Such operations exposed the Irgun to minimal risk and fitted the strategy that only a consistent campaign of harassment would convince the High Commissioner to pass the desired recommendation to the decision-makers in London. In fact, the Irgun overestimated the effect of their disruption activities, not least because most of the damage could be repaired within a few hours of most of the attacks. Some of the sabotage operations, like blowing up trains on 10 June 1946, did hinder troop movements in Palestine but only to a limited extent, since the British relied on their own means of transport. Another similar campaign took place on 13 September 1946 when 10 telephone centres and telegraph lines were attacked, cutting the British Command communications. This wave of sabotage activities was carried out after the Irgun resumed its armed revolt in the aftermath of the King David affair. The British decision to seal off the government buildings in Jerusalem (nicknamed 'Bevingrad' by the Yishuv) reflected the rise in the terrorist activities against them. The Goldsmith House, the officers' club, was also in the 'security zone' but, on 1 March 1947, it was penetrated by the insurgents. Given the security measures in the area, it was a daring attack. A truck, loaded with explosives, smashed the barrier of the premises and its passengers overpowered the guard, while others threw the devices into the building as well as leaving time-bombs in the stairwell. In that devastating attack the Irgun used four combat units. It resulted in heavy casualties – 17 British officers were killed and 27 were wounded. The government reaction was fierce: martial law was immediately imposed. The failure of this drastic measure (as discussed in a separate chapter) finally paved the way for the British decision to withdraw from Palestine a few months later.

## MILITARY FAILURES

The attack on the Ramallah broadcasting station on 19 May 1944 characterised many of the Irgun's assaults. It marked five years from the date of the issue of the British White Paper and underlined the Group's tendency to combine military and propaganda purposes in its operations. The aim was to broadcast a message to the country in three languages, denouncing

British policy on immigration. The 40 participants were divided into five units which took care of the following duties: penetrating the compound, capturing the studios and occupying them for some time; safeguarding the first unit by paralysing the enemy's fire; blocking the road to the nearby town; blocking all the other roads after the retreat; distributing weapons, transporting the insurgents and giving medical help.

The Irgun managed to take over the broadcasting studios by overpowering some of the soldiers. But despite the initial achievement, due to inexperience and technical problems they were unable to make their own broadcast and, for fear of confronting military reinforcements, the group had to withdraw. Although the Irgun hailed the attack as a success, it was in fact a failure.

Another example of an aborted attack was the attempt to rescue prisoners from the central police headquarters in Jerusalem. It was a joint action by the Irgun and the FFI whose members, disguised as fire-brigade officers, were caught in cross-fire, suffered casualties and ended up in a disorganised retreat.

On 6 March 1946, the Irgun attacked the biggest military base of Sarafand in central Palestine. The insurgents dressed up as British soldiers, but their true identity was discovered. In the midst of the attack they lost one member and the weapons they had managed to confiscate were later recovered by the police. Two other members were captured and later sentenced to death by a military court.

The attack on the police compound in the town of Ramat Gan on 23 April 1946 was one of the Irgun's biggest ever, and it too failed to live up to expectations. The method followed the pattern of previous operations. A stolen military vehicle with a dozen 'Arab prisoners' and 'British guards' entered the frontyard without difficulty. The insurgents then brandished pistols and locked up some of the policemen in a police cell. But fire from the watchtower hindered their efforts to load as many weapons as possible on to the truck. After 20 minutes they had to retreat, leaving behind three dead and one captured.

On 13 September 1946, the Irgun was responsible for a great fiasco in the town of Jaffa. An attempt to rob a bank caused Arab and Jewish casualties, which prompted angry Arab demonstrations against 'British leniency' towards Jewish terrorism. The Irgun, five days later, was forced to broadcast an apology to both communities.

The attack on the British intelligence centre in Jaffa reflected the pattern of the Irgun's operations in the early years of the revolt. Two safeguard units (whose aim was to provide cover and avoid the arrival of British reinforcement to the scene) and one of saboteurs disguised as British soldiers, were included in the mission which blew up most of the building's sections with

120 kg explosives. Due to a miscalculation, the Irgun did not have sufficient time to warn the British and in the explosion four Britons were killed and three were wounded contrary to the Irgun's intentions. A similar attack took place the same day in the intelligence centre in Haifa, but it produced negative results again illustrating the unprofessional state of the Irgun's operations.

A third operation, in Jerusalem, was also disrupted and each side suffered one casualty. The failures stemmed from many unexpected faults due to a shortage of proper military equipment, lack of experience and the fear of taking the lives of innocent people. The Irgun scored more success in the daring attack on the police HQ in Jerusalem (27 December 1945). Its members blocked the access to the compound by creating a 'fire barrier' and other units took positions in front of military bases all over the town to prevent reinforcement. The combat force broke into the target, laid explosive devices in the buildings and ran away. But, during the retreat, the insurgents bumped into a British ambush and a fierce exchange of fire took place in which seven soldiers were killed and 14 were wounded. The Irgun lost one member and another was captured. What could have been one of the Irgun's most impressive operations against the British was aborted by the Hagana in May 1947. The IZL had dug a tunnel running to the Citrus House, home of the British military headquarters in Tel-Aviv. The insurgents planned to lay a huge quantity of explosives under the security compound. The personnel were to be warned about the explosion before the building was to be blown up. But when the tunnel was on the verge of completion, the Hagana discovered it and informed the surprised authorities. On June 30 1947 the Hagana foiled an attempt on the life of General MacMillan, the General Officer Commanding the armed forces and, on 17 July prevented an IZL attack on a British army camp in the town of Rehovot.

The Irgun's military operations, some of them listed above, served their purpose to disrupt the daily life of the British armed forces in Palestine. However, its sporadic activities could not paralyse the military and civilian infrastructure of the Mandate. There were two reasons for that: firstly, British ability to recover quickly from the underground's activities. Secondly, the Irgun's fear that escalating the terrorist campaign would harm innocent people and increase its isolation within the Jewish community instead of winning it more support. In fact, the Irgun stretched its military ability to the limit, but given its very modest resources it could be concluded that the group was skilful in directing its firepower at each specific target by using its whole potential in order to make the necessary impact on each occasion.

## THE ATTACK ON ACRE PRISON

This was, beyond even British doubt, the most spectacular operation carried out by the Irgun during the whole of the Mandate period. The insurgents themselves regarded it as a severe blow to the prestige of the British Empire and described it as a brilliant act which enabled the Irgun to succeed in the very place where Napoleon had failed, when he tried to conquer the citadel in 1799.[13] It was indeed by far the most complicated attack on any of the Government installations in Palestine. However, a close examination of the operation exposed (maybe more that any of the other guerrilla assaults) the main weakness of the IZL – the inability of the Irgun, as an insurgency group, to accomplish a successful large-scale complex operation, without suffering many casualties.

The main aim of the assault in Acre was to release prisoners, but the Irgun had another reason in mind. Its command wanted to settle a bloody account with the British for the hanging on 16 April 1947 of four of their members within the prison walls. The insurgents had wanted to rescue their four convicted colleagues, especially Dov Gruner, who was captured during the attack on Ramat Gan police compound three months earlier. The relatively speedy hanging of the four caught the Irgun in the midst of its preparations, but nevertheless the desire to release other prisoners was all the greater.[14]

The Irgun had another motive: it wanted to stage a propaganda coup. The Acre fortress, apart from its Napoleonic legacy, symbolised British oppression for many Jews in Palestine. It was the central prison in the country in which many insurgents, including Jabotinsky, their spiritual leader, were jailed. Others were also hanged within the premises of the citadel and it was associated with imperial invincibility.[15] The Irgun, seeking revenge for the hangings, wanted to kidnap soldiers with the aim of using them as bargaining-cards, as they had done successfully in the past. But the military at that time would leave their camps only in convoys, sometimes escorted by tanks. 'We could attack them too, as we later attacked the troop train from Egypt', Begin wrote, 'but in those angry days that was not the retaliation we aimed at. It was our duty to pay the hangman in precisely his own coin', he wrote and while admitting inability to hit the Army which was dug into its 'hiding places', he stressed that the 'big debt remained unpaid'.[16]

The preparation for the grand attack was then already under way and the mission was the most difficult that the insurgents had yet had to accomplish. The Acre fortress was not only the site which had withstood the artillery of Bonaparte. In May 1947 the place was guarded by more than 150 armed men. At the heart of the plan lay the conviction that only full co-ordination between the prisoners inside and their rescuers outside could bring about the downfall of the fortress. The attack took place at 16:10 hours on 4 May 1947. From the roof of the Turkish Bath which adjoined the south wall of the prison, the attackers placed a charge estimated at 250lb of explosives against the other wall, breached the wall and entered the corridor inside. They then used explosives to cut the steel gates which led from the corridor into the prison yard.[17] In the meantime, several insurgents had climbed on to the prison wall by means of ladders, from the roof of the Turkish bath. To add to the confusion three hand grenades were thrown into the nearby lunatic asylum in the compound, where seven were injured. Small arms fire was directed against the prison from all sides. Following the main explosion the Arab prisoners both in the cells and in the yard panicked, apparently thinking the roof was collapsing. Two prison warders were beaten up and three Irgunists were injured. Tear gas was used by prison warders to quell the riot. At the time of the main explosion, large numbers of prisoners were exercising in the prison yard. From an interrogation of prisoners captured later the British concluded that the attack and its timing were known to them beforehand and they were making the necessary preparations to escape. The escape itself took place through the breach in the wall to trucks, reported to have been waiting on the road outside. Arms were distributed to the escaping prisoners. Whilst the main attack on Acre prison was taking place, the terrorists carried out at least four simultaneous diversionary attacks, mainly on roads leading to the town.[18] The Irgun used six units outside the prison during the operation. The first one blocked the northern road to Acre. The second broke into the perimeter wall, the third mined the road between the railway station and the fortress, the fourth mined the road from the sea, the fifth fired at the military camp housing some of the 6th Airborne Division north of Acre and the sixth bombed a bridge from the Haifa direction. Inside, four units of prisoners, fully co-ordinated with the attackers, in possession of explosives smuggled to them beforehand, overpowered their guards, bombed the cells, as well as the internal wall, and joined their colleagues outside.[19] In fact, prior to the retreat, almost everything was going according to plan – the roads were mined, the troops were stopped, military camps were under fire and the prisoners were making their way to freedom.

But good luck was not on the IZL's side. A group of soldiers, consisting of officers and soldiers from the paratroops 1st Battalion were on the beach at Acre at the time of the main explosion. They immediately formed two road blocks on which the retreating insurgents crashed. A gun battle ensued during which five men were killed and seven were captured, three of whom were badly wounded. More Irgunists were killed in the exchange of fire, including the commander of the operation, Dov Cohen, an officer previously decorated in the British army and one of the finest fighters the Irgun had. In the event, 230 inmates made their way out of the prison. Regrettably for the Irgun, most of them were neither insurgents nor even Jews. They were Arabs. Only 41 were Jews, '... a mixed bag of Stern, IZL and civil criminals', as they were described by a British intelligence report.[20] In fact there were 30 Irgun members and 11 belonged to the FFI. The group affiliation of the escapees was decided upon in advance.[21] It was, by all accounts, a very daring attack. So much so that the British believed that the Irgun was assisted by the Arabs. '... It is hard to imagine the success of the operation in a predominately Arab area without considering the possibility of Arab aid', was the verdict of British intelligence. It also assumed that 'most of the Arab escapees were gangsters who have been detained since the 1936–1939 troubles'. The British, therefore, concluded that many of the Jewish prisoners were 'front line' members of the 'criminal groups'.

The authorities were impressed, but admitted that the security forces had not done their job properly, by not having a military unit near the prison. The High Commissioner referred to the 'Acre prison incident' as a 'bad show' and ordered a special committee of inquiry to be set up, headed by the Assistant Superintendent of Police to determine how the fortress had been broken into.

He described the success of the insurgents as a result of 'lack of co-ordination between those concerned in keeping prisoners in and those concerned in keeping attackers out'. Cunningham added that 'there was also some doubt as to who was ultimately responsible' and who in fact was in charge of inspecting the security arrangements 'at such institutions as prisons'.[22] The Irgun could not have been jubilant considering that it lost nine fighters (six of them escapees), the biggest number of casualties it had suffered in a single incident to date.

Begin himself hailed the operation by saying that the 'second Bastille fell', but he admitted that 'the feeling of mourning was far deeper than the joy of triumph'.[23] Matityahu Shmuelewitz, one of the FFI's prisoners who was rescued, witnessed the ensuing battle and wrote to Begin because he believed that the brave death of the insurgents 'may somewhat ease the profound melancholy that follows the loss of friends and comrades'. He also regarded the operation as an example of the close relationship both organisations enjoyed at the time. While the British security weakness was exposed once more, the Irgun committed its main blunder by not reconnoitring the area where the attack was to take place. Had they done so, they would either have called off the operation, or have confronted the bathing soldiers on the beach. Begin listed another grave fault: the occupants of one of the forward posts were not given the trumpet signal to board their truck, and so they remained within the British ring and later came under its fire. 'Only a blind chance which could not have been foreseen, caused casualties amongst escapees and escapers', said Begin.[24] The execution of the plan itself was efficient, but the Irgun paid a heavy price for it. The complexity of the operation raised again the question of the Irgun's inability to embark on such activities while risking the lives of many people, a shortcoming that a small organisation could ill afford. Two days after the break-in, the Jewish agency accused the IZL of a display of irresponsibility and suicidal tendency. *Palestine Post*, the daily which echoed the position of the official leadership, accused the 'terrorists' of a plot to remove the democratically elected leadership and to take the political power into their own hands. The newspaper rebuked the authorities for not having 'active intelligence' and not guarding the fortress properly.[25] The Irgun commander angrily rejected the charge that it was a 'suicide mission' and fiercely attacked the 'people of defection and defeatism who exploited our spilt blood in order to pour salt on our bleeding wounds'. He pointed out that his group had never criticised the Hagana's or Palmach's operations which had turned sour in the past.[26]

The dramatic operation had its strongest impact in Palestine in the weeks that followed. In fact it was a turning-point in the Irgun's armed struggle, since it prompted a new cycle of violence in the country. The underground threatened to avenge the blood of those who died during the operation and it accused the British of maltreating the wounded who were captured and of torturing them. Three of the guerrillas who were captured during the battle of Acre were sentenced to death by a military court and their hanging was followed by one of the most significant events of that period – the execution of two British intelligence soldiers by the IZL.

## THE HANGING OF THE TWO SERGEANTS

If there was one single operation which carried the greatest trauma for the British during their three decades in Palestine, it was the hanging of the two sergeants. Even today it is still difficult to understand the magnitude of the outrage as perceived in Britain and its impact on public opinion there. Seventeen military men were killed in the 'Goldsmith House' attack and 'only' two sergeants lost their lives in that operation, but the repercussions were beyond comprehension. The hanging of the two soldiers seemed to have caused a shock not previously known.

What triggered the killing was a British military court decision to pass death sentences on the three members of the IZL who were amongst those captured during the Acre prison break-in. It was on 16 June 1947, the first working day of the United Nations' Special Committee on Palestine

(UNSCOP). The three, Abshalom Haviv, Meir Nakar and Ya'acov Wise, lived under the shadow of the gallows for six weeks, during which a vigorous campaign to have their sentences commuted was mounted and sustained by many of the leaders of the Yishuv. In the meantime, the Irgun made a few abortive attempts to kidnap British officers and four days later it succeeded in capturing two sergeants attached to British Army Intelligence in the seaside resort of Netanya, north of Tel Aviv. The Irgun's message was chilling and straightforward. The hanging of the three would result in the hanging of the two.[27] '... We shall make our gallows drunk with the hangmen's blood', was one of the warnings.[28] But while the Jewish Community was sure that London would yield to pressure, it was clear by the early hours of 29 July that the British were adamant in enforcing their tough policy, even after the announcement that they would refer the question of Palestine to the UN. The execution of the three on that day outraged even the Hagana which had assisted the armed forces in the search to unearth the two sergeant hostages.[29]

Despite the pleas of the Yishuv for mercy, the three IZL men were hanged at Acre jail, where they had been captured. It coincided with the day on which the Jewish refugee boat 'Exodus' arrived back at its port of origin in France, to which it had been returned by the British. The deportation of 5000 Holocaust survivors had eased the decision of the Irgun High Command to retaliate in kind.

After the triple hanging, it was the Irgun's turn to consider the pleas to spare the lives of its two captives. The Hagana, the Jewish Agency and the National Committee, all warned the Irgun of the outcome of a possible reprisal. But the Irgun were as inflexible as the British. Only 13 hours later, Sergeants Marvin Paice and Clifford Martin were strangled in a bunker under an isolated factory, where they had been kept captive for more than a month. Their bodies were hanged in a nearby forest and the area was booby-trapped in order to increase the number of British casualties. After their discovery, and while cutting the bodies down from the trees, a mine was detonated and the body of Martin was smashed to pieces, injuring a captain who stood in front of them.

The outrage in Palestine and Britain was unprecedented. The Jewish Agency expressed a sense of revulsion. The National Committee described it as a 'murder of innocent people by a group of criminals'. The Mayor of Netanya and one of the Yishuv's prominent leaders singled out the hanging as the most brutal crime in the liberation struggle of the Jewish people.[30] Golda Meirson (Meir) sent a telegram to the High Commissioner Alan Cunningham in which she wrote that the Yishuv had never been so ashamed. *Davar*, the organ of the trade unions, dubbed the Irgun a 'gang'. The Hagana issued a statement in which it said that the hanging was 'one of the most revolting crimes'. Rumours were spreading in Netanya of an imminent British pogrom against its residents and the community braced itself for a complete breakdown of law and order. Fearing that the security situation would get out of hand, the Hagana and the Army agreed to conduct joint pre-emptive operations whereby the British would patrol the main roads of Netanya and the Hagana would guard the rest, controlling would-be Irgun provocations.

But the inevitable British fury was expressed in Tel Aviv, where five Jewish passers-by were killed and a dozen were injured. It started on the evening of the hanging when soldiers and policemen smashed windows of shops and buses, and in return, were stoned by demonstrators. The British foot patrols then withdrew to their bases outside the city, only to be replaced by armoured vehicles whose men opened fire on bystanders.

The authorities failed to press charges against the soldiers, which indicated that they could not impose discipline on their subordinates. Cunningham, in his report to London, explained that the soldiers in question were young and 'without the benefits of long service; they have had to work in an atmosphere of constant danger and increasing tension, fraught with insult, vilification and treachery ...'. He also wrote that the brutal planned murders of two of their comrades excited the soldiers to the point of blindness to the values of discipline, reason and human behaviour.[31] In the end, two police constables were dismissed from the force, four discharged and one sergeant had his rank reduced.

The retaliation, however unauthorised, as well as the plight of the 'Exodus', did not lessen the impact of the hanging, despite the efforts of the Irgun's propaganda machine. The reaction in Britain was on an unprecedented scale, not least because of the attempt to blow up the bodies with the intention of risking the lives of more soldiers. The double killing was widely condemned in the House of Commons at an emergency debate. Some of the newspapers compared the Irgun to the Nazis. 'As a last indignity their bodies were employed to lure into a minefield the comrades who sought to give them a Christian burial', wrote *The Times*.[32] *The Daily Express* published a sensational photograph of the hanged soldiers on its front page and *The Manchester Guardian* urged the government to withdraw at long last. Waves of anti-semitic campaigns followed the denunciations and many Jewish shops and homes were attacked by angry mobs all over Britain.

In Parliament, hastily convened in the midst of the summer recess, the general sense of outrage at the Irgun was quickly replaced by a united all-party call to accelerate the withdrawal of the British forces from Palestine. The Army also came under criticism. The case of the two sergeants reflected the inability of the British Government to pursue a consistent line in their fight against the terrorism of the Irgun. A year earlier, under similar circumstances, the authorities had retracted a decision to hang two Irgunists who were sentenced to death by a military court for their participation in the attack on the military camp of Sarafand. The reason was the kidnapping of five officers and one judge who were held hostage by the insurgents. The mitigated punishment, designed to spare the lives of innocent people, prompted Churchill and Montgomery to express dismay at what they regarded as a display of weakness. The British, by passing death sentences on the three Irgunists who took part in the Acre break-in, were adamant in July 1947 not to repeat that decision, despite the campaign in the Yishuv and the abduction of the two sergeants. Some of the sergeants' colleagues raised the possibility, according to their commander, that the government's ignorance of the pair's plight stemmed from their lowly rank.[33] Menachem Begin, unusually economical in explaining the whole affair, wrote in his memoirs: 'We had warned him (the enemy) again and again and again. He had callously disregarded our warnings. He forced us to answer gallows with gallows'. He himself provided an answer of his own to the question 'Why did the British carry out these senseless execution?'. 'Maybe', Begin replied, 'there still echoed in their ears the injunction of Churchill to "act like men" and to "pursue the course of law"'.[34]

It is remarkable that the Irgun keeps insisting even today that the double hanging broke the back of the British rule in Palestine. Begin, as well as other IZL former commanders, quoted Colonel Arch-Cust, who was the chief assistant to the chief secretary of the British Government in Palestine. One year after the evacuation he said in a lecture to the Royal Empire Society that the 'hanging of the two British sergeants did more than anything to get us out'.[35]

It could be said that after the hanging of the three Irgun members, Begin had no choice but to repay the British in kind, simply because the threat to kill them was unambiguous and failing to carry it out would undermine the credibility of the insurgents.[36]

In the end, the retaliation paid off and the authorities did not execute any more terrorists thereafter, fearing a repetition of the affair of the sergeants. But Begin and his colleagues had chosen to ignore the fact that the British were already on their way out and that the killing did a lot of damage to the Jewish cause inside and outside Palestine for the following six reasons. First, it left the civilian community at the mercy of hot-headed British personnel who wanted to take revenge for the killing of their two comrades, as happened in Tel Aviv a day after the hanging. In Netanya, for example, the Irgun was accused by the Hagana of deserting the city for fear of being captured by the Army, thereby exposing the residents to greater danger. The Irgun denied the allegation, but many of its members known to the Hagana left the town to avoid capture. Second, the execution brought the Yishuv leadership and the authorities closer to the point of resuming their collaboration. General Sir John Crocker, the Commander in Chief in the Middle East, told the High Commissioner, Cunningham that he detected a readiness among many Jewish moderates to quell the growing wave of terrorism after they themselves had been shocked by the hanging. Crocker used this argument to explain his opposition to the imposition of martial law in the country, which would have harmed innocent Jews and Arabs more than the insurgents.

In the afternoon of 31 July 1947 Golda Meir, who headed the political department of the Jewish Agency (and later became Prime Minister of Israel) met the High Commissioner and informed him that the Hagana had reached the conclusion that all the forces within the Yishuv, including the trade unions, were willing to commit themselves to the struggle against the dissidents. 'We can not bear this situation any longer. They do not only kill British, and everything that we have built in two generations is in danger', she told him. Cunningham was not satisfied, reminding her that such words had been uttered by her six months earlier. He demanded open co-operation and she said that the leadership was unable to do that because a call to the community to collaborate would create a domestic debate which would weaken the strength of the anti-terrorist camp. In the end he assured her that the government would try giving her and her colleagues another opportunity to prove their ability and will to act.[37]

The meeting gave birth to what the Irgun feared most – another *Saison*, small in scale, launched against the IZL. As a result, the group's terrorist activities slowed down and the Hagana's campaign disabled the Irgun's fund-raising operations within the Yishuv. The Irgun, had therefore, to resort to bank robberies in order to finance itself. Instead of imposing martial law, and in response to the Jewish Agency pleas, the authorities arrested Revisionist leaders and a few mayors suspected of sympathising with the Irgun in what became known by the dissidents as Operation *Golda*. The British also outlawed Betar, the nationalist youth movement. Begin, for his part, accused the Agency leaders of collaborating with the 'enemy' for fear of being arrested again.[38]

Third, despite the tremendous impact world-wide, the Irgun damaged its reputation as a group of freedom fighters, more because of the booby-trapping one of the two sergeants' bodies than because of the actual hanging. Blowing up the corpse of Sergeant Martin caused a wave of disgust even in the US where the Irgun was seeking its main support. However Begin, instead of admitting that it was a mistake, simply denied the charge. In a broadcast to the nation, through the illicit Irgun radio station, he attacked those who fell victim to 'deceptive Nazi–British propaganda' and stressed that no mine had been attached to either body. According to his version, there was a mine somewhere in the forest where the two were hanged and it was meant to hit the 'living enemy forces'. However, a member of the Command admitted that the bodies were booby-trapped 'in order to cause more casualties'.[39]

The truth was that the device was not attached to the bodies of the soldiers. It was hidden in the ground just under the hanging spot and was well covered by dry leaves.[40] When the first body was cut down from the rope, it hit the bomb and caused the explosion. In this broadcast Begin chose to accuse the British soldiers of atrocities committed by them against those insurgents who were captured and injured during the Acre break-in, instead of admitting that the trap was at the least a tactical error.[41]

But the Irgun's counter-attack fell on deaf ears. In Britain and America it created the impression of pure and simple fanaticism that motivated the militant Zionists in Palestine.[42] The American Consul General in Jerusalem, Robert Macatee, reported to Washington after the hanging that '... if such generalisations are permissible, it may be well to question whether the Zionists, in their present emotional state, can be dealt with as rational human beings'.[43] Earlier, on 22 May, he expressed the view that the British were unable to rule Palestine and described the government of Palestine as a 'haunted organisation with little hope of ever being able to cope with conditions' in the country.

Fourth, the IZL was at pains to explain that the hanging was not a retaliation for the 'murder of the Hebrew underground prisoners', but the product of an ordinary legal action which was taken by the Irgun field-court. The two 'British spies' were accused of 'illegal entry to our homeland', belonging to a 'terrorist-criminal organisation', spying on Jews, possessing weapons and molesting the underground members.[44] The IZL, therefore, decided to sentence them to death and even rejected their pleas for clemency.

The attempt to over-exploit the affair for propaganda purposes was greeted with astonishment in the Yishuv and further undermined the credibility of the Irgun, so much so that Begin himself had to alter the version later on, admitting a 'certain exaggeration'. The Irgun never expressed regret about trapping the corpses, but sensing the uproar inside and outside Palestine, Begin sent a letter to the father of Paice, who earlier called on the Irgun to spare the life of his son. Explaining the reasons behind the killing, Begin blamed the British government for not showing mercy towards the relatives of the three Irgunists who had been executed before. 'Go to Downing Street and tell them there, as all British fathers should react, that their sons were recruited for the most dreadful role in world's history – tell them: you are the murderers, you have murdered my son'.[45]

Fifth, the hanging prompted the British to tighten the security around their personnel to an unprecedented level. Thereafter, no officer or soldier was allowed unarmed outside his camp or the security zone unless accompanied by at least three other comrades. In addition to that, military vehicles had to carry one armed man sitting alongside the driver.[46] As a result of these extra precautions, it was much harder for the insurgents to launch their attacks on British military targets.

Sixth, the hanging exposed the Jewish community in many towns in Britain to anti-semitic attacks on shops, houses, synagogues and cemeteries. Looting and vandalising took place mainly in Liverpool and Manchester, but also in Brighton and Glasgow. Bevin told the American Secretary of State, George Marshall, that the executions would never be forgotten and that as a result 'anti-Jewish feeling in England now was greater than it had been in a hundred years'.[47] Even after achieving independence in 1948, the state of Israel's name was tarnished and the relations between the two countries were marred by the incident. Begin himself was a *persona non grata* in Britain for nearly three decades and his first visit to the country, as head of the Opposition in 1972, was cut short because of threats on his life.

In examining the effect of the hanging on the morale of the British soldiers in Palestine and decision-makers in London, one can only refer to none other than Begin himself. Trying to explain the scale of the outrage, which surprised even the Irgun, Begin wrote a classified document which was passed on to senior members of the group. In his opinion it was the first time in the history of the British Empire that sons of the 'superior race' were hanged in a land which rebelled against its rule. Hence their shock. 'They', he wrote, 'who were accustomed to oppress and to hang, were themselves hanged according to a sentence passed on them by a court which did not recognise their legitimacy in Palestine and challenged their rule'. Begin went out of his way to regard the act as 'maybe the most revolutionary in the history of the revolutionary wars' since the oppressed deprived the oppressor of its privilege and dared hang the 'subject of the oppression'.[48] Only many years later did the Irgun recognise that such a message should have been made public instead of being used for domestic purposes in order not to lose the propaganda battle in the community.

The hanging exposed British military weakness in Palestine. This time it was Cunningham who advocated martial law as a comprehensive preventative measure despite his meeting with Meir. 'This measure now seems the only shot left in our locker', he said.[49] But his recommendation was rejected by the Army. Its commander in Palestine, Lieutenant General MacMillan, as well as the Commander in Chief of British Forces in the Middle East, John Crocker, objected that martial law would require additional troops. Both were supported by the Cabinet who refused to commit more troops to

Palestine. Fresh in their memory was the ineffectiveness of martial law in March, while already knowing full well that the UN Committee on Palestine was about to recommend the termination of the Mandate in the country in favour of a Jewish–Arab partition.

The affair, as a whole, highlighted the British failure to recognise how sensitive hanging was for the Jewish community. Previous executions could have shown the authorities that hanging united all sections of the community against them. It also produced martyrs in the Irgun, which exploited the gallows as one of the most effective tools in its domestic propaganda campaign.[50]

Again, what worked for the British during the repression of the Arab Revolt in the mid-30s, proved to be counter-productive in the Jewish sector. In itself the hanging damaged the Irgun. Luckily for the insurgents and the Jewish community as a whole, it came at a stage when the British were already losing their grip on the country. The fact that 100,000 police and troops were not enough to impose martial law on less than 600,000 Jews proved that in 1947 the Yishuv was no longer willing to tolerate the continuation of the British rule in Palestine.

If the Irgun was the catalyst of the Jewish struggle in Palestine to achieve independence from the British, the hanging served as a similar tool in the Irgun's efforts to oust them by creating uproar in Britain. This was the episode which left a traumatic mark on the mind of the British public and decision-makers alike. It has been reflected in what Arthur Creech-Jones wrote in retrospect 14 years later: '... the reprisals and hangings of the two young sergeants struck a deadly blow against British patience and pride'.[51] The British, in February of that year, had agreed to refer the Mandate to the UN whose committee recommended, a month after the fateful hanging, the termination of the Mandate and the partition of Palestine. On 26 September, the British had no choice but to comply with the UN recommendation and to announce the termination of their rule in the country by 15 May of the following year.

CHAPTER 5

# The King David Affair

If there was a single event in the Irgun's terrorist campaign which was more disastrous than any other it was the explosion in the King David Hotel in Jerusalem. The blowing up of the British headquarters in Palestine polarised the conflict yet further. It stirred up powerful emotions amongst the British who held the view that terrorism should be suppressed by all means and it caused a public outcry in London. It also drove the Irgun into a major crisis. The explosion reaffirmed the inability of the armed forces to control the country, and shed more light on the intriguing relationship between Britain and the USA on one hand and between the dissidents and the Jewish leadership on the other.

At approximately 11:45 hours on 22 July 1946, Jewish terrorists of the Irgun Zvai Leumi succeeded in entering the basement of the King David Hotel where the headquarters of the British Administration of Palestine was located. The attack began when a commercial truck drove up to the Staff Entrance of the hotel and six Jews, disguised as Arab workers and carrying milk cans filled with explosives, made their way into the hotel.

Intelligence officers who investigated the incident reported that, on being asked by the hotel reception clerk for details of their business, they produced revolvers and forced the clerk back into his office. Other terrorists rounded up the remaining hotel employees in the basement and herded them into the kitchen, whilst the other members of the gang went along the corridor towards 'La Régence' Restaurant, carrying explosives and wheeling the milk cans into which the bulk charge had been deposited.

The presence of the terrorists was detected 15 minutes later by a British signals officer, who immediately grappled with one of them but was overcome and shot in the stomach by another. When the men were leaving, after completing the laying of the charge in the restaurant, they were fired upon by policemen on the spot. At that time, the Irgun set off an explosion on the pavement opposite the hotel, which succeeded in diverting the attention of the police and military present. Only after it became apparent that six terrorists had been in the hotel basement for a length of time, did police officers start to investigate the matter. It took the British half an hour to discover that Jewish raiders had placed milk cans filled with explosives and it was too late to avert a disaster. At 12:36 hours the explosives were detonated, causing the death of 91 persons, mostly civilians of whom 41 were Arabs, 28 British, 17 Jews and five others. The blast partially destroyed the Secretariat Wing and the Defence Security office.[1]

Two days later, the Irgun claimed responsibility for the outrage in a proclamation issued by them on 24 July, in which they stated, *inter alia* 'the tragedy which occurred is not the fault of the Jewish soldiers who have orders to spare lives ... this tragedy came through the fault of the British tyrants who play with human lives. Warnings by telephone were given between 12.10 and 12:15 hours that the British had 22 minutes to evacuate the building, and therefore the whole responsibility for the loss of life falls on British hands ...'.[2]

The question of whether there was a warning given in order to reduce unnecessary loss of life has been much debated since the tragedy and continues even today. The Irgun claimed that its members first warned the hotel by telephone, then the nearby French Consulate and finally the *Palestine Post* newspaper. The British argued, after intensive enquiry, that the hotel received no warning from Irgun sources that the building was about to be blown up. Later, Begin said that he learned after the subsequent explosion that, because of the so-called 'diversionary bomb', many people tried to get out of the hotel, but British soldiers barred all exit by shooting in their direction.[3] He added that when the warning to evacuate the hotel reached a high official, he exclaimed: 'We are not here to take orders from the Jews. We give them orders'.[4]

Begin, curiously, quoted the Hagana Information Service which suggested that 'a high official had deliberately prevented the evacuation of the hotel in order, for reasons best known to himself, that a major disaster should occur'. Begin himself accepted that theory and concluded that the question remained open. He might have referred to a claim by unofficial sources that Sir John Shaw, the Chief Secretary to the British Administration in Palestine, failed to act on the bombing plan since he was waiting for information about the plan from an agent within the IZL itself. But the agent failed to make contact with the British because the IZL units who were involved in the operation allowed no one out of their sight once they had been informed that morning that D-day had arrived.[5]

The Irgun, throughout the years, went out of its way to explain the outrage at the King David by pinning the blame on the 'careless British'. The Irgun claimed time and again that the authorities, in spite of their repeated denials, were warned by the insurgents. Indeed, Edward Horne, who wrote a history of the Palestine Police Force, admitted that 'there is evidence that the Irgun were being truthful when they announced to the world that they had given three warnings'.[6] But, he argued correctly, 'the hotel was faced with 20 crucial minutes of a Comedy of Errors' which led to confusion, simply because those who were authorised to give evacuation orders did not receive the warning within the appropriate space of time. However, the fact that the Irgun released a warning did not, in any case, justify the attack on either moral or political grounds. Moreover, it called into question the wisdom behind the operation. The Irgun failed completely to realise what the outcome of such an operation would be were something to go wrong. They relied heavily on the assumption that the British would be quick to evacuate the hotel. In fact, 22 minutes could not have been regarded as a sufficient period of time for hundreds of employees to evacuate such a vast building. One should also question why the terrorists gave less than half an hour's advance notice, when they themselves later claimed that the explosive device was constructed in such a way that it would have been impossible to defuse.

Above all, the King David affair did nothing to promote the Jewish cause, or even that of the Irgun. On the contrary, the appalling casualty toll and the immense amount of damage done was greeted by the Jews with disbelief and shocked surprise. Although most Jews maintained that government policy had contributed to the outrage, the Yishuv was almost unanimous in condemning the bombing. The British themselves were also aware of the damage to the Irgun's reputation and held the view that the terrorist campaign had been tarnished and might never fully recover. They also expressed hope that even the Irgun would have learned the meaning of 'counter-productive'. At the same time they complained that, though expressing its horror, the Jewish Community did nothing to assist the police with its investigations. They added that Jewish anti-government sympathies were far stronger than their desire to see the perpetrators of the outrage brought to justice,[7] although, in this case, they were mistaken.

Indeed, it became apparent to the British that the government could expect no assistance from official Jewish sources in its efforts to round up those responsible for the outrage. It is clear that the government could not draw a distinction between the angry Jewish reaction to the explosion and the fact that the attitude of the community towards the continuation of the Mandate in Palestine had not changed. This became apparent only ten days after the attack, when Jews in Haifa were demonstrating for the release of illegal immigrants detained on board ships in the city's harbour. A member of the intelligence units regarded it as an indication that 'Jewish terrorists are allowed to proceed from atrocity to atrocity without hindrance from their own people'.[8] But that assessment was another example of the extent to which the authorities misjudged the situation in Palestine. In reality, the Yishuv denounced the explosion outright, not least because many Jews were among the casualties and on account of fears about the form of reprisal the government might take.

The attack damaged the reputation of the Irgun in Palestine and abroad and caused a rift between the organisation and the Hagana. Worst of all, it brought about the downfall of the Hebrew Resistance Movement which had united all the fighting forces in the country.

## CO-ORDINATION WITH THE HAGANA

The blowing up of the British headquarters had a direct impact on the continuation of the resistance movement, exposing the nature of the relationship between the three organisations. Most important, the attack and its aftermath revealed that the Hagana was involved in the planning of the operation and certainly knew about the intention to blow up the hotel. The Irgun itself let it to be known, a year after its implementation, that the Hagana had been involved in the plan. Already, on 1 June 1946, only three days after Operation *Agatha,* in which British soldiers invaded the Jewish Agency buildings in Jerusalem, the Hagana had given the Irgun the 'green light' to execute the plan which had been discussed long before in the joint Central Command.

Moshe Sneh, the Chief Commander, sent a written message to the Irgun and the Stern group and asked them to carry out the mission 'as it was summed up in Committee X'.[9] The Sterns were to blow up a building near by, and the Irgun had the task of hitting the King David. But due to co-ordination difficulties between the two organisations, the Sterns did not participate in the operation and the action was conducted by the IZL alone. Nevertheless, the outrage fell within the consensus of the National Resistance Movement as a whole, at least when the initial idea was discussed in the joint command. On the other hand, there was a certain amount of dissent within the Hagana. Part of it strongly opposed the action at the King David, whereas the more extreme elements, headed by Sneh, were not against it. This does not mean that the more moderate members did not support the Resistance Movement and preferred to co-operate with the government to combat terrorism. They simply viewed it as a radical departure from Hagana policy and regarded such an attack as committing an outrage along the lines of the two other groups. In fact, British Intelligence predicted that the extreme elements within the Hagana would lean more towards real terrorism and thus strengthen the ranks of the Irgun and the Stern group.[10] Sneh was in a minority in the joint X Committee which consisted of representatives of the three organisations. Weizmann, who knew about the plan, vetoed its execution and, while the Hagana complied with it, Sneh continued to consult with the IZL, although he later claimed that he had asked them to delay the operation.[11]

This does not disguise the fact that the Hagana took part in the planning of the explosion the day after Operation *Agatha*, in order to demonstrate to the British that the operation had not broken its military ability and its will to fight. However, the high toll of casualties turned out, in the aftermath of the attack, to be a political and military disaster which was to produce a profound shock in Palestine.

## THE BRITISH RESPONSE

The day after the explosion occurred, the Secretary of State for the Colonies gave the Cabinet the latest information about the event. The minister agreed with the administration in Palestine that only two alternatives remained in order to restore law and order in the country after the King David tragedy.

The first was to institute widespread searches for arms in order to break up the Jewish resistance movement. The second alternative was for the government to announce a final solution of the political problem. The Executive Council and the General Officer Commanding (GOC) the troops in Palestine preferred the second option. They maintained that in view of the outrage, 'further negotiations with the Jews seemed to be impossible' and the best course would be for the government to impose its own solution to the political problem. The Prime Minister, Clement Attlee, could not believe that the Hagana had been involved in this affair. He said that 'although there was evidence that it had been implicated in some of the earlier acts of violence, there was no reason to believe that any but the most extreme advocates of violence were involved in this latest outrage'.[12]

Attlee clearly rejected the argument for an immediate counter-action and said that it would be a mistake to rush into a widespread search for arms, 'which would be taken as a measure directed against all the Jews in Palestine'. The Prime Minister, aware of the possibility of alienating all sections of the Jewish Community, thought, on the other hand, that HMG could not, nonetheless, take a sudden decision on the political problem, before consultation with the United States Government had been completed. Attlee was in favour of issuing joint guidelines with America before resorting to any kind of action. Ernest Bevin, the Foreign Secretary, surprisingly agreed with the Prime Minister despite his well-known 'hard line' policy on the Jewish insurgency in Palestine. He attached importance to securing an early declaration by the US Government condemning the outrage at the King David and hoped that such a declaration would be made shortly.

The Cabinet as a whole was unanimous in adopting a moderate line. With regard to the question of a wholesale search for arms in Palestine, its members noted that the High Commissioner, the Chief Secretary and the General Officer Commanding were not in favour of such a course and considered that it would lead to conditions tantamount to a declaration of war. It was also agreed that this course would be directed against the Hagana rather than the dissident groups, namely, the Irgun and the Stern group. The ministers were also sceptical about the possibility of capturing those responsible for the bombing or of discovering the arms used by their organisations.

This Cabinet meeting, which took place one day after the tragedy, reflected the helpless mood which characterised the British reaction. The general feeling in London was that any military action would drive the Hagana into closer association with the terrorists. The aim was to lead the Hagana away from extremist measures and to convince them that it would be in their own interest to root out the dissidents altogether. However, this view contradicted the widespread suspicion, which also prevailed within the Cabinet, that the Hagana and the Jewish Agency were implicated in the King David affair. It was also widely believed that the British could no longer tolerate the continuous arming of the Hagana, which had been 'responsible for some outrages' in the past. The British Government, therefore, could not sit by and ignore this process which emphasised its weakness in Palestine.

The Chief of the Air Staff, Lord Tedder, expressed the view that the search for arms in Palestine would not necessarily lead to open war. He was confident that, if the search brought the Hagana into armed rebellion, the military forces in Palestine, with appropriate reinforcements, could deal with the situation. This opinion reflected the mood of some ministers, but all were reluctant to adopt radical measures for fear of further military commitment, more casualties, domestic public opinion and future relations with the USA.

The Cabinet finally agreed to put the question once more to the High Commissioner and the GOC in Palestine, and it rejected a suggestion to appeal to the more moderate Jewish elements to stamp out the dissident organisations. The argument for such an appeal was that, only with Jewish help, was there a reasonable chance of dealing successfully with these groups. However, the Cabinet felt that this was not the moment 'to place ourselves under any obligation to Jewish organisations in Palestine'.

Despite the fact that the Cabinet meeting on 23 July 1946 was devoted to Palestine as a result of the King David outrage, the ministers, shocked as they were, were at pains to state that the tragedy that the Jews had faced in Europe had 'created in them a pathological state of mind'.[13] Nevertheless, they emphasised that the Jews in Palestine should not be led to believe that terrorism provided a short cut to the achievement of their aims. Therefore, they decided to publish on the following day a White Paper declaring 'the complicity of the Jewish Agency in terrorist acts.'

The bombing of the British HQ in Palestine was widely regarded in London as a security blunder. The fact that it had been possible for terrorists to enter the lower floor of the building was an indication to the ministers that adequate security precautions had not been taken. The Cabinet therefore invited the Secretary of State for the Colonies, in association with the Service authorities, to institute an enquiry into the security precautions in Palestine. However, the ministers who participated in the Cabinet meeting the day after the explosion, did not grasp the real scale of the tragedy. When, in the following meeting, the Secretary of Colonies informed the Cabinet that the latest estimate of casualties was 65 dead and 58 missing, the general feeling was that the government could not let the organisation responsible go unpunished. In this case, it was the Irgun which admitted responsibility for the outrage in which British, Arabs and Jews lost their lives.

The High Commissioner, Alan Cunningham, had recommended a plan for widespread searches for terrorists in places where they were known to exist, including Tel Aviv. This would entail the use of a considerable number of troops, and its success would depend on sufficient information being available.[14]

This represented a form of a compromise which enabled the British to hunt down the terrorists while avoiding searches for Hagana arms in the settlements. At the same time, the High Commissioner considered that some immediate and striking action was necessary to prevent the Arabs from taking the law into their own hands following the bombing which might have demonstrated British weakness. Another reason for immediate action was the urgent need to boost the morale of the British in Palestine, which had suffered a blow as a result of the King David affair. However, the High Commissioner believed that the Jewish Community as a whole should bear responsibility for the event, and collective punishment was the logical response. To this end, he made two recommendations. First, he proposed that a fine of about £500,000 should be imposed, involving legislation to freeze the assets in the bank accounts of selected institutions, such as the Jewish National Fund and the Palestine Foundation Fund. Secondly, and more harshly, he called on the government to put an immediate stop to immigration, which would include the withdrawal of the immigration quota and the diversion to other countries of any further ships containing illegal immigrants. The High Commissioner's radical approach ignored not only the likely angry reaction of the community to such tough measures, but also the possibility that it would play into the hands of the dissidents.

He also failed to understand the mood within the British Cabinet which did not favour his proposals. In its discussions, less than a week after the bombing, there was general opinion in favour of immediate action, but not of an indiscriminate sort. Ministers felt that any measures taken in respect of the outrage should, as far as possible, be directed only at the section of the Jewish Community which had been responsible for it, namely the Irgun. 'It would be a mistake to take any step which, by affecting other sections of the Jewish Community than those responsible for the recent outrages, might prejudice the acceptance of this new policy'.[15] The disagreement between the decision-makers in London and their subordinates in Palestine reflected the latter's ignorance of political reality and global developments. Not wishing to ignore those responsible for the outrage and looking for ways to punish them, they failed to understand the political outcome of an immediate prohibition of all Jewish immigration.

The Cabinet was well aware that such a proposal 'might have repercussions on the policy of the United States Government, would cause hardship to innocent and suffering people' and was hardly consistent with the policy which would provide for the immigration of 100,000 Jews in the near future.

However, the Cabinet was strongly in favour of an extensive search for terrorists and argued for the need to direct the action only against the perpetrators of the bombing. In so doing, Prime Minister Attlee wanted to drive a wedge between the Irgun and the Hagana, who were engaged in an agreement on joint activities within the framework of the Resistance Movement. He feared that indiscriminate action would push the moderates further into the arms of the underground organisations. Indeed, as it happened, the King David affair caused the collapse of the Resistance Movement. By resisting the temptation to declare an all-out search in the Yishuv, the Cabinet, wiser than its people on the ground, contributed to the disintegration of a united Jewish front. In Palestine itself, the tragedy produced a universal reaction of revulsion and provided the opportunity, even the necessity, for the Jewish Agency to break off with the Irgun and dissociate itself from their joint revolt.[16]

The Cabinet also resisted military pressure which called for tough measures against the Jewish leadership for their alleged co-operation with the Irgun and the Stern group. The Chief of the Air Staff and other military men urged the Government to adopt a harsh attitude, convinced that a widespread search for arms would not necessarily lead to open war. The security forces in Palestine were eager to repair the damage done to their prestige following the bombing. They had been criticised by the government for not having taken the necessary precautions to prevent the terrorists from entering the lower floor of the King David building. The anger within the lower-ranking soldiers in Palestine was tremendous and created feelings of helplessness that could only have been diminished by retaliation. The Chief of the Imperial General Staff, General Montgomery, wrote two days after the incident: 'We shall show the world and the Jews that we are not going to submit tamely to violence'. He also called for action.[17] But even he could not persuade the Cabinet to his way of thinking since the latter favoured selective operations against the Irgun, on account of its claimed responsibility for blowing up the King David.

On 30 July 1946, the Cabinet invited Sir John Shaw, the Chief Secretary to the British Administration in Palestine, to give them his impressions in the aftermath of the outrage at the King David. Shaw spoke about the tension within the Arab community which had been heightened by the publication of the Anglo-American Committee's report, and by the fact that about 60 Arabs had been killed or wounded at the King David, including members of prominent families. He bitterly complained about the Hebrew newspapers which, although condemning terrorism, had not called on their leaders to assist the government in 'bringing the criminals to justice'.[18]

He then voiced the suspicion that the Hagana had been informed by the Irgun about the bombing beforehand. The Hagana had even advised the latter to alter the time of the explosion from 12.30 to 2.30 pm, when the building would be much emptier, so as to reduce the number of casualties. Like the High Commissioner, the Chief Secretary also maintained that a search for terrorists should be accompanied with sequestration of certain Zionist funds and stoppage of all immigration, which the Cabinet refused.

Shaw did not hide the fact that the demand for strong action was intended not only in order to punish the Jews, but also to avoid likely Arab outbursts. He expressed the belief that the Arab states would be less hostile than the Palestinian Arabs to the proposed settlement (which also included the admission of 100,000 Jews) for provincial autonomy. But this would be possible only if the British demonstrated that they were still in control after the outrage. 'If the High Commissioner's proposals to sequestrate Zionist funds were accepted', argued Shaw, 'this would have a stabilising effect on Arab opinion'.[19] The King David affair reinforced Shaw's opinion that the British should impose their policy on the Arabs and the Jews in Palestine, since 'it was almost beyond hope that Arabs and Jews would agree to sit around the same table'.

To a certain extent, the Secretary of State for the Colonies supported Shaw's call for drastic collective punishment and was in favour of imposing a fine on the Jewish Agency of £500,000 on account of damage to life and property caused by the outrage. However, the Cabinet was reluctant to do even that, on the grounds that the majority of the Jewish Community was in no way responsible for the King David Hotel bombing. The Cabinet also reaffirmed its conclusion that there should be no sequestration of Zionist funds, 'at the present time'.[20] The ministers, while ordering an enquiry into security arrangements to protect Government buildings in Palestine, gave their approval for a limited intensive search for terrorists. The result as we shall see was Operation *Shark*.

## THE AMERICAN RESPONSE

The bombing in Jerusalem occurred at the worst possible time for the Zionists in the United States just as they were recruiting all available allies to discredit the unfavourable Morrison–Grady Peace Plan. The heavy loss of life at the hotel swung public opinion against the Jews but not for long and the British were disappointed at the lukewarm reaction of the Administration. The Foreign Office instructed its ambassador in Washington to issue a strong condemnation and added that the British people would not understand American silence over the outrage. The ambassador, Inverchapel, had an interview with the American Secretary of State who, however upset he was about the incident, told thim that he would have to consult the President and that the condemnation might be delayed.[21]

The FO was angry at such an attitude and demanded an immediate statement from Truman. The British even tried to dictate the wording of the awaited condemnation. They wanted the President to say that 'the Anglo-American efforts were being thwarted by this stupid outrage'.[22] The two politicians met again and eventually all that Truman was prepared to say was that 'such acts of terrorism will not advance but, on the contrary, might well retard the efforts that are being made, and will continue to be made, to bring about a peaceful solution of this difficult problem'.[23] He also stated that every responsible Jewish leader joined him in condemning the bombing.

Despite the outrage in Jerusalem, the British failed to prolong American hostility towards the Zionists for more than a few days. After the war there were widespread publicity and encouragement among many American Jews, including non-members of the Zionist movement, for the activities of the dissident organisations in Palestine.[24]

## OPERATION *SHARK*

The direct and immediate outcome of the King David explosion was described by the British as the 'largest search operation ever carried out by the British Army and the police force in Palestine'.[25]

*Shark* was a compromise between the hard-liners within the administration, who advocated adopting strong measures, and the cabinet ministers, including the Prime Minister. In addition, they also took into account the political implications of any action, not least because the Anglo-American Committee was about to conclude its assessment and the British were concerned with their relationship with the USA over the Palestine question. The hard-liners, such as High Commissioner Cunningham and Chief Secretary Shaw, were strongly backed by Field Marshal Montgomery. They emphasised the need to demonstrate not only that the government did not lack teeth, but also to show the Arabs that events in Palestine were still under the control of the security forces.[26] The Arab community expected an immediate response. They put the blame for the King David affair on what they saw as 'British weakness, leniency and unpreparedness'.[27]

Operation *Shark* was also meant to satisfy the demands of the Army in Palestine, whose soldiers suffered low morale and were subject to constant frustrations which came to a peak in the aftermath of the King David affair. The general idea was not to harm the Jewish Agency, the Hagana and their respective leaders, in order to disassociate the insurgents from the rest of the Yishuv. The British were determined to bring about the collapse of the 'National Resistance Movement'. They wished to 'disengage' between the moderates and the radicals by continuing their attempts to crack down on the Irgun and the Sterns.

The operation was launched in Tel Aviv on Tuesday 25 July 1946 following preparations lasting at least three days. Its primary objective was to capture as many members as possible of the two organisations.[28] *Shark* was carried out by the 6th Airborne Division under whose command were two Infantry Brigades and a large force of Palestine police and tanks.

Approximately 15,000 troops altogether took part in the operation. The planning of the operation on such a large scale, and the concentration of troops prior to the H hour, presented a formidable task for the security forces, who wanted to check most of the 200,000 residents in the Tel Aviv area. A complete curfew was imposed on the city from the beginning to the completion of the operation. This was only relaxed for a period of two hours. All routes to the city were cordoned off and so was the entire city itself, including some of the Jewish quarters of Jaffa. The British stated in their intelligence report that the curfew was well observed on the whole by the civilian population. This was probably due to their healthy respect for the weapons of the troops and the show of force, rather than to any real willingness to co-operate. There were a few isolated incidents of curfew breaking, but in only one case were warning shots fired.[29]

In fact, the Hagana ordered all Jews to remain cool and not to resist in the event of retaliatory measures. The population was anyway outraged by the

King David bombing and had no intention other than to obey. Troops were agreeably surprised to find a considerable amount of co-operation from most citizens.[30] The British claimed that during the operation, every house, attic and cellar in Tel Aviv was thoroughly searched and 'every inhabitant, old or young, healthy or infirm, was screened by the police', in one of its many screening stations deployed all over the city.[31] Recognised or suspected terrorists, or persons who could not give a satisfactory account of themselves, were despatched to detention camps at Rafah, near Gaza, and Latrun, on the way to Jerusalem. A total of 787 males and 20 females were detained in these camps. The operation paralysed the Irgun in the Tel Aviv area and its leaders admitted that 'Shark' brought the city to a halt. CID officers armed with lists and photographs identified more than 100,000 people.[32] On one point both the British and the Irgun agreed. The insurgents did not anticipate *Shark* and were caught by surprise, despite the general expectation of some military response to the explosion in Jerusalem. The state of unreadiness of the Irgun surprised the British, who claimed, according to intelligence sources, 'that there was no indication that the actual time and date of the operation had been disclosed...'.[33]

Begin, the Irgun commander, admitted rather arrogantly, that 'had we taken it more seriously, we should all have left Tel Aviv at our leisure and waited for the military to finish their house-to-house search'.[34] He was referring to a warning which had been given to them from a 'reliable source' that the British were likely to carry out widespread searches.

As it happened, the Irgun leaders had had a meeting with the FFI chiefs the evening before the curfew was proclaimed. 'We told them of the warning, but it did not seem urgent, and neither they nor we gave it a second thought'.[35] This was clearly a failure on the Irgun's part. The organisation had no way of knowing about the operation in advance and of reading the situation properly once such a warning had been received, if as they claimed, there was such a warning.

The Irgun blunder caught most of its leaders and personnel, including those who had carried out the explosion, in Tel Aviv. This provided the British with a golden opportunity to capture the underground leaders once and for all. Samuel Katz pointed out that amongst those who were stopped were leaders and staff of the Irgun and FFI who were led to the screening stations and asked to identify themselves.[36] Most of them were picked up at random. The British regarded the operation as a 'substantial success'.[37] The intelligence unit of the South Palestine District's HQ reported that the operation was successful in arresting 787 suspected terrorists to join the *Agatha* detainees in the detention camps. 'It also provided us with a certain amount of valuable intelligence material and with several items which served as useful propaganda in the world press and broadcasting systems'.[38]

However, despite the self-congratulation which was designed mainly to boost morale and impress London, the army's achievements were very limited. It could not list the seizure of more than a handful of caches of arms, only a little forged money was confiscated and out of 767 arrests, only a few were insurgents, while most of the wanted men, who were screened, escaped detection when screened by the military. Among those who were not detected was Begin himself, who hid during the four days of the operation in a secret compartment built in his small flat. Troops were camping in the garden of his flat and at some stage they came in, made a thorough search of the house, opened cupboards, looked under beds and knocked on walls, including the walls of his compartment, but found nothing.[39]

Begin himself wrote after the operation that the British achieved little, 'with all their troops and all their detectives and all their intelligence agents and all their 'terrorist' photographs and all their elaborate identification...'.[40] Katz argued that the British operation was a fiasco and, of nearly 800 people who were led away, there was hardly anybody the British wanted.[41]

The British concluded *Shark* by stating that a number of 'top grade terrorists' had been arrested, which for them was an indication that no previous warning had been received.[42] They also claimed that during the search, certain interesting aspects of the underground movements and activities and some valuable intelligence material were obtained. In addition, five arms caches and some miscellaneous equipment and training material were also found.

In fact, the only major British success was the capture of Yitzhak Yazernitzky (Shamir), a member of the Stern Group's commanding triumvirate and an Irgun officer called Z Kromiers. Most of the 787 detainees could have been regarded as Irgun sympathisers, but they were not active members of either organisation. Taking into account that about 127,000 people were checked, this could scarcely be regarded as a success.

In all, the troops who launched the operation seized 127,000 rounds of small arms ammunition, 23 mortars and four machine guns. In the light of previous failures to seize illegal arms in Palestine, this could have been regarded as an achievement. But taking into consideration the effort and manpower which were thrown into the operation, the result was very poor. Most of the wanted terrorists who happened to be in Tel Aviv were not arrested and most of the caches were not found.

The Cabinet and the Chief of the Imperial General Staff did much to compliment the Army and the police for what they saw as a 'highly successful action'. This stemmed from the fact that the security forces in Palestine reported their achievements but not necessarily their failures.

However, Edward Horne, who wrote the history of the Palestine Police Force 33 years after the operation, took a view which reinforced the Irgun's claim to have emerged unscathed by *Shark*. He wrote that many terrorists 'slipped through the net by play-acting before the inexperienced soldiers'. Many weapons remained concealed because the troops were not searching properly and indeed did not know how to'.[43] Horne argued that the Police Mobile Force had been abolished by the time of the operation, and that 'Shark' was only half as effective as it could have been if the police had had more control over the house-to-house searches.

In short, the fact that there had not been anything like Operation *Shark* before, reflected the Army's difficulties in conducting such massive operations in Palestine. For the British, the mere fact of carrying out such an operation without inflicting casualties on either side,[44] was a success in itself. Their ability to seal off Tel Aviv before the underground organisations knew about it was an achievement for the security forces and a failure on the part of the insurgents.

Apart from the surprise factor, *Shark* was meant not only to capture terrorist leaders, but also to boost the morale of the soldiers following the King David outrage, and to make a show of force to the Arabs. The last two targets were reached, although not for long. The Army and the police emerged jubilant from *Shark*, which met no resistance, and the reaction amongst the Arabs was defined by the British as 'favourable'. The operation might be considered a success in the manner in which it was carried out, but not in the results it achieved. The events in Jerusalem and Tel Aviv could well be regarded as reflecting generally on the ability of the security forces to combat Jewish terrorism in Palestine from the time of the declaration of the Irgun's revolt.

# Chapter 6

# Propaganda and Psychological Warfare

In many ways the struggle between the dissidents, on the one hand, and the British and the mainstream Yishuv, on the other, was about propaganda. Militarily, the Irgun was not a match for the formidable forces that the government kept in Palestine during the 1940s. Being aware of that fundamental disadvantage, the Irgun, after its revolt proclamation, did its utmost to direct each of its operations at the Jewish community for the sake of winning its hearts and minds. Simultaneously, it pursued a policy with a view to tarnishing the British image abroad as much as it could.

The government, as has been argued before, could have cracked the Irgun's terrorist campaign ruthlessly and indiscriminately, as it did during the Arab revolt in the 1930s. However it refrained from doing so. The most important reason for that was the fear of incurring the wrath of international public opinion (mainly in America) and the official Jewish leadership in the aftermath of the Second World War. The British, mindful of the need to win American support for their policy in Palestine, and being, to a certain extent, dependent on the Jewish leadership, could not inflict too much suffering on the community. Ironically, they were bound to lose the war of words against the Jews in any case. Their interests in the Arab and Muslim world forced them to adopt a harsh policy towards the issue of European–Jewish immigration to Palestine. Imposing restrictions on the number of Holocaust survivors who were allowed to settle in the country created fury even within the Jewish leadership which was traditionally sympathetic to the British.

Such a 'no win' situation was fully exploited by the Irgun, active on the margins of the community, but eager to gain acceptability and legitimacy in the Yishuv. From the outset of their revolt proclamation, the Irgunists capitalised on the immigration controversy. Every refugee boat which was turned back by the British navy triggered a very noisy and emotional campaign by the Irgun, which embarrassed the Jewish Agency and increased the already existing hostility towards the government.

The main objective of the Irgun's propaganda was to recruit as many members as possible to its ranks. Needless to say, the campaign was not directed at the socialist camp, the Kibbutzim, the trade unions or the left-wing parties. In fact, the Irgun abandoned any hope of winning the support of the agricultural sector in the country. The new recruits came from the veteran urban centres, Jerusalem, Tel Aviv, Netanya and Ramat Gan, towns where oriental-Jewish families, many of them religious, were concentrated. The Irgun appealed to them as a nationalistic and militant group, as opposed to the Hagana, which represented secular socialist thinking, influenced by its East-European founding members. The Irgun's strength was its ability to accompany each of its military operations with the relevant commentary and announcements. The means of delivering the insurgents' messages were by illegal billposting, leaflets and, mainly, by radio broadcasts. These were made in Hebrew, and sometimes in Arabic and English, and were designed to influence not only the civilian communities, but also the British Government and the individual soldiers in the country.

The Irgun's own version of each and every operation was given without delay. It was a mixture of presenting facts, preaching to the enemy and vows of revenge or continuing the campaign unabated. Warnings to the armed forces or the Jewish establishment, street mourning notices about its war casualties and articles in the Revisionist legal press were part of a constant campaign which in its first phase was motivated by domestic reasons. The most pressing immediate task was to win a speedy superiority over the Stern Group, which was the only active anti-British organisation until the end of the Second World War. Badly needed support in the militant section of the Yishuv dominated the first few months of the revolt's propaganda, which was hailed by the Irgun as the best proof of their serious intent to launch an armed struggle. The fact that the first operations were ineffective was overlooked by the High Command's members. By using superlatives, so common in their daily vocabulary, they overrated the success of the campaign and kept praising the 'heroic' sacrifices of their rank and file in their struggle.

The man who was in charge of it all was the chief commander Menachem Begin. He was the prime author of most of the group publications and his writings from his hiding in Tel Aviv were broadcast by the 'Voice of Fighting Zion', which became the hallmark of the Irgun. Begin's tracts were distributed by the 'Revolutionary Propaganda Unit', which operated a network of Jewish youngsters in the main urban centres of the country. Beyond the call to remove immigration restrictions and to lift laws forbidding land purchases by Jews, Irgun propaganda was based on ideology, however vague. Begin himself outlined the manifesto of the organisation and highlighted its four main objectives: 'National Freedom';

'Return to Zion'; 'Freedom of the Individual' and 'Social Justice'.[1] These ambiguous slogans unfolded the Irgun's chief political object – to form an absolute Jewish majority in the whole of Palestine 'which would put an end to the unnatural dispersion of the people of Israel'.[2] This was to be achieved by a massive immigration to Palestine.

By stressing that point, the Irgun did not differ from the other moderate elements within the Jewish community, but the means of achieving that aim, as explained by Begin himself, were different. In his opinion the need for armed struggle was based on the experience of the Jews since the British presence in Palestine. 'The attempt to restore the land of Israel to the Hebrew people by land purchases and commercial means have failed, as well as the struggle by means of moral and political argument'.[3]

The Irgun held the view that the British had no intention of abandoning their grip on Palestine, on the pretext of doing 'justice' to the Arabs. Therefore any attempt to adopt 'persuasive' measures in advance was doomed to fail. Such thinking was partially dominated by the belief that Arab terrorism, during the revolt of the 1930s, played some part in reinforcing British determination to suspend Jewish immigration in 1939 and to adopt a harsh attitude towards the issue thereafter.[4]

Begin laid down the necessary conditions under which creating a Jewish majority might be achieved. The first one was 'a continuous liberation war'. The second was 'incessant preparations for the decisive movement'. The third, from which we can learn about the importance he attached to propaganda, was to 'raise the problem into an international issue and to win over political support'.[5] Begin was well aware of the political impact which the Irgun's activities had outside Palestine, especially in Britain and the USA. This was exemplified on 15 October 1944, eight and a half months after the Irgun revolt proclamation, when he spoke to his district commanders, summing up the influence of the IZL's first military activities on Western public opinion. 'In total contradiction to the past', he said, 'we have taught the world that the Jews are capable of resisting oppression. We have proved that the community can launch a rebellion on a large scale'.[6]

Begin overestimated the magnitude of his armed struggle. After the British Governor of Jerusalem argued that the attacks caused nothing but damage to the Zionist cause,[7] Begin was quick to conclude that public opinion in England was influenced by the Irgun's first violent acts. 'The important press preaches to the authorities about the seriousness of the situation', he said in that meeting which was designed to boost the morale of his subordinates.[8] As he had throughout the whole campaign, the Irgun chief commander, quoted the British press to reinforce his claim over the effectiveness of the revolt. *The Times* warned that if the situation was allowed to continue, anarchy was inevitable and 'such words make their own impression on the reader'. *The New Statesman* called for an immediate political solution to the problem of Palestine and *The Economist* clearly admitted that the Jewish Brigade was set up, within the British Army, to quieten the radicals, who opposed terrorism.

Begin also claimed credit for what he regarded as tremendous support among the decision-makers in America which manifested itself in President Truman's new policy to lift his objection to an unlimited Jewish immigration into Palestine. Seeking impact abroad, as that meeting showed, was a prime target of the Irgun's armed rebellion, but more pressing was the need to enhance the group's political grip in Palestine. Here came the second phase of the propaganda battle. After averting the danger, in the first six months of the revolt, that young Jewish militants might move to the Stern Group, the next task was to confront the mainstream Yishuv. The latter, represented mainly by the Jewish Agency and the Hagana, waged an unprecedented war of words against the Irgun. The insurgents were accused of embarking on an adventuristic campaign which might have lost the community the goodwill of London. Moreover, they were blamed for the possibility that the British would suspend immigration as an immediate punitive measure for the terrorism in the country. The major accusation levelled against them was that they were planning to dominate the Yishuv and take its leadership by force.

The Irgun, fearing that its opponents might be able to tarnish its image at such an early stage, was therefore eager to challenge what became throughout the remaining Mandate years a central issue in the community's domestic political confrontation. The socialist camp stopped at nothing in its efforts to portray the Irgun as a bunch of trigger-happy hooligans who would inflict calamity on Jewish hopes of a national homeland. Many of its attacks concentrated personally on Begin himself. At another meeting that he convened with his colleagues in November 1944, Begin complained that his rivals had spread rumours that he was an employee of British intelligence. 'The propaganda campaign against us is very strong', he said, 'but we shall respond to it only with political arguments. The situation may escalate, but we have to ignore the results and beware of provocations.'[9] Consistently suspected of its motives, the Irgun was on the defensive. The Hagana dragged it into a domestic propaganda confrontation and the only way for it to climb out of the 'trap' was to concentrate on the anti-British armed struggle. The British, not fully aware of the unrest among the Jewish youth, played down its bitterness on which the Irgun wanted to capitalise. Britain was an easy target for the dissidents' attacks due to its policy of immigration. The deportation of the illegal refugees arriving in Palestine from Europe became the centre of the IZL psychological warfare and served to justify its terrorist campaign.

Menachem Begin masterminded the propaganda war. He left the military aspects of the struggle to members of the High Command and devoted himself to his writings and broadcasts. Almost every word expressed by the Irgun during the revolt was written by him. In fact, members of the 'Revolutionary Propaganda Unit' acted as distributors of Begin's pamphlets and had little or no say in the direction of the campaign. Samuel Katz, head of the unit, said that Begin was at the central core of the Irgun. 'He presided directly over the political department, with its branches of propaganda, of information and of exhortation to the people at large and the world outside.'[10] Katz was responsible for disseminating information in English about the IZL. He published a monthly bulletin called *Irgunpress* and wrote booklets on the group's background and the purpose of its struggle. He also translated the Irgun broadcasts into English and provided the formula for the propaganda publication in French, Italian, Greek and Bulgarian. But as we have seen Katz and the unit he headed were dominated by Begin, who issued written statements every day, sometimes more than one or two within the space of a few hours. Begin's work was the main inspiration for the 'Voice of Fighting Zion' and his articles, hailing his men or damning the enemy, were published and distributed regularly. Domestically, Begin had to manoeuvre between the Sterns' constant reminders that the Irgun co-operated with the British during the war and the Hagana's allegation of a plot to seize political power. Begin's initial preferred strategy was to ignore both sides and to concentrate on military activity, but since the Irgun's first attacks on government buildings lacked political impact, he had to respond to the criticism of both the Hagana and FFI. The British, on the other hand, were not provoked at all by the revolt proclamation and this fact reinforced its hollowness. They seemed neither to take it seriously nor to combat it. Regarding the Irgun as a minor and non-representative terrorist group, they left the arena open to its increasing rhetoric.

Frank Kitson, one of Britain's most notable experts on counter-insurgency operations, has roundly condemned British apathy in the conduct of its psychological operations overseas. 'They seem to persist in thinking of psychological operations as being something from the realms of science fiction, when it has for many years been regarded as a necessary and respectable form of war by most of our allies, as well as virtually all of our potential enemies . . .'.[11]

This argument was well reflected in Palestine. Apart from their dismissive attitude, the British thought of the IZL as a terrorist group only, unaware that it could provoke a growing erosion of their grip on the country. The complacency of the authorities was mainly based on the fact that the official Jewish leadership, with whom the British were dealing, strongly disassociated themselves from the use of violence. The insurgents, for their part, by flooding the streets with posters and leaflets, made serious efforts to drive a wedge between the population and the Mandate rule. Gradually its campaign gathered momentum.

That is not to say that the British ignored the Irgun altogether, but they played down its potential importance. They failed for the most part to grasp the full meaning of the Irgun's skill at using the holocaust for promoting its aims. The guerrillas made the most of the Jewish mass-extermination and continuously blamed the British for completing the unfinished task of the Germans. The 'boat propaganda' was its best psychological weapon and it was widely used whenever a ship carrying refugees was stopped by government forces on approaching the shores of Palestine, and turned away. The Irgun gave many incidents full exposure for the benefit of the press. A photograph of a child, who died in one of the shaky craft, was distributed under the title 'gassed by the Nazi-British'. The holocaust survivors were the subject of most of the Irgun statements throughout the last remaining years of British rule in the country.

Apart from the use of the secret radio station and the poster campaign, the Irgun maintained close contacts with the foreign media. Many of the insurgents, even Command members, briefed international journalists on a regular basis and were skilful in knowing how to provide the press with 'good stories'. So effective was its use of correspondents that Moshe Shertock, head of the political department of the Jewish Agency, made a direct appeal to the journalists based in Palestine. On 11 June 1947 he asked them not to report the Irgun activities 'in terms of glorification'. He explained it on the ground that positive coverage encouraged the terrorists and undermined efforts to isolate them and deny them public sympathy.[12]

The Irgun, in its contact with the media, placed much importance on the accuracy of its reportage. Although its 'propaganda of allegation' was exaggerated, the underlying facts were presented accurately and information which could have been subject to refutation was avoided. Marek Kahan, one of the Command members who was in charge of the Irgun's bulletin called *Herut* ('Freedom'), said that his colleagues' work was done by sticking to Begin's 'Iron Rule' which forbade them to use unsubstantiated information. Kahan admitted, though, that sometimes they relied on the revolutionary literature of the Bolsheviks and the tactics they applied before the October revolution.[13]

Moshe Gold, one of editors of *Freedom*, which was posted on the street walls as well as being handed to the public, said that the 'mission was guided by constant educational writing, and not by inflaming feelings or by voicing many slogans'. He added that the attention was focused on one goal throughout the years of the campaign – the right of the Jewish people to their own freedom in the state of Israel.[14]

Gradually, the Irgun learned to exploit all the possible opportunities which enabled it to promote its campaign: speeches of convicted insurgents during their trials; statements made by those condemned to death; meetings with overseas delegations, including UN representatives; personal letters to international leaders and messages aimed at the 'British soldier in Palestine'.

## THE PROPAGANDA DIRECTED AT THE BRITISH FORCES

When the Irgun addressed itself to the British forces, it adopted the 'soldier to soldier' approach. Statements made by the insurgents were worded in a personal style in order to convince the individual of the futility and the fruitlessness of his presence in Palestine. The IZL used to publish appeals to the soldiers after each successful operation in which British soldiers were killed or wounded. That approach was exemplified in one of the first pamphlets issued on 6 October 1944. 'The struggle is not directed against you', it said, '... we appreciate that you shed your blood on many fronts and in many countries. We know that many among you condemn the official hypocrisy and many are looking, as we do, for a better world ... (but) now we are fighting against a regime based on bad faith ... this little country belonged to us, it was promised to us, it is the only haven for millions of homeless Jews ...'.[15]

While stressing that 'it is this regime of oppression against which we are fighting', the pamphlet went on to make a distinction between the soldiers and the 'mercenaries and instruments of this regime' (i.e. the police and the CID, nicknamed by the Irgun the 'Palestine Gestapo') who are not 'strong and courageous enough to overcome the revolt of free men, so they resort to you soldiers ...'. Then came the typically repeated questions: was it for this purpose that you left home and joined the army? Does your duty consist of oppressing Jews in their homeland? Don't you realise the humiliation to which you are subjected by participating in such police action? Is this your kind of war, which is being called by your politicians a 'war of liberation'?[16] Another example of the way the Irgun directed its psychological campaign towards the individual soldier, could be seen in a pamphlet written in March 1945, as follows:

> We, members of the National Military Organisation (NMO) in the land of Israel, address you as soldiers address soldiers. You joined the armed forces, left your homes and families, exposed your life to danger, determined to defend your country against the enemy of yours, the monstrous enemy of all humanity – Hitlerite Germany...

In November 1945, the Irgun published a 'letter to a friend from a Jewish ex-serviceman' in which the British soldier was told: 'I have seen you in the street and felt like having a talk with you. I wonder whether you realised why you have been sent here. When soldiers are sent overseas, they naturally presume that it is to fight an enemy. It has occurred to me that someone may have tried to tell you that I am your enemy. You must not believe it. We are not your enemies. We are only stretching forth our hands to give refuge to the starving survivors of our people ...'.[17]

Such statements were usually published after the Army had mounted mass-searches, imposed curfews or applied other counter-insurgency measures which caused suffering to civilians. The Irgun liked to call the armed forces 'soldiers on leave', drawing a line between them and the civilian administration. The distinction between the conscripted soldiers and the British Government was made in an attempt to convince the individual soldier that the Hebrew underground did not have any intention to harm him, if he refrained from implementing the 'government policy of oppression'.

Most of the Irgun's verbal and written attacks were not aimed at the Army but at British Intelligence, the police, the High Commissioner and the government in London. The reason was not necessarily tactical. The Irgun, at least during the first years of its self-proclaimed revolt, wanted to get rid of the 'imperialistic' nature of British rule in Palestine.[18] The army, especially after the war, was not included in that category and did not represent the 'traitorous regime' in the eyes of the insurgents. For the Yishuv, the British troops were an army of liberators who had fought the Nazis successfully, and the IZL was very reluctant to be seen as its enemy. Later, when the clashes between both sides intensified, the Army did not escape the terrorist campaign, but in the propaganda war it was singled out as an element which was forced to pursue London's policy in the country, against its will and its moral values.

Begin, embracing that tactic, did not hold the Army responsible for the plight of the Jewish refugees, despite the fact that the navy was blocking their entry into Palestine. He chose to describe them as tools in the hands of the oppressive regime, since they had to obey its orders. Hence the tendency to compare only the civil administration to the Nazis. Such a repeated comparison was well reflected in a statement issued by the Irgun on 29 June 1946, when a British counter-offensive was launched against the United Resistance Movement. 'The oppressive hand of the enemy', it said, 'the teacher of Hitler and the executor of his plans, has been raised against the Jewish people. The existence of the nation is at stake'. In that statement, titled 'Mobilise the Nation', the insurgents voiced the demands which represented their views at the time. They included the establishment of a

'Hebrew Provisional Government', followed by the forming of the 'Supreme National Council' which was to have acted as provisional parliament. A call for a Jewish army and supreme military command was also made.[19]

These demands were not fulfilled by the British, nor were they expected to do so by the Irgun, but they were part of the guerrillas' propaganda campaign to win support at home, by portraying itself as a responsible political movement, not a terrorist group. This is why the insurgents, being so mindful of their reputation, were determined to demonstrate their political character time and again. In a message to the public, after being accused by the Jewish Agency and the Hagana of adopting violent methods, Begin wrote: 'The Irgun is not a 'terrorist' organisation. It does not commit acts of violence for the sake of violence. Its aims are political – the freeing of Palestine from foreign domination . . . When it fights, it fights for political purposes and in a legitimately political manner. It regrets every casualty it is forced to inflict, and inflicts no more than is forced upon it. It proclaims its friendship for the British people, as for every other people on earth . . .'.[20]

Another message best illustrates the 'soldier to soldier' approach adopted by the Irgun:

> We will fight you. It can not be helped. Nor does it help to speak about 'law and order'. Law and order means each shall rule in his own house and live on his own soil. That right is our cause for which we are ready to fight to the last. Where is yours? Bevin's stupidity? Oil? Their Lordships' income? Is that worth dying for?'.[21]

## THE IRGUN'S USE OF THE COURTROOM FOR ITS PROPAGANDA CAMPAIGN

As the armed revolt took shape, the insurgents were instructed by the High Command to increase the propaganda factor of each operation. Members, if arrested and brought to trial, were told not to co-operate with the legal system, not to recognise the authority of the British military court, and to use the defendant dock as a platform for denouncing the government. Some examples demonstrate the ability of the Irgunists to turn court hearings into 'show trials' in front of the watchful eye of the national and the international media. One defendant A Moscovitch made a political speech in which he reviewed the British attitude towards the Palestine question and chose to quote Lord Wedgwood who said in 1942 that he would like to urge all Jews in the Land of Israel to 'acts of violence, to acts of rebellion, for they

*Irgun Commander, Menachem Begin, after his emergence from the Underground.*

*The office in Haifa of the Deputy Police Superintendent of Palestine's North District after a car loaded with explosives was detonated against a wall. Two British and two Arab policemen were killed and approximately 100 police and civilians were injured.*

*The Inland Revenue Office in Jerusalem, bombed by the Irgun on 20 November 1946.*

*Irgun members on the rooftops of Tel Aviv on its border with Jaffa at the end of 1947. Although this confrontation was mainly with the Arabs, the British were also involved and all sides exchanged fire.*

## To The British Soldier In Palestine!

We, members of the National Military Organisation in Erets Israel address you as soldiers address soldiers:

You have joined the armed forces, left your homes and families, exposed your lives to danger not as mercenaries, but as free and proud men determined to defend your country, against the enemy of yours, the monstrous enemy of all humanity — Hitlerite Germany.

The Hebrew Youth, however, was for 5 Years denied the opportunity. In spite of its most ardent desire, to fight our mortal foe, as it was robbed of the basic idea which inspires all nations participating in this glibal war, the idea, that the goal of its fight and sacrifices is a free homeland.

The „political gamble" so cinically conducted by unsempulous politicians and so hipocritically camouflaged with fine phrases about „Justice" and „Freedom", resulted in our case in the following: that thousands of young Jews of Erets Israel who voluntarily joined the Army have been degraded to auxiliary services in the desert and elsewhere instead of taking part, under their national banner, in the military operations on the many battlefields of the world; that the gates of our homeland, which must be a homeland for every Jew, have been shut and barred in face of the unprecedented massacres of our brethren in Nazi-Europe; that five millions of Jews — our parents, brothers, sisters and children — who, were it not for the bad faith of your politicians, should and could have been rescued, were exterminated in the European slaughter-houses.

This is the tragic situation we face and it imposed on us the necessity of starting a struggle for the liberation of our own country and for the rescue of our persecuted nation. It is not only our natural right, but above all our sacred duty to rise and fight, even with the cost of our life, in order to put an end to our people's sufferings, in order to give it, after so many ages of dispersion and persecutions, its home, so that it may live in peace, security and honour.

This struggle is not directed against you. We appreciate that you shed your blood on many fronts and in many countries; we know that many among you condemn the official hypocrisy and many are looking — as we are — for a better world in which every nation and every individual will be given an opportunity of free and undisturbed development.

Nor is this struggle historically directed against your country. No Jewish Government will pursue any other policy than that of friendship with the British Commonwealth and with other free nations. But friendship must be mutual.

Now, we are fighting against a regime based on bad faith, on repudiation of solemn pledges and international obligations, a regime of treachery and oppression. This little country belongs to us. It is our old historic motherland, dreamt of by tens of generations, sacred by the blood of heroes and fighters. It was promised to us. It is the only haven for millions of homeless Jews.

The declared aim, however, of your rulers is to prevent our people from repatriation and restoration: their policy is to keep by force the door of our country closed to the survivors of the Nazi massacres; their decision is to impose on us the status of a permanent minority, the well-known „existence" of a GHETTO.

It is this regime of oppression we are fighting against. And we are determined to continue our struggle, if necessary, to the last man in our ranks. And so is every free and proud Jew in Erets-Israel.

But it appears that the mercenaries and instruments of this regime, the police and C. I. D. men—those „heroes" of the Palestine Gestapo who succeeded in evading the dangers of the battlefield—are not strong enough and not courageous enough to overcome the revolt of free men. So they resort to you, soldiers on leave from the war fronts, in order to be assested in their „noble" job. Recently, in Jerusalem, Tel-Aviv and Petach-Tikva, units of the Army took part in mass searches, chasing Young fighters, who shed their blood for a Justa Causa of no precedent in human history.

We are, indeed, proud of the fact that the Government of oppression has been compelled to bring in brigades and divisions, tanks and planes in order to try — in vain! — to destroy the spirit of freedom of the regenerated Hebrew Youth. But we are bound, on th other hand, to ask you:

Is it for that purpose, that you left your home and joined the Army? Does your duty consist in oppressing Jews in their homeland? Don't you realise the humiliation to which you are subjected by participating in such police-actions? Is THIS your task in this war, which is being called by Your politicians „war of liberation"?

THINK OF IT!

HAIRGUN HATZVAI HALEUMI
B'ERETS-ISRAEL
(National Military Organisation)

*Irgun notice.*

*Mining of a train in the Sharon district.*

*The British Headquarters in Palestine at the King David Hotel, bombed 22 July 1946.*

*The damaged Inland Revenue building.*

*British Officers arrest Irgun suspects.*

*Searching for guerrillas and weapons in Jerusalem.*

*British mine detectors in Jerusalem.*

*Searching for the two sergeants in Netanya.*

*Evacuating Ramat Gan Police Station.*

Curfew in Tel Aviv. Armoured cars of the 6th Airborne Division.

Goldsmith House, in Jerusalem's security zone. Bombed by the Irgun, 1 March 1947.

*A casualty is helped from the wreckage of Goldsmith House.*

*The funeral at the military cemetery at Ramlah of the officers killed at Goldsmith House.*

sometimes are acts of salvation ...'[22] He added: 'From past history you know that whenever a white oppressor comes across a white oppressed, the former must withdraw. We belong to the international family of resistance'. Another Irgunist, I Ganzweich, explained his reason for joining the struggle. 'How does it come about that a Jewish fighter from Poland is on trial, not before a German court, but a British one? Only a year ago, I and my brother were your allies. Together we killed Germans ...'.[23] D Kirpitchinkoff spoke of the legal background to the 'rising against oppression'. He told the court that 'science and history teach us that when two legal principles collide, the higher one always get the upper hand'. He then presented the question 'which of these principles is the higher? Is it the British law in Israel? Or is it the consciousness of justice of the Hebrew population?' And facing the judges he answered: 'Your duty is to do justice, to restore to us our stolen homeland ...'.[24]

One of the favourite tactics adopted by the Irgun members was to demand the rights of prisoners of war during their trials. In June 1946 no less than 30 men, who were caught in a military operation in south Palestine, claimed this status. One of them, M Binden, told his judges that complying with the Irgun demand would be more in the British interest than his. 'After all, gentlemen, we are prepared for everything, for every sacrifice ... Our determination can be compared only to that of the Russians in their defence against the German invaders of their homeland ...'.[25] His speech reflected the Irgun fatalistic view, which conveyed to the authorities in court, that they were 'taking part in a struggle with no other alternative' and 'with nothing to lose but our lives'. Binden was not alone in expressing despair and indifference to life. Other Irgunists also said that they fought in the profound conviction that if they did not succeed in their war, there would be 'neither life nor future for them'.[26]

The intensification of the armed struggle against the authorities caused some key Government officials to make anti-semitic remarks, which were widely exploited by the Irgun's propaganda machine. The most disastrous one came from Lieutenant General Sir Evelyn Barker, GOC British Troops in Palestine, who called on his soldiers after the King David explosion 'to punish the Jews in a way this race dislikes most – in the pockets'.[27] But the Irgun alleged, on its clandestine radio, that another such remark was made by a president of a military court. He was accused by the IZL of having told some officers 'what a pity one has not done with the Jews in Palestine what was done with them in Europe. I could then leave this damned country and return to England'.

Such remarks gave the Irgun inevitable ammunition for its propaganda efforts and it was not lost on the insurgents in the dock. C Luster confronted the same court president. 'The Holy land', he said, 'became a 'damned country' because the Jews live in it ... and if you hate us, how does your conscience allow you to be the judge of the Jews? And if a judge has a hostile attitude to the accused, it is his duty to ask to be released from his function'. Luster declared: 'You are perfectly free to return home and not only you alone. Take away with you all your army and police, and all your officials, who too would probably like to go home ....'.[28]

Some of the most effective statements were made by the IZL who were sentenced to death by the British military courts. They were widely publicised and won immense popularity for the Irgun even among its opponents who admired their courage in the court-room, as well as in the death cell.

One of them was Mordechai Elkahi, who was in the Irgun 'flogging squad' which used to catch British personnel and whip them, in retaliation for similar preventative measures. He and two of his colleagues claimed in court that they were badly beaten after their capture and maltreated in prison. 'An enemy who does what was done to us is not an enemy. It is a filthy gang, lacking all human feeling, or human dignity, which threatens the foundations of human civilisation'.[29]

In May 1946, Moshe Barazani and Meir Feinstein, members of the IZL and FFI respectively, caught the imagination of the public when they blew themselves up in their prison cell in Jerusalem with a hand-grenade smuggled by colleagues only hours before their execution. In court, a few days earlier, Feinstein said: 'How blind you are, British tyrants ! Do you think you will frighten us with death? We, who for years listened to the rattle of the wheels of those trucks that bore our brothers, our parents, the best of our people to a slaughter which has no precedent in human history...?'.[30]

Captured members of the Irgun were also encouraged by the High Command to portray the British as a power which oppressed freedom everywhere, not only against Jews in Palestine. Abshalom Haviv, hanged with two of his friends, for his participation in the attack on the Acre Fortress, voiced the Irgun's support for the Irish struggle. He told the court: 'You will probably remember that in Ireland too you seized a small country and captured people by force of arms and deceit in the name of religion and under the cover of 'law and order'. When the sons of Ireland rose up against you, you tried to drown the rising against tyranny in rivers of blood, you set up gallows, you murdered in the streets, you exiled, you ran amok, and believed, in your stupidity, that by dint of persecution, you would break the spirit of resistance of the free Irish ...'.[31]

The most famous and controversial insurgent was Dov Gruner, who was wounded and captured by the British during the Irgun attack on Ramat Gan police station. He was a Holocaust survivor and his refusal to appeal against the death sentence passed on him, won his case world-wide publicity.[32] Gruner was tried at the military court of Jerusalem which was packed with newsmen from all over the world. He told the court on 1 January 1947: 'When a regime in any country is transformed into a rule of oppression, it ceases to be lawful. It is the right of the citizens – moreover it is their duty – to fight this rule and overthrow it . . .'.[33]

The plight of Gruner caused an emotional reaction in the Jewish community which was united in calling on the British to mitigate the sentence. His case was debated also in the House of Commons on 28 January 1947 and was subject to bitter arguments between the government and the opposition benches. A British officer wrote after the war that out of all the people, British, Jews and Arabs, who were involved in Palestine affairs during the post-war years, only a few won as much publicity as Gruner, 'whose name has become known all over the world in three months'.[34]

Before and after Gruner's eventual hanging on 15 April 1947, the Irgun launched a massive propaganda campaign which portrayed him as the solitary soldier who stood against the entire British Empire. In a broadcast addressed to him before his death, the Irgun declared: 'Everybody wants your life. Churchill, who for damned British 'prestige' is willing to sacrifice millions of people, and the British 'socialist' government who wants to see your blood shed. All this Empire, its ministers, commissioners and armies, stood against you . . .'.[35]

The Gruner case, as well as other hangings of Irgun's members, vividly illustrate the insurgents' ability to create a show trial out of every legal procedure against them. They were prepared for the task in the event of their capture. Their speeches were distributed all over the country and were broadcast by the underground radio station.[36] The Jewish youth in Palestine were impressed by the insurgents' acts of heroism. Their willingness to sacrifice their lives, their skill in making political statements and the courage they demonstrated while singing the national anthem on their way to the gallows, won them the admiration of the Irgun's most bitter opponents in Palestine.

But despite the success of its psychological warfare, the Irgun remained a minority within the Jewish community in Palestine. More youngsters joined the group in 1946 and 1947, but sympathy was not translated into mass mobilisation. The Hagana's hegemony was not seriously challenged and the insurgents were sometimes at pains to justify some of their activities, such as the King David blast or the hanging of the two sergeants. The level of moral support for the Irgun was swinging from one extreme to another and was subject to the way the British were conducting their policy on Palestine. From their initial unhappy experience, the dissidents learned that if they wanted the public to be aware of their existence, they must accompany their rhetoric with military operations. The failure of the first year of the revolt created a vacuum which the Irgun could not fill with bill-posting and broadcasts only. The propaganda campaign failed in the absence of terrorist action. That is why each operation was followed by a blaze of publicity. The Irgun, consistently made attempts to explain the motive behind each act and to inform the public about the extent of its success.

Begin, aware of the underground's weak position in the community, tried, sometimes desperately, to use every opportunity to voice the Irgun's political views in Palestine and overseas. Most of all he wanted to rid the Irgun of its terrorist image. He therefore frequently reacted to international developments. Begin wanted to prove himself as a statesman and behaved like one in July 1945 when the Labour Party won the general elections in Britain. The Irgun, responding to the community leaders' calls, declared a cease-fire in order to give the new government in London the opportunity 'to prove whether it is their intention to fulfil without delay their public undertaking'.[37] Being on the sidelines of Jewish–Palestinian diplomacy efforts, the Irgun strongly wanted to involve itself in the political debate on the future of the country. For that purpose it issued memoranda, declarations, messages and communiqués and simultaneously made attempts to get in touch with international institutions and foreign governments. One of its principal targets was American public opinion, and members of the High Command, including Begin himself, met clandestinely with representatives of the United Nations Special Committee on Palestine.[38]

One of the achievements of the Irgun's propaganda machinery was its relative success in equating anti-Zionism with anti-semitism, although the constant attempt to brand the British as no better than Nazis did not win much approval. The man who 'helped' the British to play into the hands of the insurgents was none other than the Foreign Secretary himself. Ernest Bevin did not choose his words carefully when he referred to the Palestine question. His occasional anti-Jewish remarks were seized upon by the IZL and became a central issue in its public preaching. When Bevin accused the Jews of 'jumping to the head of the queue' with regards to immigration, the Irgun reacted swiftly. This was also the case with General Barker's remarks. The Irgun went out of its way to leak and publicise widely the General's 'Order of the Day' in which he instructed his men not to deal with the Jews in the aftermath of the King David affair. Barker, in many ways, came to the Irgun's rescue in one of the worst moments of its armed struggle when it had the impossible task of justifying the explosion in Jerusalem. 'I am determined to see them punished and to make known to them the disgust and the contempt we feel towards them', he told his soldiers. Barker's mistake was that he failed to make a clear distinction between the insurgents and the community as a whole. His remarks aroused a wave of outrage all over the world and the Irgun made full use of them, especially in America.[39] As well as relying on British mistakes, the Irgun concentrated on military operations with the clear aim to diminish British prestige in the country. It would be fair to argue that on many occasions the Irgun embarked on armed attacks against British targets only for the benefit of public relations. Such were, for example, the flogging activities and even the Acre fortress break-in. That pattern of the campaign was not lost on the Hagana which accused the insurgents of 'adventurism' and readiness to sacrifice their own people for the sake of publicity.[40]

It is self-evident that the circumstances in post-war Palestine could not have been better for a guerrilla organisation which launched a major propaganda campaign against a 'foreign ruler'. Despite that advantage, the Irgun lacked the ability to convince the majority of the Jewish section in Palestine that its strategy was the right one. Many people were impressed by the bravery of its members, but they maintained all along that the policy of the IZL was dangerous. The group's psychological assault also failed to make an impact on the individual British soldier. Ironically, the Irgun's cause was more popular in the United States and the campaign launched there on its behalf was one of the most effective propaganda exercises of modern times.

## THE IRGUN'S CAMPAIGN IN AMERICA

The American public's disapproval of British policy on Palestine owes much to the activities carried out on behalf of the Irgun in the United States. It was, by almost all accounts, the most effective Jewish political campaign for the Zionist cause between the two world wars.

Acknowledging the importance of the future American role in the Middle East and recognising America's ability to apply pressure on the British Government, the insurgents were determined to do everything in their power to influence the political mood in the States. Various committees, set up by the activists, managed to win the support of many decision-makers within the Administration, Jews and non-Jews alike, who assisted them in promoting the Zionists' national aspirations. Politicians, film stars, writers, poets, artists, trade unions and spiritual leaders were recruited by the committees and massive public support was won for the Irgun's armed struggle in Palestine and for the efforts to save the remaining European Jews from the German extermination.

The Irgun's first delegation to America, small in number and lacking funds, came with the aim of collecting money and winning moral support. It established a body called 'American Friends of Jewish Palestine', but its success was very limited.[41] One of the reasons for this was the hostile attitude of the Revisionists who feared competition and expressed concern at the possibility of losing control of the Irgun's activities abroad. The Revisionists, who had established themselves in America as far back as 1939, were totally subordinate to Jabotinsky who urged American public opinion to help him establish a Jewish army inside the British forces. The outbreak of war emphasised that need more than ever before. The death of Jabotinsky in summer 1940 delivered a blow to these Revisionist efforts. At the same time, however, it relieved the small Irgun delegation in the USA of a heavy political burden. The group, which was led by Peter Bergson (and included S Merlin, Y Ben Ami, O Hadani, A Ben Eliezer, B Rafaeli and E Lankin) decided to adopt Jabotinsky's ideas of forming a Jewish Army. Without losing much time, they set up the first of three committees, which they called the 'Committee for the Jewish Army'. This committee was established on 4 December 1941 in Washington, under the presidency of Dr. S Choresh, the head of the Karangi Institute. Bergson said that the aim of the new body was to mobilise 200,000 Jewish soldiers in Palestine and elsewhere. The campaign was conducted under the slogan 'Jews fight for the right to fight'. Senators and trade union leaders were asked to send telegrams to British members of Parliament, urging them to 'take advantage of the Jewish manpower' available to the Allied forces.

At first, many Americans leaders hesitated to join the campaign. But, surprisingly, after the Japanese attack on Pearl Harbor on 7 December 1941, they changed their mind. This event in the Far East increased American readiness to support the Jewish cause. As a result, many prominent people supported the idea of a Jewish army, including judges, bishops, authors, ex-generals and admirals, state governors and businessmen. The activities of the committee intensified after a few months and, in Bergson's own words: 'gradually and imperceptibly, from a mere Irgun delegation, we became a politically effective force'.[42] Although operating without co-ordinated plans (the Irgun in Palestine was relatively inactive at the beginning of the 1940s), the committee, taking full advantage of the war, started its activities with considerable success and regarded itself as the 'political wing of the IZL'.

However, because of the need to come to terms with the nature of American public opinion, it soon had to change its strategy. Bergson, the chairman and figurehead of the committee, confirmed that the Japanese attack had changed everything. 'Before that we regarded ourselves as Zionists. But we failed to take into account the difference between a Polish Jew and an American Jew. We were all Zionists, every Jew, wherever he lived.

When a Jewish activist and businessman approached us and advised us to change the name of the committee to 'Committee for a Palestine Army', we dismissed it out of hand on the grounds that we were all Zionists. After the Japanese attack on Pearl Harbor, when Jews were recruited to the American army as ordinary American soldiers, we knew he was right'. According to Bergson, they added another line to the initial title and called themselves 'Committee for the Jewish Army of Stateless Palestine'.[43]

The change was not one of semantics, but of substance. This alone created a deep and bitter confrontation between the Committee and the Irgun during the Begin-led anti-British revolt in Palestine. The ideological rift was intensified towards the end of the war when the committee made a clear distinction between American Jews on the one hand, and Jews in Palestine and East Europe on the other, by indicating that the latter were stateless and homeless.

The fact that these Jews, unlike the American ones, lacked self-determination, made the Committee feel that they could talk on their behalf. And in order to distinguish between religion and nationality they coined the term 'Hebrew People' and claimed that every Jew who wanted to be called 'Hebrew' was Hebrew, even if he lived in the United States. It was, more than anything, a tactical change. But it enabled the Committee to ask for the support of many non-Jews who became even more influential in the struggle of the Jews for a state of their own in Palestine. However, the first news from Europe about the horrific scale of the Holocaust changed the nature of the Committee. On 17 November 1942, it had already organised a petition signed by 3000 American leaders, demanding that the government declare the 'moral rights of the homeless Jews in Europe and Palestine'.[44] The petition was the cornerstone of an aggressive, ambitious and skilful campaign, which included mass rallies, radio broadcasts, meetings, newspaper advertising and constant pressure on the Administration to do its utmost to stop the extermination of the Jews in Europe.

The group had two main objectives: to make every American citizen aware of the Jewish plight and to lobby the decision makers in Washington. In the space of a few weeks, its leaders met ministers, members of Congress, senators and other senior officials. They drew the attention of President Roosevelt to the events in Europe so forcefully that at one stage he himself complained about their noisy campaign on Capitol Hill.[45]

Bergson and his colleagues called for an urgent conference to mobilise all efforts to save the Jews from the Nazis. After four intensive days of debate, a new body, the most important to date, emerged – 'The Emergency Committee to Save the Jewish People in Europe'. The new committee started to bombard the media and the public with endless communiqués, bulletins, pamphlets and pleas. It recruited the author Ben Hecht, who joined the campaign and wrote articles attacking those, who in his opinion, remained indifferent to the German atrocities. Another recruit, the artist Arthur Szyk, with his visual expression of death camps, ghettos and the Partisans' heroism in the European forests, made a great impact on the public. The daily newspapers and the radio stations devoted much space and air time to the issue. The committee initiated many media programmes in which the extent of the extermination was brought to light. Slogans were broadcast to awaken the conscience of the listeners[46] and accusations that the Administration was not doing enough were frequently made. Millions were informed by the committee about the existence of the gas chambers for the first time.

One of the Bergson group's outstanding achievements was to recruit Christian leaders to the task of the salvation of the Jews. On 6 October 1943, the Committee organised a mass rally in front of Capitol Hill, in which hundreds of rabbis from all over the country participated. The demonstrators were led by Henry Wallace, the Vice President, together with senators and congressmen. Four days after the rally 6000 churches declared a Day of Intercession as a gesture of goodwill, calling upon all believers to pray for European Jewry. A few weeks later, on 22 November 1943, the leader of the American Labour movement, Dean Alphang, accused the Governments of the USA and Britain of 'collaborating in the crimes', by maintaining a conspiracy of silence. He blamed President Roosevelt for what he called 'tragic incompetence'.[47] Another prominent American figure was the Congressman Will Rogers, who flew to London to seek British co-operation in saving the Jews. He came back empty-handed, but the committee continued to send delegations of American public figures to Britain.

One of the biggest assemblies initiated by the Committee was held at the Carnegie Hall in New York in honour of Danish and Swedish efforts to save Danish Jews. It took place on 3 October 1943 in the presence of Sigfrid Undset, the Nobel Prize winner for literature, and the actor Orson Welles. Hollywood actors and actresses were much sought after by the committee and Marlon Brando was one of its many supporters. He volunteered to star in the Ben Hecht play 'We Shall Never Die', which was performed in Madison Square Garden, attracting 45,000 spectators at its first performance.[48] The same show was also presented in Washington, where it was seen in Constitution Hall by members of the Cabinet, including Frank Voks, First Secretary of the Admiralty and a warm supporter of the Committee. In the audience there were more than 100 congressmen, 25 senators, all the ambassadors (except from Great Britain), High Court judges and others. Among those present was Eleanor Roosevelt, the wife of the President.

When only the hope of sparing the lives of the 600,000 Hungarian Jews remained, the Committee organised its biggest petition. It was signed by 500,000 Americans and was handed to the majority leader of the Congress by a special delegation composed of Jews and Christians alike.[49]

## A CONFLICT WITH THE JEWISH ESTABLISHMENT

In spite of its success, the Committee's campaign was characterised by bitter confrontation with the official Jewish leadership in the USA. The Bergson group insisted that one of the major and damaging obstacles to its operations was the attitude of the Jewish establishment in the country. Not only, he claimed, did they fail to assist the Committee, but they even blocked the group's attempts to rescue European Jewry. This was done by putting pressure on the Administration to oppose the committee's activities. Y Ben Ami, one of the group founders, said that the issue on which the State Department and the Jewish leadership were in complete agreement was 'the mutual wish to silence us'. He also claimed that leaders like rabbi S Wise and N Goldman did not like the fact that the Committee was a 'baby composed of a lot of non-Jews'.[50]

Indeed, there was constant friction between the leadership and the Committee, acting on behalf of the Irgun in America. There were several reasons for this tension. First, the Committee's huge success overshadowed the long-serving official establishment. Second, the noisy and aggressive style of the Committee caused irritation in the community. Third, the Zionist movement in America, like everywhere else, was made up of figures whose ideology was far distant from that of the militant right-wing Revisionists. Needless to say, they did not approve the Irgun's use of violence in Palestine, instead supporting the Jewish Agency.

Both sides also differed on tactical issues. The official leadership concentrated its efforts on helping the East European Jews to emigrate to Palestine, while the Committee maintained that they could only be saved if they were admitted as quickly as possible into any possible country, including the USA. Another controversy arose when Bergson refused to attack Britain, because it was fighting the Nazis, even though it was denying the entrance of Jews into Palestine and hindering the aims of American Jewish leaders. This decision created bitter opposition even from the Revisionists, who argued that, because Britain was eager to win American assistance, it was logical to launch a campaign against the British in which the demand to open the gates of Palestine to Jewish refugees would be made public.[51] One can blame the American Jewish organisations for not putting enough pressure on Washington decision-makers during the war, in order to persuade the British to change their immigration policy. But that leadership consisted of many groups which were, by their nature, very slow to react and were partially paralysed due to domestic conflicts and personal animosities. Bergson, who labelled most of them as 'criminals', said that they also sabotaged his efforts to create a special body within the senate and the congress with the expressed aim of saving European Jewry. He accused G Blum, the chairman of the Foreign Affairs Committee in the senate and himself a Jew, of blocking the bill to implement such a body. Blum was subject to pressure by Rabbi Wise, who also spoke against the bill in a committee of inquiry, set up despite his opposition, to examine the implication of the bill. Bergson claimed that church leaders were very outspoken in favour of the mission 'while Mr Blum tried to bury it in his Committee'. Subsequently, the Senate under the chairmanship of Senator Connolly (Texas), together with the leader of the Senate, Senator Berkly, saw the bill through the Congress extremely quickly. Thus, on 22 January 1944, the 'War Refugee Board' came into being in a statement by President Roosevelt. This was considered as one of the greatest achievements of the 'Committee for Saving European Jews'.

The initiative, which could not be attributed solely to the Committee's activities, rounded off a series of dialogues with the Administration, which began on 16 August 1943 when the Committee met G Hall, the Secretary of State, and submitted to him a detailed plan for the establishment of a special government board to save the Jews. On 11 November 1943, Senators Gillet and Topet, and Congressmen Rogers and Baldwin, submitted the bill which called upon the President to appoint a committee, which would formulate a plan 'to bring about the rescue of the Jewish remains from Nazi-German destruction'. The bill was unanimously accepted and confirmed on 20 December 1943 by the Foreign Affairs Committee, headed by Senator Thomas, himself a supporter of the group.

All along, it was difficult for the Zionist movement in America to tolerate the activities of Bergson's men: young, energetic, aggressive and arrogant. All were newcomers from Palestine, who acted against conventional rules, refusing to co-operate with the existing organisations and launching a campaign outside their sphere of influence. The rift between the two sides grew until it reached a point at which the Jewish leaders refused to communicate with the Committee's members at all. The few meetings which took place between them turned into stormy sessions of mutual accusation. In one of them Rabbi Wise claimed that Roosevelt told him that, if the political campaign for a Jewish Army was not stopped, he would outlaw the Zionist movement altogether.

Jewish resentment of the committee also had other grounds, which stemmed from the way its leaders were dealing with prominent Americans.

Bergson was not always scrupulous in his methods. Only at times did he trouble himself to secure the individual agreement of each signatory to a new advertisement. His group's stormy relations with Truman is another example. Truman, as a senator, was a member of the Committee for almost a year until he resigned abruptly in May 1943 in protest against the group's forthright condemnation of American policy with regard to the European Jewish refugees. In his letter of resignation Truman warned Bergson not to make further use of his name for any purpose in the future. He wrote: 'This does not mean my sympathies are not with the down-trodden Jews of Europe, but when you take it on yourself without consultation to attack members of the Senate and the House of Representatives who are working in your interests, I cannot support that procedure'.[52] Bergson was convinced that the Jewish leaders, out of concern for their position and relationship with the Administration, were reluctant to devote themselves to the task of saving European Jewry by demanding their entry into America. Bergson quoted William Allen Hart, one of the biggest publishers in the USA, who complained about the indifference of New York's three million Jews towards the Holocaust. He told him: 'If the Irish were being exterminated, there would be no window left in any Government building, let alone the British Consulate in the city'.[53] Indeed, the Jewish community was very slow in responding to the dramatic developments in Europe and Palestine. One of the reasons for their weak stand was the fear that, by pressing the government to influence British policy in the Middle East, they would be accused of trying to push America into the war. The leadership was concerned that this would result in waves of anti-semitism in the country. But even after America had entered the war, official Jewish policy did not change until much later.

The leaders did not wish to damage either the Allies' military efforts or Anglo-American relations. One of them, Louis Dembitz Brandeis, Associate Justice of the Supreme Court, said in 1941 that anti-British propaganda against the 'White Paper' at that time would be regarded as an 'anti-American act'. Another judge, Felix Frankfurter, refused to approach the British Embassy in Washington to demand that refugees aboard the ship *Patria*, which was blown up in the port of Haifa, would be allowed to stay in Palestine. His explanation was that he 'did not want to sabotage the Anglo-American relationship'. That attitude changed slightly during the course of the war, when the leadership concentrated on demanding the defence of Palestine and the formation of a Jewish Army within the British military framework.

However, despite the constant friction, the announcement of the setting up of the 'War Refugee Board' was welcomed by the Jewish leadership and the Zionist Federation in the USA, including those who had fought the

Irgun delegation bitterly before the war. They expressed the opinion that the American decision had brought some hope to the task of saving the Jews. At the same time they voiced reservations on the nature of the decision and the circumstances under which it was made.[54] The main reservation derived from the fact that Palestine, as a shelter for Jewish refugees, was not mentioned at all in the declaration approved by the President.

Various organisations accused Bergson's group of omitting this point intentionally. The emergency Committee did not try to deny it. Its members argued that mentioning Palestine would arouse political controversy which might slow down the process of the rescue operation. Sadly, the setting up of the Refugee Board and all the other activities in the USA were insufficient and came too late to save even Hungarian Jewry from the Nazi extermination plan. These powerful Jewish organisations in America had failed to exert their considerable influence to put more pressure on the Allies. Although the Allies could not have done much to avert the Holocaust, they could have tried to diminish its scope; for example, allocating some air squadrons to hit the railways leading to the concentration camps.

## THE COMMITTEE FOR NATIONAL LIBERATION

The Bergson group's policy of establishing *ad hoc* committees was repeated on 18 May 1944, when it set up the Hebrew Committee for National Liberation (HCNL), succeeding, but not necessarily replacing, the previous organisations.

After operating on behalf of the Irgun (though without its direct blessing), campaigning for a Jewish Army, organising illegal immigration to Palestine and lobbying for the rescue of European Jewry, the group decided to concentrate its efforts on its last remaining aim – an independent Jewish state in Palestine.

Contrary to the other campaigns, this one did not meet with serious problems. Most of the people who supported the first committees were also united behind the demand to let the Jews have a state of their own. Even the Jewish leadership, under the trauma of the Holocaust, did not interfere. Bergson thus needed to use no more than the existing structure, which had had so much success in the past. He and his men had only to change the theme of their struggle.

The Irgun's anti-British revolt of February 1944 carried the ideal background for the demands of the new Committee. The HCNL advocated the idea that an armed rebellion was the only way to achieve independence. Since the war was nearly over and the task of defeating the Germans was accomplished, the committee had no difficulty in directing greater propaganda against London than had been possible before. Its support for the Irgun was much stronger and more vocal, relying heavily on the insurgents' activities in Palestine. At that time, the activists on the committee often defined themselves as the political wing of the Irgun in the USA. Simultaneously, another body, 'The American League for Free Palestine', was established to co-ordinate the activities of all the committees which were still in operation. Bergson and his colleagues regarded this umbrella organisation as a kind of government in exile, along the lines of various liberation groups which existed around the world during the war.[55] From 1944 onwards the committee launched regular attacks on Britain. Its propaganda campaign held London responsible for closing the gates of Palestine to Holocaust survivors and did not hesitate to justify the Irgun's terrorist activities against the Mandate authorities.

The fact that many more American Jews joined the last committee made the latter's support for the Irgun even more significant. The group monitored all the operations of the Underground and widely publicised them. Its leaders even dared to call on Prime Minister Winston Churchill to pardon the two Stern Group members who assassinated Lord Moyne on 6 November 1944. The petition sent to London was signed by senators, congressmen and intellectuals (including the leader of the majority in the Congress, Doc MacCormack, the Italian conductor Arturo Toscanini, the Norwegian novelist and Nobel prize winner Sigrid Undset, the leader of the Labour movement Dean Alphang and the American novelist Louis Bromfield). They deplored the act, but declared that the two youths had been driven to desperation by 'agony, despair and death of millions of Hebrews in Europe'.[56] Pardons were also called for in America for Irgun members awaiting the death sentence in Palestine, and American diplomats asked the British to improve the living conditions of the insurgents detained in camps in Africa. The Committee, which daily informed the public about the armed struggle in Palestine, was also believed to be instrumental in putting pressure on President Harry Truman (who had taken office in April 1945) to demand the immigration of 100,000 Jews into Palestine by the end of August 1945.

At the same time, the League initiated a visit to London by an American delegation to meet with the Foreign Secretary Ernest Bevin. They also had talks with Harold Laski, the chairman of the Labour Party, George Hall, the Colonial Secretary, and many Members of Parliament. While in London, the delegation conveyed its views to the Anglo-American Committee on Palestine.[57]

The Hebrew Committee for National Liberation used to divide its activities into separate large-scale campaigns, concentrating on one issue at a time. On 22 March 1945, it denounced the British decision to exclude the East Bank in Transjordan from Palestine. On 23 February 1946, the League called for a special conference in New York, in which an appeal to open Palestine to Jewish refugees was made to the British. Two more mass rallies were organised against Bevin's policy on Palestine. Two of his 'anti-semitic' remarks raised a tremendous uproar in the USA[58] and were fully exploited by the committee, which redoubled its efforts to widen the scope for the support of the Irgun.

Events in Palestine led the Committee for National Liberation and the American League for Free Palestine to identify fully with the Irgun's campaign of violence to the extent that the President of the League even defended the controversial bombing of the King David Hotel in Jerusalem. A delegation of the League visited Palestine only two days after the explosion on 23 July 1946 and met with the High Commissioner and the Jewish community leaders.

The visitors' support for the Irgun deepened the rift between Washington and London on the Palestine question. The Committee, apart from recruiting prominent Americans and getting them to condemn British policy in the Middle East, continued to organise and finance illegal immigration to Palestine. One of the ships acquired by them was named *Ben Hecht* after the author and was captured by the British army with 626 refugees on board whom the British deported to detainee camps in Cyprus. Ben Hecht himself[59] wrote a letter to the 'Terrorists in Palestine' from his hospital bed, where he was recovering from serious surgery.

'The Jews of America', he wrote, 'are with you. You are the champions Everytime you blow up a British arsenal or wreck a British jail, or send a British railroad sky-high, or rob a British bank the Jews of America make a little festival in their hearts . . .'.[60] In Palestine the message was distributed by the Irgun to the population at large, but it infuriated London. The Foreign Office issued a protest to the State Department, blacklisted Ben Hecht and accused him of 'inciting to kill British officials and soldiers in the Holy Land'.[61] However, the Committee's success did not result in improving its relations with the Irgun in Palestine. On the contrary, the IZL accused Bergson and his colleagues of not sufficiently assisting the military campaign in Palestine and of deviating from its policy. Moreover, both sides were divided on the controversial issue of possibly establishing a provisional government in exile.

## THE RIFT BETWEEN THE COMMITTEE AND THE IRGUN

The original Irgun delegation to the USA, as already pointed out before, had set up various committees to promote a Jewish Army, the saving of European Jewry and for statehood, each with its own objective. But the activities of those bodies were in sharp contrast to the initial mission they were instructed to carry out – to win direct political support for the Irgun and to raise funds in order to maintain the insurgents' activities in Palestine. The disobedience of the Bergson Group (as was reflected in the use of the term 'Hebrew People'), aroused bitterness within the Irgun command which blamed its men in America for abandoning their commitment to assist the organisation. The friction between both sides increased from 1944 on, when the Irgun launched its terrorist campaign against the British forces.

Samuel Katz, a member of the IZL High Command and in charge of propaganda, said that the committees were not necessary as organising illegal immigration was a project which had already been run by the Hagana. In his opinion the task of the group in America was to alert public opinion to the plight of the Jews in Europe and Palestine. Since that had been achieved by the group and the Zionist movement as a whole was no longer isolated in the USA, there was no need, in his opinion, to carry on with their various political activities when the armed revolt in Palestine was starved of money and weapons.[62] Katz touched on one of the main causes of resentment between them. The Irgun was outraged to learn that the committee had no intention of diverting the funds raised to Palestine. Instead, the IZL claimed, the committee had acquired ships for the refugees and used its financial resources to strengthen its position in America.

Ya'acov Meridor, the Irgun's transitional commander before Begin took over, was even more outspoken. He alleged that the Committee for National Liberation was created by a few people who 'thought themselves exiles and left the country because they feared to face the danger of being imprisoned' by the British.[63] Others argued that the propaganda build-up of Bergson and his friends appeared to smack of personal ambition for the future, rather than total commitment to the armed struggle.[64] The accusations were not entirely groundless. The Hebrew Committee, 'flushed with their remarkable success in gaining support for their Emergency Plan'[65], failed to realise that, once the struggle with Britain had started in Palestine, all efforts should have been directed to winning it. Eliyahu Lankin, another command member, who was active mainly in Europe, took upon himself the task of mediating between the Underground and the men overseas. He said that 'some of the money raised did not reach the Irgun, and was spent on the noisy publishing style of the Committee'.[66] The latter pointed out, in return, that Begin deemed the activities of the Committee second only to the military struggle in Palestine. They added also that Begin resented funds which were spent on what he regarded as 'gestures'. In reality, the 'Americans' not only refused to bow to Irgun discipline, they did not even accept the Irgun policy on priorities. That attitude contributed to the HCNL's success, but as Katz recognised, 'though sympathy for the Irgun was widespread in the USA, they received practically no help from the American Jews'.[67]

One of the main issues which divided the Irgun and the Committee was the latter's persistent efforts to establish a provisional government in exile. The HCNL's activists drew up a plan in which they emphasised the urgent need for the Hebrew people to take immediate steps towards a permanent internal solution of their national problem. The plan, eight pages long, accused Britain of violating its Mandatory commitment to help the Jews create their own homeland.[68]

It called, therefore, upon the 'Hebrew People' to convene an assembly to form and proclaim a provisional leadership (in Palestine or in exile) which would be the governing body of the country, until a representative government of Palestine was elected under UN supervision. In outlining the aims of such a government, the committee called for free elections, concluding treaties with the British on the withdrawal of their troops, and the signing of peace agreements with the neighbouring Arabs. The HCNL clung to the theory that it was essential to set up a provisional government, but they admitted that only the Irgun could provide them with the political backing vital for the achievement of that goal.[69] Menachem Begin did not reject the idea out of hand, but neither did he like it. His attitude towards the plan was clearly reflected in a letter he sent to the Committee in America. He tried to explain how dangerous the implementation of the plan could be due to the delicate fabric of the relationship between the Irgun and the official leadership. 'A civil war can break out at any time, within weeks or months, I have no doubt that your campaign in the United States is one of the factors inhibiting the plotters', he wrote. 'But we can not jump the gun.... We can not give the inciters the excuse to claim that we are not fighting the British but the Yishuv. Consequently, there will be no hasty formation of a provisional government.... We will do so only if we are sure of the participation of others, or if there is no choice left'.[70]

Yizthak Ben Ami, one of the HCNL leaders in America who met Begin at his underground flat in January 1947, said afterwards that Begin himself promoted the idea of a provisional government, but backed down because 'he was afraid to be accused by Ben Gurion' of attempting to take over the community's leadership.[71] Indeed, the Irgun commander, aware of the hostility towards him within the Zionist establishment, believed, correctly, that sponsorship of such a government would have forced the Irgun into a bitter struggle with the Jewish Agency which could escalate into a full-scale civil war. 'From beginning to end', Katz said, 'the Irgun exerted itself to avoid such a conflict'.[72] Unsurprisingly, the Irgun did not approve of the idea, not only because it did not find it practical, but also because of the suspicion with which the Committee had been treated by the High Command. But the notion of a government in exile indicated how out of touch its advocates were with events in Palestine. The Jewish Agency opposed it simply because it regarded itself as a semi-official government in dealing with the British authorities in the country. Begin was not only worried about the possible outbreak of a civil war but, as he put it several times to the Committee, he also wished to avoid a situation in which the guerrilla activities would depend on the approval of such a government. Bergson, for his part, bitterly argued that Begin misled his group by promising to form such a body, though in reality he had no intention of doing so.[73]

Instead, Begin tried to impose discipline on the Committee. On 1 May 1946 he obtained the agreement of Samuel Merlin, one of the HCNL's leaders, to co-ordinate operations with the Irgun and to resume the traditional contacts with it by restoring them to their pre-war pattern. As a result of that meeting, a compromise was reached by both sides according to which 'the Committee for National Liberation was to handle the political propaganda of the Irgun in exile.'[74] Otherwise, every other aspect of the struggle would be taken care of by the special unit of the Irgun which was to deal with the diaspora. Begin, through his activists in Europe, was careful not to voice opposition to the idea of provisional government. On the contrary, Article C of the agreement with the Committee indicated very clearly that the 'immediate task of the Irgun's representatives in exile is to convene a national convention of the people of Israel in order to create a Provisional Government, which would consist of all factors that agree with the definition of the ultimate aim and regard that government as an efficient means of achieving it'.[75] Begin, in order to dominate the committee and have it under his control, was even willing to support the terminological argument that 'Hebrew People' was a political definition which included all Palestine Jews and all diaspora Jews who regarded Palestine as their homeland and wished to liberate it and live there.

The Irgun's influence, especially during the peak period of the revolt, became considerable and even Bergson could not ignore it. The driving force behind all the political activities in America, he was approached by two of his colleagues in December 1947 and agreed that the HCNL would cease its independent existence, at least officially. However, at the practical level, its leaders continued to carry out their campaign without obeying orders from the Irgun from then until the establishment of the State of Israel in May 1948. The agreement could not heal the rift between the two bitterly divided sides. The Irgun recognised the fact that the various committees were very successful in America. This view was expressed by Lankin who admitted that the Bergson Group had influenced public opinion in the USA, which in turn played a role in inclining the British to terminate their Mandate in Palestine. Lankin was right in arguing that the group 'exploited the name of the Underground for its own end without the authorisation of the Irgun', but at the end of the day it worked to the mutual benefit of both.

However, constant friction and personal confrontation between Begin and Bergson overshadowed some of the essential differences in their positions. Bergson was in a position to dictate terms. The Committee for a Jewish Army, for example, was his brainchild and even Irgunists admitted that his group scored 'the most striking political success ever achieved by any Jewish organisation in the US'.[76]

The success strengthened Bergson's position and made him reluctant to accept any outside guidance, even from the Underground in Palestine, whose name he so often used in his propaganda campaign. The setting up in 1944 of the War Refugees Board by President Roosevelt, was largely regarded as the product of his efforts and was highly praised, despite its limitations, since it helped to save many Jewish lives in Europe. Bergson's group had emerged in America at the right moment and the task of awakening Americans which it took upon itself shook the Jewish community and the public at large out of their state of apathy. The aggressive fashion in which it conducted the campaign added many people to the list of those who were hostile to its leader. When Bergson secured the support of the war minister, the naval minister, leaders of powerful trade unions and other prominent figures in the country, he caused a great deal of jealousy among the Jewish leaders. They denigrated him and even tried to take him to court to have him deported.[77] One of them, Nahum Goldman, told his colleagues on 28 September 1944 that Roosevelt had said to him that 'Hitler would have been glad to pay for Bergson's anti-British propaganda'.[78]

Bergson and his aides aroused much hostility within the Jewish establishment. Not only did they accuse it time and again of abandoning European Jewry, but their success also underlined its incompetence. They gave the community leaders a fascinating lesson in professional propaganda, attracting many youngsters to the Zionist movement and winning supporters for the Irgun's cause within the Administration, all of which made them at times a somewhat 'embarrassing ally'.

Listing the activities of all the Bergson committees in the USA does not mean that they were the only effective bodies which fought for the rescue of the Jews in Europe. There were other groups which enjoyed even better access to influential Americans. But the committees, in their three different forms, were the first to raise the issue of the Holocaust and to shake public opinion with regards to both Jews and non-Jews. Acting as a catalyst, they refused to obey the authority of the local Jewish leadership and zealously maintained their independence. Bergson and his colleagues gained large followings in Congress, introduced congressional resolutions, cultivated many officials in Washington, and in 1944 performed their boldest act by opening a Hebrew embassy in the American capital. The group owed its success to its aggressive manner and to the many Christians who were involved in its activities. Placing concern over the situation in Palestine in second place, and acting in isolation from the Irgun, contributed also to its considerable achievement. This was highlighted on 2 January 1944 by the decision of the White House to set up the 'War Refugee Board'. Unfortunately, this decision, although it enabled the admission of displaced people to America, came too late to stop the massacre of the Jews in Europe.

# Part Two

# BRITISH COUNTER-INSURGENCY

CHAPTER 7

# The British View

By the end of 1943 the British had not ruled out the possibility of an armed Jewish revolt in Palestine, but regarded its probability as small and not imminent. However, following the illegal immigration efforts and the seizure of some British weapons during training, the government's representatives warned that the situation needed careful monitoring. They concluded therefore, that they must keep sufficient troops in or near Palestine to be able to deal with any trouble that might arise.

General Sir Henry Maitland Wilson, the commander of the 9th Army, voiced his suspicion on 1 July 1943 that the final objective of the Jewish Agency was to build up an army for its own ends. 'These actions are always conditioned by the desire to ensure that all Jewish soldiers are loyal firstly to the Agency, and secondarily to us', he wrote to London.[1]

At the end of that year, intelligence reports warned of an armed revolt, in which the Jewish Agency would take part. 'Zionists would make the best case to justify the use of force in the eyes of the world opinion', they wrote.[2] They also predicted on 12 December that a possible confrontation might stem from the immigration question. The reaction of the Jews as well as the Arabs seemed certain to be heading for a collision, whatever the attitude of the British Government. The fierce Jewish opposition to the 'White Paper' policy, even among the moderate leaders of the community, was regarded by the British as a factor which would justify the use of force, not only as a means of self-defence, but also as an instrument to build a Jewish Army.

Furthermore, intelligence reports indicated that the Zionists might welcome and even provoke angry Arab reaction to Jewish immigration in order to 'legitimise their illegal activities'.[3] The British believed this might provide the conditions for a revolt. The British Foreign Secretary, while visiting Cairo and Jerusalem in June–July 1943, voiced this concern when he stated categorically that the British 'must damp down the present Zionist agitation'. He emphasised that the British were not going to leave Palestine until the problem was settled. 'We will not be influenced by force ...' he said.[4] The British apprehension derived mainly from the knowledge that a

Jewish fight within the Yishuv would begin when the war against Germany ended. The Jewish Agency did not make a secret of its intention of exploiting the confusion of the post-war period and presenting the British government with a *fait accompli* with regard to the issues of immigration, army and statehood. The Mandate authorities were aware of such a development, in which the Arabs might also be embroiled.

At the beginning of February 1944, the headquarters of British Intelligence in Palestine considered the possibility that the Jews of the Yishuv might use force to achieve their political aims even in 1944. This possibility was made apparent by some of the political activities of the Yishuv which included a propaganda campaign, political pressure, and military training, as well as resisting searches and in general, hardening its attitude towards the continuation of the Mandate.[5] The key to the achievement of the political aims of the Jews in Palestine was unrestricted immigration or, as the Biltmore Programme put it, 'that the control of immigration should rest with the Jewish Agency'.[6] As a result, British fears of a possible Jewish revolt in Palestine were directed towards the official moderate leadership of the community and not the Irgun or other radical elements in the Yishuv. Because of the growing evidence that events in Europe and the question of Jewish immigration would lead to an inevitable confrontation with the Government in Palestine, the British focused their attention on the Jewish Agency.

It is true, however, that British Intelligence took into account the possibility that 'radical elements, in particular the Stern Gang'[7] would heat up the atmosphere in the Yishuv, inclining it towards a revolt, but the official leadership was seen as the only body which could mobilise the Jewish Community.

Even the first Irgun attacks, in February and March 1944, on the immigration and income tax offices in three of Palestine's main cities, failed to make the desired impact on the government. The CID dismissed their significance out of hand and the general impression was that the Irgun was capable only of bombing empty headquarters. The attacks were thought by the British to be of a symbolic nature for domestic political consumption. But the sporadic strikes continued. On 19 May, the Irgun attacked the central broadcasting station in the Arab town of Ramallah to mark the fifth anniversary of the White Paper. In July, two police constables were murdered. But even these events did not alarm the authorities. The High Commissioner did indeed express some concern in a message to London in which he pointed out that 'available information indicates that the security position may be deteriorating' and that the 'outlook is not encouraging'.[8] But even that warning failed to draw the attention of the Government, heavily preoccupied with the final stages of the war in Europe, until an attempt on the life of the

High Commissioner himself was made by the Stern Group.

It was just 10 days after High Commissioner MacMichael's telegram to the government that his car was riddled with bullets on the Jerusalem – Jaffa road by terrorists who opened fire with automatic weapons, wounding the driver of his armoured car, but 'miraculously leaving him only slightly grazed'.[9] After the assassination attempt, British reactions to the continuing violence hardened. They arrested 18 insurgents on 16 August 1944 and conducted a massive search operation in the town of Petach Tikva, described by the police, not without reason, as 'full of terrorists'.[10]

On 14 August 1944, another intelligence report warned for the second time that the security situation in Palestine was deteriorating. It indicated that the attempt on the life of the High Commissioner was its most serious manifestation. The authorities held the view that 'the policy adopted by the Irgun Zvai Leumi and the terrorist Stern Group is believed to be gaining adherents, particularly from the youth element in the country'.[11] The report continued that the actions of the Underground could amount to the beginning of a war of liberation in order to allow the entry of the Jewish refugees to Palestine. The British reached this conclusion simply from manifestos issued by the Irgun and Hagana in which they condemned the immigration limits imposed by the White Paper. This, the British feared, might develop into a situation in which the Jewish Agency would feel obliged to co-operate with the radicals when 'there may be a further slide of public opinion towards supporting a policy of action'.[12]

## BRITISH RELIANCE ON THE JEWISH LEADERSHIP

The most significant of the Irgun operations thus far was their psychological victory over the British soldiers who were warned not to approach the Wailing Wall on Yom Kippur (the Day of Atonement). This was part of the insurgents' diversionary tactics which allowed them to attack four government fortresses in Bet Dagon, Katra, Haifa and Qalqilia (see Chapter 2).

Those attacks damaged British prestige and also created anxiety amongst the Jewish Agency leaders who feared a fierce reaction against the Yishuv. But the Jewish fears were groundless since the British did not seek to pursue a policy of vengeance even two days later when Constable J T Wilkins was shot dead in a Jerusalem street by Stern Group gunmen. However, the worst was yet to come. On 25 October, the Mandate authorities took a far-reaching measure against the Irgun. They deported 251 members of the Underground movements to Eritrea in Africa, including some prominent members of the Irgun High Command. Most of them remained in the African camps until the formation of the Jewish State. The deportation was the most serious attempt by the High Commissioner to hit the Irgun, but it was also his last. On 1 November 1944, he was replaced by Field Marshal Gort, who was faced six days after his appointment with the worst terrorist attack yet. This took place on 6 November, when two members of the Stern Group assassinated Lord Moyne, British Minister of State in Cairo and a close friend of Prime Minister Winston Churchill. Moyne was believed by the Underground to have been responsible for the policy of curbing Jewish immigration to Palestine.[13]

The Yishuv was outraged by the assassination. The Jewish Agency was appalled. With world-wide condemnation of the murder, the Jewish community in Palestine feared severe retribution from London. This had been reflected by Churchill in an emotional speech in the Commons warning that 'these harmful activities must cease and those responsible for them be radically destroyed and eliminated'.[14] However, the Jewish Agency was quicker than the British to react, and its leaders, during the convention of the Trade Union Federation, announced their 'Saison' plan to destroy the separatist groups (See Chapter 3). The assassination had not been approved by the Irgun. On the contrary, its leaders feared that the event would disrupt their own operations and give their enemies a pretext to crush the group, still in its embryonic stage. As Begin himself recalled, 'This immediately became the signal for an all-out crusade by the Hagana and the Jewish Agency for our destruction. The official leadership made full use of the foreboding occasioned by the death of Moyne to launch a large scale attack on the Irgun.'[15]

The British, for their part, gave the Hagana and the Jewish Agency the chance to crack down on the terrorists and isolate them from the Jewish population. Lord Gort, 20 days after taking over the High Commission, made it clear that 'helping the government to maintain law and order must rest with the Agency'.[16]

This attitude emphasised the over-reliance of the authorities on the Jewish leadership throughout the 1940s, despite British suspicion of the leadership's motives. Lord Gort, in one of his first despatches to the Colonial Secretary, wrote that 'the issue for Zionism today is clear cut: it is whether the Jewish Agency can regain the control it has lost or whether the smoke of the assassins' pistols will win the day'. But he expressed doubts as to the will or the capability of the Jewish leadership to fight terrorism. Two weeks after Moyne's death, Gort formed the impression, in spite of his short stay in Palestine, that the Jewish Agency was always attempting to pin the blame for terrorist activities on to the Irgun and the FFI. 'In practice', he stressed, 'supporters of terrorists are to be found in all sections of the Yishuv'.[17] The Administration's continued reliance on the Agency, rather than the search for independent means to destroy the dissidents, was subject to controversy. Lord Killearn, the ambassador to Egypt, complained about what he called 'our leniency to the terror' which had led to Arab loss of confidence in the British following Moyne's assassination. Killearn told the Foreign Office that Britain is 'losing its credibility in the Arab world' and that it should react immediately when events were still fresh in people's minds.[18] He did not share Gort's view of giving the Jewish Agency the task of combating terrorism. He strongly recommended that all irregular Jewish groups should be disarmed and called for the 'suspension of pending action to complete the immigration quota as laid down in the White Paper'. Killearn maintained that the urgent need to eliminate terrorism should precede the search for a solution for the future of Palestine. For that purpose, the Government should mobilise all its military power, including the air force, the navy and the infantry.

The ambassador in Cairo was one of the most outspoken British senior officials who had serious reservations about the government's policy on Jewish terrorism. He was also one of the few British who predicted an escalation of the violence in Palestine. On 23 November 1944 he wrote to London, stressing that the Middle East, especially Egypt, was confidently waiting for an effective action 'to eradicate this gang of terrorism'. Killearn asked: 'Is it really conceivable that we are still not going to do so? Despite Lord Moyne's murder? Despite knowledge of their guilt? And that we are going to postpone action until yet another outrage occurs?'[19] However, the administration was impressed by the Yishuv's outrage at the murder and the measures announced by Ben Gurion to terminate the guerrilla activities. They believed that 'at present, Jews seemed to have been shocked by the death, and they are in the mood in which they are more likely to listen to Weizmann's counsels of moderation'.[20] The Cabinet even decided against issuing public warnings, wholesale arms searches and stopping information. The Foreign Office told Killearn that a police force of sufficient power was capable of breaking the 'criminal gangs'.

Even the Prime Minister Winston Churchill, who had threatened to change his policy on the Middle East after the assassination of his close friend, expressed disapproval of drastic action against the Jewish community as a whole. He was not willing to go further than punishing the insurgents and refused to suspend immigration because he believed that this would 'play into the hands of the extremists'.[21] Radical steps, he feared, would cause unbearable hardship to the moderates to the benefit of the separatist groups and, in the long run, would unite all the Jews against His Majesty's Government. Churchill suggested further retribution against the terrorists and severe punishment for those who carried weapons with them. Indeed, the war which the Jewish Agency declared on the terrorists and the shock with which the Yishuv responded to the murder in Cairo, coupled with the

British measures, brought a period of quiet to Palestine. Gort was, therefore, able to write to the Colonial Office on 12 December 1944: 'The police force is doing its best and we did not list any special events'.

## THE AFTERMATH OF THE MOYNE ASSASSINATION

'If a barometer could be made to register the rise and fall of pressure of the political atmosphere of Palestine, it would be a hard worked instrument, for it would swing with an irregular rhythm from 'Set Fair' to 'Stormy'. Each time the clouds come circling up, it seems as if the storm must break, yet hitherto they have always dispersed, leaving behind, not the freshness of rain washed air but the sultry tenseness of an unfulfilled thunderstorm'. This is how the British intelligence headquarters described the upheavals in Palestine at the beginning of 1946.[22] The events of the period under review were the destruction of some police and military installations on 27 December 1945 (about a month after Lieutenant General Sir Alan Cunningham had relieved Lord Gort as High Commissioner) and the intensification of illegal immigration activities. As before, the administration looked to the Jewish Agency to impose law and order within the Yishuv. The High Commissioner summoned David Ben Gurion and Moshe Shertock (Sharett) and they, on behalf of the Zionist leadership, expressed regret at any loss of life and promised to act against terrorism. It is interesting that, although the British believed in the sincerity of the Jewish Agency and their opposition to violence, they always treated it with varying degrees of suspicion. 'As always in Palestine', said a forthright intelligence report, 'sanity and self-interest are nicely balanced against fanaticism'.[23]

The willingness of the Zionists to take action against IZL and Stern, the British maintained, was not because they wanted to obey the instructions of the Government, but because of their own political motives and interests. At the same time, they detected a process of radicalisation in the Jewish Community in Palestine. The British were surprised to find that the Community let its political judgement be clouded by what they called 'a blitz of propaganda' which did not help it to see that terrorism could prejudice their hopes. The British intelligence listed six chief factors which brought about such a trend in the attitude of the Yishuv.

1. Disillusionment with His Majesty's Government on the question of settlements and immigration.
2. The belief that the Arabs had succeeded in forcing the promulgation of the 1939 White Paper by a three year rebellion. The Jews' conclusion was, therefore, that with a better armed and

organised force they might be equally successful using the same means.
3. A real hatred of the Palestine police, fed also by organised propaganda.
4. The belief that a Jew should not be handed over to the British, even if he was a criminal.
5. The conviction that the British were profoundly untrustworthy and that their political negotiations were doomed to fail.
6. The feeling that the Jews had lost so much in the Holocaust that there was little further left for them to lose.

Indeed, the British captured the mood of the Jews in Palestine correctly and spotted the real threat to the stability of the Mandate – the possibility that, in the absence of a political solution, the majority would slip out of the Agency's control into the hands of the extremists. The British knew that the Yishuv was generally more radical in its approach than its leaders and concluded that losing the co-operation of the latter would get the country embroiled in a cycle of violence.

## THE BRITISH RESPONSE TO THE UNITED ARMED CAMPAIGN

The first waves of organised violence against the British authorities by the Hagana, IZL and FFI created strong echoes in Great Britain. The press immediately drew a distinction between the much condemned terrorism of the Irgun and the bombing of the bridges by the Hagana, an operation which did not result in British casualties. The pro-Labour *New Statesman*, for example, associated the Hagana's involvement with the violence with Bevin's anti-Zionist policy, which rejected the demand to admit 500,000 Jewish refugees into Palestine. The magazine expressed the widespread belief within the British administration that Jewish frustration over immigration had widened the confrontation between the British and the Jews. That conflict was not only confined to the dissidents. On 6 July 1946, the British cabinet discussed the recent attacks in Palestine which included the bridges across the river Jordan, railway workshops in Haifa and the kidnapping of British officers. The High Commissioner, who took part in the meeting, called for vigorous action and urged the government to refuse to conduct any further discussion on the subject of the admission of the 100,000 Jews into Palestine until the kidnapped officers had been returned. He also called for an immediate action against the illegal Jewish immigration and the Jewish Agency's alleged co-operation with the dissidents. However, the Government was reluctant to act, for the same reasons which had prevented it from doing so on previous occasions. The Secretary of State for the Colonies recalled that the Cabinet had not so far considered the moment opportune to take extreme measures against the illegal organisations in Palestine, but admitted that the situation was becoming more serious.[24] Although in his view it was necessary to take firm action, he did not advise the acceptance of the High Commissioner's first recommendation. He explained his refusal to continue negotiations with the Americans over the possibility of admitting the 100,000 immigrants to Palestine. 'To break off the negotiation at this stage', he said, 'might imply that this decision had been taken and would also have a very unfortunate effect in America'.

But the Colonial Secretary could not ignore the fact that this time his government confronted not only radical minority groups but also the Hagana, backed by the Jewish Agency. Moreover, he was aware that the patience of the administration was running out and the troops in Palestine could have taken matters into their own hands. He was also subject to pressure from the Secretary of State for War and Chief of the Imperial General Staff. The latter emphasised at the same meeting that if the existing state of affairs continued, it would be difficult to control the Army. He therefore demanded that greater freedom of action be given to the High Commissioner and the Commander in Chief. Those recommendations were supported by the Foreign Secretary. He took the view that strong action should be taken, but did not ignore the need to enlist the support of the US Government for that action. The Prime Minister himself joined this call and there was general agreement that the situation called for firm action. The Cabinet was concerned mainly by the activities of the National Resistance Movement, although the first priority was given to the freeing of the officers kidnapped by the Irgun. The main concern stemmed from the possibility that, without drastic measures, the Hagana might bring itself closer to the militants and embark upon terrorist activities. Therefore, the Cabinet decided to inform the United States about its forthcoming plans and at the same time instructed the High Commissioner in Palestine to break the illegal organisations rather than to compel individuals throughout the country to surrender their arms. The joint terrorist activities led the British to conclude that the Yishuv was unwilling to co-operate with the authorities in order to bring about an end to the violence. Such a realisation was supported by the Army in Palestine. A secret military memorandum, covering the events of summer 1946, claimed that 'not even in the face of the worst outrage in the recent history of Palestine, or the brutal murders which have characterised the last month, has any attempt been made by the mass of the Yishuv to fight terrorism ... The Yishuv takes anything but a negative stand ...'.[25]

The Cabinet wished to deliver a severe blow to the Jewish Agency, which it found to have been 'under the control of the extremist elements' at the early stage of its co-operation with the terrorists. Hence its determination to damage its nerve-centre by raiding its headquarters in Jerusalem and arresting some of its prominent members. With that decision the British laid down the basis for what came to be called Operation *Agatha*.

## OPERATION *AGATHA*

Despite the fact that the operation was aimed solely at the Jewish Agency, one cannot ignore the underlying British intention of destroying the Irgun by undermining the leadership which co-operated with the separatists. The government's main fear was that the insurgents would attract defectors from the Hagana. 'The terrorist groups are growing in size', warned British Intelligence during the second half of 1946' with recruits from the more hot-headed and impatient members of the Hagana'.[26]

The authorities were convinced that by inflicting a severe blow on the Jewish Agency, they would drive a wedge between the Hagana and the Underground organisation. 'Since the end of the war', wrote the intelligence unit of the 6th Airborne Division to London, 'Jewish illegal armed organisations in Palestine have been conducting a campaign of violence, terror, sabotage and murder'. Between 1 November 1945 and the end of June 1946, 47 incidents of a major nature occurred, resulting in the deaths of 18 British Army personnel and the wounding of 101, as well as nine Palestine police killed and 63 wounded.

In addition, during this period, sabotage reached the value of over £4m. In June 1946 alone, damage to bridges blown up in Palestine amounted to £250,000. The High Commissioner, who found the situation intolerable, together with the Chief of the Imperial General Staff, put pressure on the government to allow the armed forces to act in the heart of the Jewish headquarters in Jerusalem. It was deemed necessary to occupy the Jewish Agency building in order to search for incriminating documents. Another of *Agatha*'s aims was to arrest certain members of the Jewish political bodies who were considered either to have been implicated in recent terrorist activities or responsible for inciting such actions. Search for arms and other members of the illegal organisations, including the Palmach, was also part of the operation.

On 29 June 1946, the Army closed the borders in Palestine, cut off the telephone service to all the Jewish settlements and started its most extensive search campaign in the country. The 17,000 troops captured more than 300 rifles, 425,000 bullets, 8,000 hand grenades, 5,200 mortar bombs and large quantities of explosives. Searches were conducted not only in the Jewish

Agency buildings, but also in the Tel Aviv headquarters of the Palmach and the Trade Union Federation (the *Histadrut*). Two thousand people, among them members of the Agency's executive, and hundreds of Hagana recruits were arrested. Many documents, mostly in Hebrew, were removed and curfews imposed over all the Jewish areas of Palestine. It was indeed the largest ever operation of its kind and it caught the Yishuv by surprise despite its efficient intelligence. However, the operation failed to achieve its major objective: to isolate the militants and to bring about the creation of a more moderate leadership. The British themselves admitted ten days after *Agatha*, that 'the operation has temporarily lost us what friends among the Jews we still have'.[27] They also predicted that it would certainly drive some into the ranks of the terrorists, although there was some hope that for others it might serve as a warning against violent action.

Despite the fact that *Agatha* was the biggest British military operation in Palestine, it was limited in its objectives. The British wanted to enforce law and order by neutralising the Hagana and disarming it. This was not feasible, as Lieutenant General Sir Evelyn Barker, GOC British Troops in Palestine, explained: 'The Yishuv will arise against us. They are also determined to hold on to their arms for self-defence, and there is a certain degree of right on their side.'[28] In his opinion, the Hagana needed reorganisation and not disbandment. Barker and many of the British decision-makers in Palestine tended to draw a distinction between the Hagana and the Palmach, its spearhead squads, which was called 'the real enemy of law and order'. The British made it clear throughout the operation that *Agatha* was not directed against the Jewish Community as a whole, but solely against those few who were taking an active part in the campaign of violence. The High Commissioner in a telegram to the War Office stated also that the *Agatha*'s activities did not constitute reprisals or punitive measures. 'They are being undertaken against one section of the Jewish Community merely because it is from that section that present violence has emanated'.[29] He added that *Agatha* would cease at the earliest possible moment after its objective was achieved.

The desire to bring the Hagana as close as possible to the government was so great that the British considered the possibility of making the organisation part of their own police force.[30] This might well have been because of the concept that without the support of the Hagana, it would have been much more difficult, if not impossible, to impose law and order in Palestine. This attitude was strengthened after a search in Kibbutz Yagur, where many arms caches were discovered amid fierce resistance by the local population, who confronted the army almost to the point of an armed offensive.

'This wild vituperative campaign', British Intelligence reported, 'has served to show that the Jews are quite unbalanced, dangerously emotional and psychologically insecure. This may be the result of centuries of persecution. It makes them no easier to deal with.'[31] The British did not delude themselves that *Agatha* would stop Jewish terrorism in Palestine. The operation might have paralysed the Hagana and the Palmach temporarily, but General Barker himself predicted that 'further recruits for the Irgun will be found from Palmach members whom we have not picked up'.[32]

The police expected more trouble from the Irgun, such as kidnapping, in view of the severe sentences passed on the group personnel captured during May 1946. Barker indeed envisaged that the extremists would treat *Agatha* as a declaration of war against the Jewish Community and react accordingly. He was proved to be right, because only three weeks later came the bombing of the King David Hotel.

CHAPTER 8

# British Measures Against Terrorism

The British Government and the security forces in Palestine tried a great variety of counter-measures to combat terrorism. They exiled insurgents, they imprisoned many of them, hanged almost a dozen, set the whole Yishuv against them, imposed martial law, conducted search operations, committed 100,000 troops to the military effort – and yet failed to win the war against them.

The reasons for the failure were a mixture of military incompetence, political indecisiveness, Jewish hostility and the inability to uproot terrorism in the heavily populated urban areas of Palestine. Conflicting attitudes in London added further difficulties to British attempts to enforce law and order in the country. As stated earlier, the British played down the first acts of violence following the Irgun's declaration of revolt on 1 February 1944. The first actions of the Underground failed to win the full attention of the authorities, mainly as a result of military ineffectiveness of the attacks. However, this was not the case on 6 November 1944, when two members of the Stern Group (Lehi) murdered Lord Moyne, Minister of State for the Middle East, in Cairo.[1] The Colonial Secretary, Oliver Stanley, argued that the government should consider the effect of the murder not merely upon Palestine, but upon the Middle East and the rest of the world in general. He suggested, therefore, a full-scale search for illegal arms and the suspension of Jewish immigration to Palestine.[2] Stanley, as well as other British during the crucial years of the Mandate, expressed the hope that a harsh response would induce the Jewish Agency to assist the authorities in fighting the terrorists.

Lord Gort shared his superior's concern, but being the High Commissioner and thus more familiar with the reality in Palestine, he doubted whether this was the best response. He maintained that an arms search would demonstrate the determination of the Government to fight the insurgents, but failed to take into account the consequences of failure. Indeed, all the search operations which took place in the country ended in various degrees of failure which resulted in further damage to British prestige.

## THE OPTIONS: SEARCHES, IMMIGRATION SUSPENSION AND COLLABORATION

Stanley's tough line was also adopted by Brigadier I Clayton, Moyne's advisor on Arab affairs, and Lord Killearn, the British Ambassador to Egypt, who similarly lobbied for an aggressive response.[3] Their views were supported by members of the Eastern Defence Committee. Lord Gort, under pressure from Cairo, changed his mind, and became convinced that searches were necessary, not because they proved effective, but because they were vital for maintaining the morale of Palestine's security forces. At the same time, he hoped that the drastic measures would help to bring about pressure on the Hagana to uproot the Stern Group, responsible for the murder of Lord Moyne.[4]

Killearn, outraged by the assassination in Cairo, continued to press for action and demanded severe punishment as the only way to uphold Britain's status in the Middle East. In a telegram to the Foreign Office, he wrote: 'Please forgive me if I speak strongly, but we are playing with fire; on that let there be no illusion. It has taken the murder of one of our most distinguished public men to arouse us to our responsibilities and to indicate the direct results of our over-patience'.[5] Two days later, he sent another telegram in which he wrote: 'The eyes of the Middle East and certainly Egypt are upon us, confidently awaiting effective action to eradicate this gang of terrorists. Is it really conceivable that we are still not going to do so? Despite Lord Moyne's murder? Despite knowledge of their guilt? I do most earnestly beg you with all the force at my command that we hesitate no longer to take drastic and immediate practical steps to round up the Stern Gang'.

But these arguments failed to persuade either the Prime Minister or the military establishment in London. Winston Churchill opposed a major arms search because it would strike the moderate section of the Yishuv whose sympathy he wanted to win.[6] The Joint Planning Staff of the Chief of Staff supported the Prime Minister simply because they estimated that two or more divisions would be needed for the operation and its chance of success was anyway in doubt.[7]

On 23 November 1944, the Colonial Office recommended the introduction of compulsory registration of arms, a measure supported by the High Commissioner, and called for the imposition of collective fines on the community and the deportation of Jewish leaders. But faced with a shortage of military personnel, the initiative came to nothing. On 27 November 1944, the Cabinet met to consider the entire matter. Its conclusions reflected the views of the Prime Minister and the Chiefs of Staff, who did not approve the wholesale disarming of the Jews. The Cabinet stated that searches were rarely productive; secrecy as to the action contemplated was difficult to maintain; mistakes were made by troops and bad feelings engendered. The Cabinet accepted the military's view that such tasks were best left to the police. The soldiers already in Palestine would support the police when needed. Jewish immigration should not be suspended, nor should military reinforcements be transferred to Palestine.[8] The Colonial Office wired Lord Gort: 'No systematic searches for arms should at this stage be undertaken ... You are at liberty to carry out local searches for arms.'[9]

The Irgun, at this point, was almost ignored because of the responsibility claimed by the Stern for the killing of Moyne. The Foreign Office, feeling obliged to satisfy Killearn's demands for tough action, informed him on 30 November that efforts had been made 'to round up the Stern Gang and other terrorists'. Arrests were also made. The Irgun was not mentioned.[10] London, confused as to the right approach to the increasing wave of terrorism in Palestine, delivered contradictory messages to the Middle East. On 27 November, the same day that the Cabinet decided against adopting drastic measures, the Secretary of State for the Colonies urged Gort to tell the Zionist leader Chaim Weizmann that, if terrorism was not stopped, Jewish immigration would be suspended.

The War Cabinet decided likewise: 'Further support must be given to the efforts to break up the terrorist organisations and hunt down members of the murder gangs'.[11] The High Commissioner in Palestine was in a dilemma. If a wholesale search for arms was undertaken, he anticipated quick and widespread Jewish reaction in the form of active armed resistance. This was likely to lead to the discovery of a substantial quantity of weaponry, but it would be at the cost of undesirable unrest and military confrontation which would include the Hagana as well.

However, if the authorities were to ignore the terrorist campaign which had been highlighted by Moyne's assassination, they would suffer a blow to their prestige. It would encourage the separatists to continue their violence and would ruin their reputation amongst the Arabs in Palestine and Egypt. Neither of the two alternatives was satisfactory and much as the British wanted to choose the first one and re-assert their authority in the country, they were unable to do it militarily. Arms searches on a large scale or the stoppage of immigration required reinforcement of personnel, and this was contrary to the wishes of London and out of the Army's reach. The Colonial Office even considered the removal of certain Jewish units from Palestine before the situation there deteriorated.[12] The idea was rejected but later, during 1946, the Government exiled many of the dissidents to detainee camps in Africa.

As we know, Moyne's assassination was not approved by the Irgun, and was strongly condemned by all sections of the Yishuv, which feared that the Government would inflict punishment on the Community. The ground was therefore prepared for a period of collaboration between British Intelligence, the Hagana and the Jewish Agency. London chose a policy of restraint, and enjoyed the co-operation of the moderates, which under British pressure, hunted down suspected terrorists and handed them over to the police. The number of guerrilla activities was diminished as a result of the so-called 'Hunting Season', but not because the Army or the police had improved their performance. Britain was preoccupied with post-war priorities and Palestine was regarded as a staging post to which troops were sent either for training or regrouping. Plans for reorganisation were shelved. Countering urban terrorism remained a police matter and the relative calm during the start of 1945 deluded the British into believing that the problems facing them in Palestine could be suspended for the immediate future.

The British could not find the right response to the assassination of Lord Moyne and the War Office was also at odds with the Colonial Office on this issue up until 1945. The Eastern Department of the War Office created some doubts about the public warning by the Colonial Secretary that should further outrages occur, Jewish immigration into Palestine would be suspended. The Department maintained that 'it is not only the Jews who are capable of staging outrages and it might almost appear as an invitation to the Arabs to do something which would stop the hated Jewish immigration'. The War Office, it will be remembered, had suggested taking far more drastic action by announcing that 'in view of the outrage which has occurred, further Jewish immigration into Palestine is suspended'.[13] This would prevent a situation in which either the Arabs or the Jews could try to take the law into their own hands by attempting to influence events for as long as threats remained unfulfilled.

At its meeting on 22 November 1945, the War Cabinet recognised that the stoppage of immigration would cause outrage and controversy among the Jews. Therefore, it diluted its recommendation by stressing that such a declaration should be accompanied by a statement that this would in no way affect the temporary transfer of refugees from Europe to the Middle East.

The War Cabinet also criticised those responsible for Palestine, expressing surprise that no suggestion had been made of mass arrests and interrogation of all persons suspected of involvement with illegal associations in the country. Such an act, in its opinion, would greatly impress public opinion. The War Cabinet, as well as the Chiefs of Staff Committee, voiced its support for harsher measures against the insurgents and even opposed the High Commissioner in Palestine, who expressed the hope that the Jewish Agency would co-operate with the British against the terrorists by themselves arresting them. 'It would make HMG lose a great deal of face in Arab eyes ...', it said. On the other hand 'it would seem to show that there are some elements in the Jewish Agency which could help a great deal more in the search for terrorists if they cared to do so'.[14]

## EXILE IN AFRICA

The most effective counter-measure taken by the British against the Irgun was the deportation of hundreds of insurgents to the Empire's colonies in Eritrea, Sudan and Kenya. It started on 20 October 1944 when 251 men, held on terrorist charges at Latrun prison, were transferred by air to Eritrea without advance warning. Six more groups were flown to Africa in the following month. It was, in the words of Begin himself, 'one of the most serious measures that the enemy had taken against us, apart from the nightmare of the hanging'. He had no doubt as to the motive behind the deportation: 'to break the spinal cord of the fighters and to extinguish the flame of the revolt'.[15]

The move confronted the Yishuv with a dilemma and was deplored even by the opponents as an attempt to rob a Jew of his basic right to live in his homeland, even behind bars. But the diminishing power of the Underground, as a result of the African exile, indirectly helped the Hagana to re-assert its rule over the Community while the armed struggle was gathering pace.

The plight of the insurgents at the African detention camps was highlighted on 17 January 1945, when the Sudanese guard in Eritrea shot dead three prisoners and injured 17. The killing triggered off a wave of protest in Palestine. Jewish Agency leaders met the High Commissioner, demanded an inquiry and called on him to put an end to the exile. This was at the time when the Irgun was joining forces with the Hagana and the Stern group against the authorities. The Irgun considered a retaliation for the shooting, but the Hagana urged against it, threatening to break up the partnership. Finally, the Irgun agreed and restrained itself. The British, for their part, agreed to dismiss the Sudanese guard and ten days later transferred the camp to a new site, in Sudan, 600 kilometres from the capital Khartoum.

One of the reasons for the exile was the British fear that the insurgents would try to attack prisons in Palestine in order to release their colleagues as they were to do in Acre in May 1947. While that fear could have indicated British weakness in safeguarding its law-enforcement institutes in Palestine, it was a convenient way to detain terrorists at a low financial cost. The Irgun might have taken pride in such a motive, but the issue was more complicated. A meeting held in Government House in Jerusalem on 20

December 1945 was indicative. The Chief Secretary recalled the circumstances which had necessitated the first deportation two months earlier. In his words there was a 'sharp increase in terrorism and sabotage of troops locally'. He singled out two difficulties which had prompted the authorities to resort to such a far-reaching move: 'We had been largely dependent upon information given by the Jewish Agency. The screening had consequently been poor, and full re-examination of each case had been necessary'.[16] Both the IZL and FFI prisoners made many attempts to escape even from the African detention centres. But, while succeeding in making their way outside their camps to freedom, they failed in most cases to reach safety and often went missing in the African jungle. The inability to find outside contacts revealed serious Irgun shortcomings, for it made no efforts, during a three year period to establish a network (with or without the involvement of the local Jewish community) to help the escapees. The same criticism was echoed even by Ya'acov Meridor, second in command to Begin, who spent most of the armed struggle years in African detention. He argued that the revolt could have been much more effective if the prisoners could have participated in it, either by being in Palestine or in Europe, where weapons for the Irgun were collected in earnest. 'In Africa', he added, 'was the concentration of the best men of the Irgun'. The detainees, Meridor implied, were simply abandoned.[17]

The African exile was a severe blow to the Irgun, since the mass expulsion had deprived the guerrillas of their leadership and isolated those in exile from the events in Palestine. Whereas, had they been imprisoned in their own country, there would have been some possibility of their release by military or political means, their exile in Africa cut them off completely from the struggle until Israel became independent in 1948.[18] Bearing in mind the failure of the insurgents in their plans to resist the deportations, it is easy to see the exile as a clear example of how the British could have gained the upper hand over their adversaries.[19]

## CONFRONTING A JEWISH UNITED FRONT

The establishment by the United Resistance Movement of an armed front on a formidable scale was a blow to the British authorities and their efforts to isolate the 'dissidents'. The British concern was focused on the Palmach which consisted of 2000 full-time people, and on the Hagana itself, believed by the British to contain 8000 front-line men.[20]

At a meeting of the Defence Committee on 5 November 1945, the Chief of Staff was asked to consider whether the time had come to request the Commander in Chief in the Middle East to demand the surrender of illegal arms in Palestine. The Commander in Chief replied that, rather than take action forthwith, the government would wait 'until terrorist activities make such a course obviously necessary and justifiable'.[21] He pointed out that searches for arms would in any event be violent and lead to considerable bloodshed. He and his colleagues were waiting for the psychological moment to take drastic measures. Such a moment arrived in June 1946 after a series of attacks had taken place in Palestine in which bridges over the Jordan river had been blown up, the railway workshops in Haifa had been severely damaged and five British officers had been kidnapped from the Officers' Club in Tel Aviv. The acts had been carried out by the Hagana, FFI and Irgun respectively, as part of their joint operations and dealt a severe blow to the military authorities. The High Commissioner called for rigorous action by the government and urged it to refuse to conduct any further discussion on the subject of the admission of a further 100,000 Jews into Palestine until the kidnapped officers had been returned. He added that he should be authorised to put into effect, at whatever time he thought appropriate, the full plan drawn up locally against the Jewish illegal organisations and the Jewish Agency.

However, in spite of these terrorist acts, the British were not prepared to react and were reluctant to sabotage their talks with the Americans, which had just begun, about the implications of admitting 100,000 immigrants to Palestine, as President Truman had requested. The British wanted to avoid creating an unfavourable impression in America. Field-Marshal Montgomery, the Chief of the Imperial General Staff, who had adopted a consistently tough line, warned that if the existing state of affairs continued, the troops in Palestine might get out of hand. He suggested that the time had come when greater freedom of action should be given to the High Commissioner and the Commander in Chief. This view was supported by the Secretary of State for War.[22] The Foreign Secretary also took the view that strong action should be taken and emphasised the importance of enlisting the support of the US Government for such action. The Government was well aware that its prestige in Palestine might be damaged, especially from the Arab point of view. The Cabinet feared that the Arabs would take to the streets and use whatever arms they had. Breaking the illegal Jewish organisation was therefore seen as the top priority.

London was eager to show that it did not wish to appear to discriminate against the Jews in favour of the Arabs, but made clear that only the Jews had effective illegal organisations. However, the factor which later played the greatest part in the Government's retaliatory policy measures was the insurgents' link with the Hagana which was itself controlled by the Jewish Agency. Therefore, while anti-Jewish feelings were mounting in England, the Government instructed the armed forces to prepare themselves secretly to attack the Yishuv at its most vulnerable point – the Jewish Agency itself. Thus Operation *Agatha* (described in Chapter 7) came into being.

## THE CIVIL-MILITARY CONTROVERSY

On 24 July 1946, two days after the King David explosion, the Commander in Chief for the Middle East, Lieutenant General Sir Miles Dempsey, sent a telegram to the War Office, in which he wrote that he had instructed General Evelyn Barker, the GOC in Palestine, to take over 'a suitable area in Jerusalem as a British cantonment from which all civilians will be excluded'. This 'enclave' was later nicknamed 'Bevingrad' by the Jews. He also instructed him to institute a continuous series of raids on towns and villages with the object of collecting terrorist arms and ammunition. Tel Aviv was to be the first objective – namely Operation *Shark* (see Chapter 5). The order included taking over the Jewish Agency buildings in Jerusalem and arresting certain Hagana officials.[23] But Dempsey, eager to get Palestine back under control, suggested a series of punishments for the King David outrage. He asked for the War Office's permission to divert all illegal immigrants, when caught, to another country, and to deport the Jewish leaders who were behind bars as a result of Operation *Agatha*. In addition, he recommended the imposition of a heavy collective fine on the Jewish Community for the benefit of the dependants of the murdered persons and for the repair of the physical damage caused.

However the Colonial Secretary was adamant that those in the Yishuv who were not responsible for the outrage should not be punished. He rejected outright confiscation of Jewish funds and suspension of all immigration to Palestine, not least because it would clash with the Anglo-American discussions on the issue of Jewish immigration. In a telegram to the High Commissioner for Palestine he advised the military authorities 'to secure any known arms dumps which might be used by the Irgun, while avoiding a widespread search throughout the whole Jewish community'.[24] Cunningham was not, therefore, given the green light, except for a limited action which would be confined to one place at a time and be directed only against the Irgun.

When the Cabinet summoned Sir John Shaw, Chief Secretary to the Government of Palestine, on 30 July 1946, he expressed the fear that an Arab outburst might follow the outrage at the King David, not least because 41 Arabs had been killed in the explosion. He said that the majority of the Jews were shocked by the bombing and had openly declared their support for the Government. He then spoke about the joint anti-British activities of the three organisations and suggested that the Hagana had known about the plan to blow up the hotel. 'There was reason to believe that the Irgun had informed the Hagana authorities beforehand of their plans', he told the ministers.[25] Shaw supported Cunningham's view that the Government should accept the idea of seizing Zionist financial assets. This, in his opinion, would have a stabilising effect on Arab opinion.

The general feeling in the Cabinet was that, due to the damage caused to life and property by the recent series of outrages, and the connection between the Hagana and the other organisations, some fines should be imposed on the Jewish Agency. Fines amounting to at least £1m had been imposed on the Arabs during their 1936–39 revolt. But the Government was very reluctant to do this in Palestine even after the King David explosion for fear of pushing the Hagana further into the arms of the dissidents. This reflected the Mandate authorities' view that it was unable to fight the terrorists without the co-operation of the Jewish leadership and the local population.

Heavy fines were strongly objected to by the Chief of the Imperial General Staff who argued that some of the Yishuv leaders had already taken the militant side. In his assessment at the meeting of the Defence Committee held on 20 November 1946 he decided that the situation was 'rapidly deteriorating' and demanded immediate action. 'It would be impossible for the Army to play an effective part unless it could be given the authority to act fully as an aid to the civil power for the purposes of maintaining law and order in Palestine. The only means of stamping out this type of warfare was to allow the army to take the offensive against it'.[26] Field Marshal Montgomery was referring not only to the King David affair, but also to the general security situation in Palestine, where 76 men of the Army and 23 police had been killed or wounded since 1 October 1946 in the space of seven weeks. During this period sabotage of property continued and rail communication came to a standstill. He pointed out that the Army had in the past gained the initiative against terrorism when it had been permitted to attack the illegal organisations in the country. Since then, it had been forced to adopt a defensive role which had seriously increased the strain on its morale. The Palestine Police were 50 per cent below strength and they needed 3000 recruits to reach their full requirement. Montgomery feared that more soldiers would take the law into their own hands as a result of frustration, as they had already done in some isolated incidents.

The Secretary of State for the Colonies agreed that the situation in Palestine had deteriorated. However, he did not think that the position of the armed forces in their capacity as an aid to the civil power had changed since the Cabinet decision in June. His description of the situation was more muted. While agreeing that the total number of incidents had increased, he noted that 'they were of a less serious character than previously, though the total of casualties was still large'.[27]

At that meeting the Prime Minister admitted that British strategy in combating terrorism had failed. He referred back to June, when the Cabinet had agreed to authorise the High Commissioner to take such steps as he considered necessary to break up the illegal organisations in Palestine. For that purpose the government had given him the green light to launch Operation *Agatha*, which included searching the Jewish Agency premises and arresting its leaders. Attlee, at that time, had told the Cabinet that, when this authority had been given, the ministers had been assured that the power of these illegal organisations would be seriously weakened. Now it appeared that the action had not achieved this objective since terrorist activity was increasing. Attlee expressed a sense of helplessness, uncertain what else could be done. Because there had been no change of policy regarding the role of the Army since the Cabinet decisions in June, he asked the Chief of the Imperial General Staff what further measures were required.

Montgomery replied that the Army had been prevented from carrying out searches for arms or from taking pre-emptive steps against the insurgents, based on intelligence information. Owing to political restrictions, he argued, the armed organisations had been allowed two months of re-organisation, after a period during which military action was to have 'destroyed the organisation of the Hagana and Irgun'. The Prime Minister was not impressed by Montgomery's eagerness to prove that giving the Army a free hand would improve matters in Palestine. He said that the Cabinet had authorised the High Commissioner to institute a widespread search for arms, which he had discontinued after a period of time as a result of the limited nature of their success. He was referring to Operation *Agatha* (against the Jewish Agency) and *Shark* (against the Irgun). He then said that the authorities in Palestine had confined their counter-insurgency activities to areas where terrorist incidents had occurred. This authority had never been withdrawn, he told Montgomery, nor had instructions been given to block preventative action.

The High Commissioner was allowed to use the armed forces at his disposal as an aid to civilian power for the sake of maintaining law and order in Palestine. In this statement, the Prime Minister contradicted both Montgomery and the Colonial Secretary who maintained that the armed forces had been prevented from playing an effective role in Palestine. The fact was that the army had never been specifically forbidden from acting offensively against terrorism.

The Commander in Chief in the Middle East, Lieutenant General Sir Miles Dempsey, criticised the High Commissioner for not giving the military more freedom of manoeuvre.[28] He referred to his inability to carry out retaliatory action against a population which was indirectly linked to an outrage and complained that conditions created by the situation 'hold the Army back'.[29] In response, the GOC, General Barker in Palestine, sent a personal telegram to the Commander in Chief in the Middle East, in which he wrote that no action that could be taken by the military alone could stop terrorism. He said that action must always be supported by a policy 'which is not existent at present'.[30] He was referring to the possibilities of a complete stoppage of immigration or refusal to continue negotiations as a means of stopping terrorism. 'We have apparently not made sufficient use of our political weapons, nor does it seem that we ever intend to do so', he commented.[31]

Field-Marshal Montgomery, in Palestine towards the end of November 1946, said at a meeting at Government House in Jerusalem that political restrictions on the Army affected its ability to maintain law and order in the country. He complained that the absence of clear guidelines from London made life very difficult for the security forces in Palestine. In his opinion, if a political solution was not forthcoming, it would be necessary to take strong military action in the country.[32] It was quite clear that Montgomery, as well as Dempsey, tried to put the blame of the Jewish terrorist activities on the civilian authorities in Palestine and to make Cunningham the scapegoat for the situation. They were hostile to the High Commissioner's opposition to 'collective punishment' and ignored his warning that indiscriminate retaliatory measures would push the Jewish moderates into the arms of the terrorists and punish innocent people.

Cunningham, aware of the onslaught against him by the military, was furious and demanded an apology from Montgomery. The latter told him in Jerusalem on 29 November that he, Cunningham, was reluctant to give the army a free hand because he feared the Zionist reaction. The High Commissioner felt that he was the one who was most familiar with the reality in Palestine. Montgomery, indeed, took his words back and conceded that advancing the military option would not be effective, given the type of urban terrorism in existence, which the soldiers would find very difficult to combat.[33] Montgomery failed to recognise the complexity of the Jewish-Arab conflict and its difficulties which were different from those with which he had been dealing before as a military commander. He was supported by General Barker, who maintained that only a political settlement would solve the problem. As far as Montgomery was concerned, most of the counter-insurgency operations were designed to raise Army morale, rather than to target the elusive terrorists. Palestine, therefore, had witnessed a confrontation between the military and the civil administrations. Needless to say, the Colonial Office supported the latter and the War

Office endorsed Montgomery's assessments.

The Chiefs of Staff Committee submitted a report for the Cabinet Defence Committee in which it argued that 'the only measure of combating terrorism is a policy of constant harassment which will keep the terrorists on the move and thus disrupt their plans. It is inevitable that in the course of such action, certain law-abiding Jewish citizens may be molested, but it may serve to bring home to them the fact that terrorism does not pay and that the community itself should give practical effect to their denunciation of the terrorists'.[34] Montgomery told the Cabinet that in the last few weeks searches in Palestine, carried out without specific evidence but on general suspicion, had been very effective: a number of suspected terrorists had been arrested and a quantity of arms and documents had been obtained. He was satisfied that with suitable power, the military authorities would take the initiative against the terrorists. Then they would be able to bring terrorism under control and restore the confidence of the Jewish community in the government. The Cabinet agreed that 'leniency towards the terrorists would not strengthen the influence of the Jewish Agency'.[35] The British military establishment ignored the political circumstances in Palestine altogether and isolated the terrorist incidents from the question of Jewish immigration. It believed that hurting the population would deprive the insurgents of their popular support. The truth was that the majority of the Yishuv did not back the Irgun, nor did it support the British Government. Past operations, such as *Agatha* and *Shark*, which had caused great inconvenience to the public, had not proved a success, and contrary to the military argument had not won the British any support in the country.

The Colonial Secretary at that time, Arthur Creech-Jones, argued that the security problem should also have been considered from the political point of view. He stated that adopting aggressive tactics would upset the political balance and hinder efforts to reach a settlement in Palestine. In order to resolve the impasse, Cunningham was recalled to London and on 3 January 1947 he again confronted Montgomery. The High Commissioner said with great confidence, despite the attacks on him from the military, that he could not see that it was worthwhile 'turning areas upside down where there was no indication of the presence of terrorists'.[36] Montgomery remained resolutely opposed to Cunningham. He was adamant in his claim that by giving a free rein to the Army, it would be able to impose law and order in Palestine. The Chief of the Imperial General Staff advocated worldwide arms searches and used the phrase 'turning the place upside down', without even waiting for evidence of terrorist complication. He believed that, although the Jewish Community would indeed be upset by having its life disrupted, it had wearied of the disturbances and would agree to co-operate in putting an end to terrorism. He played down the possibility that the Hagana might join the battle, saying that he would welcome the opportunity to fight them.

However, he made an error of judgement by comparing the situation in Palestine to the Arab revolt of the 1930s which the British were very successful in putting down.[37] Montgomery believed that the partition of Palestine between the two communities should be enforced on both Jews and Arabs. He ignored the view, expressed by Cunningham and Creech-Jones, that such an attitude could involve the Yishuv in an all-out war against the British. Such a confrontation, they argued, would spread throughout the country, affect innocent people and destroy any hope of a political solution.

Montgomery's arguments finally won the day, although not entirely. Twelve days after the meeting, on 15 January, the Government endorsed a draft, prepared by the Chief of Staff but qualified by Cunningham. It included an order to take immediate steps to maintain law and order in the country and the Army was given the powers it wanted to defeat terrorism. However, Cunningham insisted on inserting his own reservation that 'there can be no question of taking reprisals which merely bear hardly on innocent people'.[38] The outcome of the 'new policy' was the imposition of martial law on 2 March 1947.

The debate was marked by many operations launched by the British at the end of 1946 and the beginning of 1947. Their success was marginal. These were Operation *Noah* in Netanya, Operation *Ark* in the Yemenite Quarter of Rishon LeZion, Operation *Lobster* in Tel Aviv, Operation *Mackerel* in Rehovot, Operation *Lonesome* in the Montefiore Quarter of Jerusalem and Operation *Cautious* in the Hatikva neighbourhood near Tel Aviv. All in all, of the thousands who were screened, only a handful of suspects were arrested and few arms were seized. The terrorist campaign of the Irgun continued throughout 1947 despite these military efforts and reached a new peak prior to the British decision to quit Palestine. One of the operations, *Cantonment*, was a pre-emptive action, taken by the British to defend their families in anticipation of more disturbances. It consisted mainly of moving them around in the country and evacuating them abroad. The security forces were worried that 'reaction to recent measures taken up by the government of Palestine to maintain law and order, have brought about a situation in which the security of the British subjects in the country against attacks and kidnappings is now a matter of prime importance'.[39] Martial law, as indicated, did not fulfil British expectations, but it was the least the Government could have done to apply economic pressure on the Jewish Community. After the lifting of the law, less than two weeks after its imposition, the authorities maintained that it should be reintroduced in a flexible manner and occasionally in selected areas.

As an alternative, the authorities considered the implementation of regulations contained in Article 6 of the Palestine Order of 1937. This related to the withdrawal of all civilian government services from the area to which they were extended. There were two reasons behind this conclusion. First, since terrorist activities were directed against the government, its services could not be maintained with reasonable security for the civilian officers operating in areas where terrorism was in evidence. Secondly, only 'strong economic pressure and coercion' could make the Jews aware that they could not expect to continue normal social and economic life 'as long as they have in their midst murderers and saboteurs ...'. Yet the British admitted that even those measures would not solve the problem as illustrated in the following statement: 'By controlling movement and communication, the regulations are preventative, and by restricting economic life they are coercive, but they will not in themselves stop terrorism'.[40] The High Commissioner told the Cabinet that after two weeks it was clear that they had reached the limit of their usefulness. Substantial relaxation would otherwise have been necessary, and increasing unemployment might have provided further recruits for the terrorists. There was also a serious risk of alienating the sympathy of the Trade Unions Federation, which was disposed to co-operate with the government. However, despite shortcomings in the policy, Cunningham had no doubt that the results achieved had been beneficial.

After the imposition and lifting of martial law in 1947, which had not ended in success even on the Government's own admission, the British continued to search for the right answer to the problem of terrorism in Palestine. They examined the possibility of setting up special summary military courts, but rejected the idea on the grounds that the existing military courts were satisfying the demands of the security forces. They also considered reducing the time allowed for appeal against death sentences so as to prevent the taking of British hostages. Then a new approach was adopted by the Palestine Police – appointing select squads to mix with Irgun and Stern Group members with the aim of eliminating them. But the new tactics had to be shelved due to a public outcry at the killing on May 1947 of a 17-year-old billposter who was allegedly tortured to death.[41]

The security forces in Palestine, as well as the High Commissioner, were eager to show London that they were capable of reducing the scale of terrorism in the country. Whenever there was a lull in the insurgents' activities, they were quick to point out that they had the upper hand. They also put emphasis on boosting the morale of the Army and police as an aim which justified a pre-emptive operation against the terrorists.

On 16 May 1947, at a security conference held in Jerusalem, the army expressed satisfaction that the 'railways were in operation again', after a long period of disruption caused by the Irgun's sabotage campaign. However, the disappointing results of martial law encouraged the Irgun to intensify its activities. The first half of 1947 was marked by the kidnapping of soldiers, assassinations of policemen, flogging of British personnel, dozens of attacks on economic targets, and, on 4 May, the stunning break-in at the Acre prison, described by Creech-Jones as a humiliation for the government.

## HANGING, KIDNAPPING, FLOGGING AND COUNTER HANGING

Having failed to eliminate terrorism by their policy of arrest, exile, martial law and co-operation with the Jewish majority, the Mandate authorities turned in 1947 to their last resort – the death sentence.

In fact, the first Irgun member had been sent to the gallows in the summer of 1939,[42] but this was because of his attempts to attack Arabs at a time when the Irgun itself hardly existed and was not in any way hostile to London. Again, at the end of 1944 the British had hanged the two FFI members who had assassinated Lord Moyne, although the sentence took place in Cairo.

The Government was reluctant to exercise its power to hang the insurgents, bearing in mind the repercussions of such an act on the Jewish Community in Palestine and public opinion elsewhere. But, faced with growing criticism by British and Arabs alike for failing to punish the terrorists severely enough, it changed its mind about the death penalty. The Government hoped that by such extreme action it would demonstrate a 'firm and hardening attitude on our part',[43] although it did not delude itself that hanging would deter the underground organisations.

In fact, that policy was first reintroduced on 7 March 1946, when the Irgun launched one of its most spectacular attacks, this time on Sarafand, the biggest British military base. As a result of the attack, two of the Irgun's members were captured. On 15 June 1946, a military court sentenced them to death and two days afterwards the organisation kidnapped five British officers in Tel Aviv. The Irgun, threatened to execute the officers if the sentence was not commuted. On 3 July, after consultation with London, the authorities yielded to the ultimatum and the sentence was reduced to life imprisonment. The Irgun, for its part, released the officers and hailed it as a victory over the Empire, but the British strongly denied that the mitigation was the result of fear of retaliation. Yet, the episode further diminished their prestige and enhanced the Irgun's position in the Yishuv.

On 23 April 1946 the Irgun members attacked the well fortified police station of Ramat Gan in order to get hold of its arms store. The attack failed and one of its participants, Dov Gruner, who was later to become a household name in the country, was wounded and captured. He was sentenced to death in a well known trial which he turned into a political platform from which he accused the government of responsibility for the plight of the deported Jewish refugees. Gruner won sympathy in Palestine and also in America mainly because of his adamant refusal to ask for parole in order to save his life. After 105 days, marked by constant demonstrations and other political protests designed to save him from the gallows, he was hanged with three other Irgun members who belonged to the 'flogging squads'.

These squads had been set up by the Irgun's High Command after a British military court sentenced a 17 year old Irgunist to 18 lashes for his part in the attack on the Jaffa Bank on 13 September 1946. Begin saw the flogging as an unforgivable act, designed to humiliate the Jews, and regarded it as a form of anti-semitism.[44] He published a warning to the British authorities and demanded that they should not carry out the flogging.

*Herut* (Freedom), the organ of the Underground, threatened to retaliate in kind. The paper used typical Irgun terminology and wrote that the British would be mistaken if they treated the Jews in the same way as the 'natives in their colonies without being punished',[45] that is, with impunity. When the Irgun learned that the British had ignored its warning, it captured a British major in the town of Netanya and gave him 18 lashes. They also caught two soldiers in Tel Aviv and humiliated them in the same way in the local municipal zoo.

Thus, what should have been, by logical accounts, a marginal episode in the history of the Mandate period, was enlarged to a confrontation between the government and the Irgun, which exploited it to the full for its own propaganda motives. While the Army was announcing a wide search for the IZL's 'flogging squads' by sealing urban districts and setting up road blocks, the retaliation by the Irgun was greeted in London by uproar. The government was attacked by the press and Parliament, and on 29 December Churchill demanded in Parliament a firm hand to deal with the terrorists in Palestine. The main reason for his critical speech was the decision to commute the flogging punishment of two more Irgun members following the Irgun reprisal. He said that, if the British had changed the sentence only because some officers were kidnapped and lashed, this proved their lack of will to fight what he termed 'a minority of desperate fanatics'.[46]

Two other death sentences were passed on Irgun member, Meir Feinstein (for his part in the attack on the train station in Jerusalem), and Moshe Barazani from the FFI (for possessing a pistol). However, on the night of 20 April, a few hours before their execution, the two blew themselves up by means of a hand-grenade smuggled into their death-cell by friends outside.

The hanging and flogging created an outcry within the Yishuv. Although the Irgun was criticised by the bulk of the Jewish press 'for sacrificing their members'[47], the general feeling was that the British should review their policy in Palestine and induce the withdrawal of their forces from the country. The Irgun was not able to save its members from the gallows in spite of its threats. After the hanging of four of its members, it was determined to seek revenge, but could not find its desired victims because the Government had instructed its soldiers to take extra precautions and to move only in convoys. The Irgun's High Command, for its part, set up 'field courts' and announced that executions of Jewish insurgents would be met by the same measures.[48] The Irgun then ceased its activities for 12 days. The lull caused speculation in Palestine as to its possible reasons and created hope amongst the British that the insurgents, licking their wounds, might have changed their strategy. In fact it was only a preparation for the IZL's biggest operation yet – the break-in at the Acre prison (described in Chapter 4).

The operation caused outrage in the House of Commons and its members expressed the view that it was no longer possible for the Government to impose order by force. The call for evacuation from Palestine was intensified. Ironically, in their classified correspondence, the authorities in Palestine praised the Irgun for the way it executed its plan. The general opinion was that of all their operations, the one in the Acre citadel had been the most daring. The Army concluded that the perpetrators had an accurate knowledge of the prison buildings and the daily routine. The attack was indeed a military humiliation for the British, despite its mediocre results, not only on account of the prisoners' escape, but because of the insurgents' ability to penetrate the citadel by co-ordinating the operation with their fellow-prisoners. The security forces were severely criticised for having failed to foil the attack and the High Commissioner was at pains to explain that the break-in reflected the difficulty that his men were facing. Cunningham said that no amount of soldiers or policemen would be able to defend the country from attacks on buildings, railways or pipelines, which could be executed at any time, day or night – a situation that had existed for many years.[49] In the same report, the High Commissioner indicated that the 'dissidents in Palestine are trained with the same underground stratagem which was used by the European Underground in the Second World War'. The Irgun itself made clear in its 7 May broadcast that it regarded the operation as a success: 'We had the advantage of complete surprise. We had safeguarded the rear with formidable fire-power and only an unpredictable coincidence caused us heavy casualties'.[50]

## BEVINGRADS AND FAMILY EVACUATION

Parallel to the drastic measures that the British Government had taken against the insurgents, it had also adopted defensive steps to safeguard its armed forces and their families in Palestine. At the end of 1946, 591 more policemen were brought to the country and the Palestine Mobile Police (PMP) was annexed to the General Police in order to increase co-ordination.

After the King David explosion on 22 July, the Government had created 'security zones' (nicknamed 'Bevingrads') in the three major towns, by sealing off its own premises. As a result, it confiscated shops and offices owned by Jews and evacuated hundreds from these areas. These precautions were designed to prevent terrorists attacks on Government buildings, but the British, in fact, put themselves under virtual siege. In January 1946, anticipating a wave of insurgency activities against them, the British declared Operation *Polly* in which they evacuated all women, children and other subjects whose presence in Palestine was not vital. The evacuation order was given to enable the security forces to continue maintaining law and order in the country without hindrance. In fact, the decision reflected the fear of further terrorist attacks which the government would be unable to control. 'It reflected the increasing helplessness of the government and the armed forces to fight the Jewish extremists without full freedom of action'.[51]

While transferring 1800 people by train from Haifa to Egypt, the British extended their 'Bevingrads' in Jerusalem, Tel Aviv and Haifa. The declared intention was to maintain the 'security zones' for six months, although this never materialised. The mass evacuation boosted the Irgun's morale. The organisation saw it as proof that its strategy had paid off. Its members responded on 18 February with a campaign of mining and sabotaging economic and military targets, among them the bombing of the Kirkuk–Haifa oil pipeline two days later.

The failure of the Army's efforts to prevent the chaos that the Irgun wanted to inflict on the country was most graphically illustrated by the IZL's terrorist attacks on the railway system. The British concluded at the height of that campaign that the only answer to the mining was foot patrols, covering most of the trains' routes. At an evening security conference in Jerusalem the High Commissioner admitted that 'at present we are defeated on this matter' and urged the Army to find a 'workable plan'. The GOC agreed with that assessment, but he maintained that 'even by using more men, it would be impossible to prevent mining completely'. So grave was the situation that one of the possibilities which was considered was to keep the railways open for short periods during darkness. One other suggestion was to inform Arab villages that rewards would be given to them for the exposure of terrorists. The 'epidemic' of attacks on trains necessitated an increase of troops in the country, but the Army's response to Cunningham's request was negative. The authorities, in the end, found a solution to the 'mine outrages'; they instructed the armed forces to sweep the sides of roads for mines and patrol them carefully, since, in the words of the GOC, 'the terrorists tactics were always the same'. In total, the terrorist damage to the railways was valued at £325,000 and the loss of traffic to £100,000 a month. That solution was typically defensive and only partially tackled the problem. Such ineffectiveness characterised also the need to reduce dissidents' attacks by vehicles. The High Commissioner considered another unsatisfactory proposal: to issue a card for display on windscreens with the name and photograph of the driver on it. The scheme was not fully implemented and it fell a long way short of preventing attacks on the armed forces from fast moving stolen cars.

As the question of Palestine was about to be debated at the United Nations, the Underground intensified its activities against the Mandate authorities. On 1 March the IZL delivered a blow to the British by attacking Goldsmith House, the officers' club in Jerusalem, which was located inside the military zone. It was one of the most devastating terrorist outrages, not least because it resulted in the death of 17 soldiers and officers and injury to 27 others. The building was reduced to rubble after explosives were thrown through the windows. The attack was in response to what the Irgun saw as a 'political waiting game' by Bevin who had, in its view, made his intention clear in the UN not to abandon the Mandate in Palestine.[52] On that day the Irgun carried out 16 other operations.

The Goldsmith House incident prompted the decision to impose wide-scale martial law 24 hours after the attack. The law was applied in Tel Aviv (Operation *Elephant*) and Jerusalem (Operation *Hippopotamus*) and reflected British determination to fight the Jewish Underground. As mentioned previously, martial law was imposed for only 16 days during which the Irgun and the Stern Group continued, albeit separately, to attack military camps, vehicles, trains and banks all over the country. Altogether 20 such attacks took place in that period.

The failure of martial law, despite the authorities' efforts in Palestine to portray it as a relative success, did not go unnoticed in London. Churchill voiced the main opposition to the Government's policy, questioning the wisdom of the continuation of the Mandate and calling on Attlee to quit Palestine if he was unable to maintain law and order there.

In Palestine, Churchill said in another parliamentary debate, the British 'keep three to four times more soldiers than in the whole of India'. In a motion of no confidence on 12 May, he reminded the government that

Palestine had cost London £82m during the last two years, and kept 100,000 Britons away from their families and jobs. The Opposition leader's views were supported by the majority of the press, while public opinion increasingly demanded that the Mandate should come to a speedy end. The mood was intensified by the low morale of the security forces who had also lost the campaign of psychological warfare mounted against them by the Jews of Palestine.

## MARTIAL LAW

Imposing comprehensive martial law on the Yishuv on 2 March 1947 was the British military's last resort, having failed to cope with the increasing number of terrorist activities in Palestine by all other means. This unprecedented step was designed not only to strike directly at the Underground movement, but also to harm the economic interests of the Jewish Community, so that its moderate elements would be willing to co-operate with the authorities.

Martial law contradicted the principles upon which the Mandate had been given to the British to manage the affairs of Palestine. In the event of such a law, the army was to take over the administration of the country from the civilian authorities and the military Command would assume the authority of the High Commissioner. The War Office would be responsible for the country's external affairs, taking over all responsibilities from the Colonial Office.

The armed forces were not able to supervise the imposition of the law all over Palestine, so the government restricted its actual implementation to the suspected 'terrorist' areas – Jerusalem and Tel Aviv. The idea of a comprehensive campaign had, therefore, to be abandoned. By declaring martial law the British transferred the responsibility for law and order from the civilian administration to the military authorities in the country. According to British law, unless it was imposed throughout the country, it could have been challenged through the Civil Courts, which would remain in operation in those parts of the country not under martial law. (However, another form of rule existed: 'statutory martial law' which was the name given to exceptional powers which could be assumed by the Crown, but could not be challenged in the courts).[53]

The imposition of martial law involved the withdrawal of all Government services from the affected areas, paralysed their economic life and caused large-scale unemployment. No Government revenue could be collected, civil courts were closed and the police and the military were able to conduct a thorough search for known terrorists which ended in 78 arrests. The daily life was also disrupted because the military commander of each area was empowered to close banks and control all movement of traffic. Only a few days after the beginning of the operation, the Government was informed by its intelligence services in Palestine that there was 'an encouraging degree of co-operation from the Jewish Community'. Yet, despite this optimistic note, the high degree of anticipation and the human resources which had been invested in the operation, the High Commissioner and the local military authorities decided within a very short space of time that martial law had reached the limit of its usefulness.[54] The measures were withdrawn on 17 March, two weeks and a day after they had been proclaimed. The government was at pains to explain the sudden removal of this stringent policy. The Colonial Secretary, Creech-Jones, told the Cabinet on 20 March that, from the beginning, martial law itself 'had not been supposed to bring terrorism to an end, and some outrages, involving loss of life, had since occurred'.[55] But the authorities had not intended to remove the law so soon, hoping, through its imposition, to inflict maximum damage on the terrorists. The fact that it lasted only two weeks was in itself an admission that British expectations of its potential had been too high. Equally, the need to resort to such drastic measures in the first place was a clear indication that the British had exhausted all other methods of counter-insurgency at their disposal in Palestine.

A meeting of all the major decision-makers in Palestine, which took place on 5 March 1947 in Jerusalem, reflected the confusion and uncertainty which surrounded the implementation of martial law. The difficulties underlined the difference between the British success in suppressing the Arab revolt in the 1930s and the obstacles facing them with regard to the Jewish Community in 1947. Unlike during the Arab rebellion of the 1930s, when a strict control of the movement of vehicles had been imposed, the British were unable to apply the same rigorous measures in 1947. Such measures required combined efforts and a comprehensive organisation of pass control offices which the armed forces were unable to provide in the short space of time required by the Government. The special circumstances made the task too difficult to accomplish. For example, the question of stopping Jewish bus services within Jerusalem was raised, but the Inspector General of Police considered that this would affect government officials and unnecessarily dislocate the administration, an opinion which was also supported by the Chief of Staff in Palestine.[56]

However, the sudden imposition of martial law stunned the Jewish Community which had not prepared itself for such a harsh move. In the words of an inspector of the CID, the Jews were 'shaken rigid'. The Intelligence Department of the 6th Airborne Division reported that 'their feelings were outraged' and that the fact that the majority of the community was forced to suffer was for the Jews 'scandalous and unbelievable'.[57]

Indeed, on the third day of its implementation, it was generally realised that all business had virtually come to a standstill in the area affected. It was a deliberate tactic. The British knew that such an action would not stop terrorism. What they wanted to achieve was maximum damage to the livelihood of the Yishuv; they hoped to deter the community from assisting the underground by driving a wedge between them and trying to prove that their interests were mutually contradictory. The British did not try to conceal their desire to see the Jews suffer financially and, in a rather anti-semitic remark, they stated 'that the making of money is almost a second religion with the Jewish race'.[58]

The new restrictions did indeed impede industry in the directly affected areas and severely curtailed activities there. The British predicted, therefore, that prolonged imposition of martial law, would cripple the economic structure of the country as a whole. The Jewish Agency was appalled by this prospect. Golda Meir feared that the Community would be economically ruined, and that, under the strains arising from the new situation, individuals might be tempted to collaborate with the British.[59] Equally, the leadership feared that some sections of the population might be pushed into the arms of the dissidents, as a result of the hardships. It also expressed the view that certain sectors of society might blame their current troubles on the Agency's absolute unwillingness to co-operate with the Administration. The military expressed confidence that if martial law continued for any length of time, action would have to be taken by the Jews themselves, 'unless they wish their economy to break down entirely'.[60]

As already indicated, the British knew that this was not the way to stop violence, but they hoped that a ruined economy would plunge the Yishuv into a state of turmoil in which public resentment would reduce the scale of terrorist activity. However, in spite of the restrictions, acts of sabotage and murder continued on an increasing scale, mostly in south Palestine. The Irgun also carried out attacks in Haifa, Jerusalem and Rehovot on 5 March and 8 March, infiltrated the British security zones and attacked targets within them.

The military admitted that the action of the Underground became more irresponsible as the days went by. 'The illegal forces are going all out to 'thumb their noses' at the authorities and their fellow countrymen', wrote one of the army intelligence units. In their report they added that searches, martial law, and anti-semitism throughout the United Kingdom were all the 'cost of a considerable number of murders of troops, who are unable to hit back directly'.[61]

The British had been ambivalent about the chances of martial law even before its implementation. The Chiefs of Staffs Committee examined the possibility of imposing the law for six months over the whole country. They studied a report by the Joint Planning Staff, prepared in consultation with the authorities in Palestine. Cunningham drew his colleagues' attention to the report's assessment that martial law might result in a demand for a great increase in military staffing. Previously, the Cabinet had been advised by the GOC that there were sufficient forces in Palestine to fight either the Jews or the Arabs, but not both simultaneously.

In discussion, it was pointed out that if martial law was declared, large numbers of troops would be employed on 'static duties', cordoning off certain areas, whilst, in addition, the military authorities would become entirely responsible for the administration of Palestine.[62]

At a security conference which took place in Jerusalem on 21 March 1947, the Chief Secretary said that he did not feel that martial law had been fully exploited, drawing attention to the fact that the telephone service had been allowed to continue. The Inspector General of Police replied that the service had not been discontinued in the hopes of obtaining the co-operation of the inhabitants 'which could more easily be achieved if communications were not disrupted'.[63]

Like the Chiefs of Staff Committee, the High Commissioner in Palestine considered the possibility of imposing martial law for six months. But the idea was not well received in Britain, not only because of the inevitable need to increase the number of soldiers in the country, but also due to their inability to predict the outcome of the policy, even after its first week in force. None of the decision-makers was certain about the impact of the law on the local population or on the underground organisations. But there seemed to be agreement with the General Officer commanding in Palestine, who said that 'the severer the measures, the shorter the time required for imposition'.[64] Therefore, it would have been unwise to impose it for as long as six months.

Indeed, a few days after the law came into effect, the British optimistically noted that statutory martial law had born fruit. Areas involving half of the Yishuv were 'sealed off'; all civil administration was withdrawn; no contacts between areas inside and outside were possible; transport facilities were severely restricted; the postal and telegraph system were put out of action and business was virtually at a standstill. The British were quick to comment that the harsh measures had shown immediate results. In a secret memorandum, the military reported on their effect: 'Jews received a severe shock; considerable financial loss running into millions; unemployment; organised labour realised the need for stopping outrages. Lifting done at psychological moment and probably no drift from Hagana to the dissidents. 78 extremists apprehended; more to come; signs of greater co-operation from Yishuv as a whole'.[65]

Ben Gurion, the head of the Jewish Agency, was also appalled by the situation. In a letter to Attlee on 15 March he wrote about 250,000 Jews in Tel Aviv and 30,000 in Jerusalem who were 'isolated from all normal contact with the outside world, facing a complete breakdown of the mechanism of civilised life.'[66] He reaffirmed the British assessment and expressed concern about a crippled industry and paralysed trade and predicted that unemployment would threaten 'to become catastrophic'. He also added that martial law cut off employees from their places of work and children from schools. But much more important, he stated clearly that the restrictions had not affected the terrorists, nor stopped their outrages. Instead, they had 'increased the resentment of a hard hit population, created fertile soil for terrorist propaganda and frustrated the Community's attempts to combat terrorism by itself'. The Jewish Agency concluded, two weeks after its imposition, that martial law was futile and senseless, 'unless', in Ben Gurion's words, 'it meant to punish the whole community, ruin its economy and destroy the foundations of the Jewish National Home'.[67]

The Jewish establishment was indeed right. Despite reports of crippling Jewish business, the financial losses, unemployment and the disruption of daily life, martial law did not stop the outrages. The violent activities even increased. The British themselves recognised this and concluded that 'if kept too long, it will turn the whole Yishuv against us and will considerably aggravate the internal security situation'.[68] The Government decided to lift martial law because, in the High Commissioner's words, it 'had reached the limit of its usefulness'. The new measures ended in failure. There is no doubt that martial law appealed to the Mandate authorities as a drastic step which would curb terrorism through inflicting hardship on the Jewish Community. It also offered an acceleration of action by the military. In addition, it enabled the authorities to set up summary military courts with the power to pronounce the death penalty, to ensure quick execution of their rulings and avoid dangerous delays resulting from appeals to the Privy Council.

However, the disadvantages were far greater. The retention of martial law for a long period would have meant economic ruin for the country, involving the British taxpayer in the expenditure of millions of pounds. After being in force for only two weeks, it had already aggravated internal security and, instead of dividing the Yishuv, it had united it against the British. There was also the fear that the Arabs would become involved in the new development and might have seized the chance actively to oppose the government, by taking advantage of the army's preoccupation with the Jewish Community.

The problem for the British was that, in spite of being aware of the disadvantages of martial law, they realised that they did not possess any alternative measures with which to combat terrorism. As a result of the very limited success that they had in the early days of the law's imposition in Tel Aviv and Jerusalem (when 78 dissidents were arrested), they concluded that martial law could be effective only if introduced for a short time and in a restricted area. The lesson of that experience was that, if possible, the Army should be kept flexible and avoid committing itself to heavy static duties.

In a secret memorandum issued in Jerusalem on 23 March 1947, the Government strongly recommended that civilian rule should continue. Intensification of counter-insurgency measures could make outrages as difficult as possible to perpetrate, and should be carried out in the form of curfews, road blocks, patrols and rigid control of civilian transport. It also recommended reimposition of statutory martial law in the main Jewish centres, in spite of temporary financial loss to the authorities in Palestine. The memorandum echoed the demand of Cabinet Ministers to introduce summary courts, that would have the power to impose the death penalty without giving the individual the right of appeal. However, the best proof of the claim that the new measures were unsuccessful was the continuation of terrorist attacks on British targets all over the country.

Ironically, the insurgents benefited from martial law, a fact recognised even by the Government. In a report by the Chiefs of Staff Committee, written after the lifting of the law on 23 March 1947, it was stated that 'they (the Irgun and Stern) wish to force us to employ sterner measures which can be presented as punitive against the Community, thereby swinging moderate opinion against us and obtaining more recruits for themselves'.[69]

The idea of imposing martial law for six months was, therefore, dropped on moral, military, financial and practical grounds; morally, because the British thought that it would be an unjust burden on innocent Jews and Arabs alike; militarily, because it would require a great increase in military staffing and would involve the War Office and the GOC in the entire administration of the country; and financially, because the damage to the economy and unemployment would create a loss of revenue to the administration itself. At the end of the day, statutory martial law, introduced as an experiment, was lifted after two weeks at a psychological moment, chiefly for fear of a drift from the Hagana to the dissidents which might well have occurred if the restrictions had remained in place for a longer period.

This was contrary to the British hope that hardship might have driven the Yishuv to stop the terrorism. The Cabinet discussed the subject with Lieutenant General Sir Gordon MacMillan, who had replaced Barker as GOC British Troops, and with Cunningham, the High Commissioner. The men on the spot told the ministers on 27 March 1947, that the measures had reached the limits of their success after two weeks. The Cabinet then approved the military's recommendation not to impose martial law over the whole country and for a longer period.[70]

The Government was at pains to explain the reasons for ending the martial law and restoring normal administration after an interruption of two weeks. According to senior official sources the decision was 'experimental' and based upon evidence that 'sections of the Jewish Community are now more prepared to co-operate with the Government in restraining terrorist gangsters'.[71] In spite of relatively satisfactory remarks made by British administrators in Palestine as to the achievements of the two-week martial law period, the Cabinet finally admitted that the new measures had ended in failure. In a discussion which took place on 20 March 1947, there had been a considerable measure of criticism of the decision to halt martial law after such short a period, with no apparent gain to the security of the country as a whole. The general feeling was that the imposition of martial law for this limited period and over a very small area of Palestine had been of little value, 'in that it left us in a relatively worse position than we were in before, without any firm plan for suppressing the acts of terrorism which were continuing to occur. Furthermore, the economy of the whole country had been considerably upset with its consequent dislocation to essential services and the loss of revenue and trade'.[72]

The Cabinet itself reiterated the assessments of the Chiefs of Staff Council and even went so far as to say that 'the withdrawal of martial law after so short a period had given an impression of weakness and must have encouraged the Jewish Community and the terrorists to think they had successfully resisted it'. Nevertheless, the Cabinet did not reject the validity of martial law in principle. It regarded it as potentially one of the most flexible of government systems. In August 1947, renewed imposition of martial law was again under consideration after the hanging of the two sergeants by the Irgun, but was rejected on the grounds that it would delay the withdrawal of British troops from Palestine.[73]

The lifting of martial law after only two weeks made the Irgun jubilant. They saw it as further proof of the British realisation that Palestine was ungovernable and their attempts to remain there were unsustainable. Martial law was regarded as the most drastic measure imposed on the Yishuv as part of the British attempt to combat the insurgents of the Irgun. Its failure reinforced their belief that nothing could stand in the way of victory. The Irgun maintained that the purpose of the law had been to break the spirit of the Jews by prompting them to become informers against the fighting Underground. Part of the policy, according to the Irgun, was to isolate Jewish centres from one another and from the outside world and to destroy Jewish economic life. The insurgents claimed however that, during that period, they had delivered a heavy and widespread series of blows to British objectives.

Following the lifting of martial law, the Irgun issued a communiqué in which it explained why the Government had not been able to sustain the measures, citing international public opinion, the continuation of attacks on the Army, the support of the local population, and bitterness and frustration amongst the military rank and file. The Irgun, in its pamphlet, thanked the public for assisting its men during those two weeks: 'From the depth of the Underground, we send our greetings to the poor of our people who, subjected to the severest of tribulations, courageously stood the test'.[74]

CHAPTER 9

# Morale and Public Opinion In Britain

The pace of the eventual British withdrawal from Palestine was dictated partially by the ability of the Government to contain the terrorist campaign in the country and to confront public opinion at home. The military difficulties which faced the armed forces in Palestine resulted not only in a severe blow to their prestige, but also in a low degree of morale which affected the psychological well-being of the soldiers, both individually and collectively. During the years 1946 and 1947, which saw a substantial increase in anti-British guerrilla activities, daily life for the soldiers stationed in Palestine became quite unbearable. Their movements were restricted, their friends were assassinated and the general Jewish attitude towards them was very hostile. The Army itself admitted to some of the difficulties of being confined to their barracks: 'the troops are living under conditions which are lacking in adequate sports facilities and sufficient entertainment'. The Headquarters of the Southern District indicated in one of its quarterly reports that morale amongst the troops was 'generally high', but acknowledged that conditions were poor and that there was a 'certain amount of resentment at not being able to visit Tel Aviv and other towns at weekends'.[1]

Although Southern District headquarters described morale as satisfactory, at about the same time (September 1946) the Headquarters in the Jaffa–Tel Aviv District informed London that 'morale both with officers and ordinary soldiers is particularly low', the reason being that Tel Aviv had been under curfew and out of bounds for some considerable time. The soldiers, owing to the numerous incidents, were confined to their quarters.[2]

While the men's psychological attitude had been affected by the terrorist campaign, the British recognised that one of the principal factors which tended to lower morale was the deteriorating relationship between the soldiers and the Jews. 'The attitude towards the inhabitants has become increasingly anti-Jewish', the Southern District Headquarters commented in October 1946. While officers informed their superiors that 'confidence in military leaders remains high' and that 'the state of discipline remains good', individual units complained of isolation and lack of freedom.

The Army felt that taking firmer steps in dealing with terrorism would help to increase morale. This was partially true, since a series of successful attacks by the British had a positive impact on the soldiers, especially after the King David outrage. On the other hand, the intensity of the operational and security measures kept the soldiers on constant alert and reduced their free time. Growth of anti-Jewish feeling amongst all ranks and the heavy burdens imposed on them by additional duties resulted directly from attitudes adopted by the terrorists who determined the pace of the struggle.

Summing up the state of the Army's morale during the last three months of 1946, the Southern Palestine District Headquarters wrote that discipline 'is good within unit lines, but poor when troops are off duty in public places'. The report also indicated that 'insufficient pride has been shown by some officers'.[3] The report referred to the deterioration of attitudes towards the Jewish population. It added that cordial relations existed with the Arab population, which improved as Jewish terrorist activities continued. The Army, while emphasising time and again that 'confidence in the military is high', made a point of hinting that there were some doubts within the ranks as to the effectiveness of the political leaders. One of those who advocated the need to take more aggressive counter-insurgency measures was the Chief of the Imperial General Staff, who saw a direct correlation between Army morale and the success of the terrorist campaign. Montgomery claimed that deeds, not declarations, would lift the spirits of the soldiers in Palestine. He maintained that if, however, there were to be any new policy, 'the policy declared should be followed to its ultimate end as any modification of a policy, once embarked upon, would be detrimental to morale'.[4] Political restraints imposed on the Army, caused deep frustration amongst the soldiers. The troops were troubled by the feeling that they had been set up as a target for Jewish terrorism and prevented from reacting in the manner in which they had been trained.

An inside view of the morale of the British Army was given after the King David affair by Lieutenant Colonel Martin Charteris, Chief of Military Intelligence in Palestine from September 1946.[5] According to Charteris, the attitude of the average soldier was conditioned not by politics, nor by imperialist ambition, but by more trivial issues, such as the date of his demobilisation, the comfort of his camp, the amount of time spent on guard patrol and the 'uncomfortable hours erecting barbed wire and even more uncomfortable hours living behind it'. The soldier was a 'bird of passage', waiting to go home. Palestine was a 'fatigue' for the conscript and for the regular. It was another job of imperial policing, which interfered with the real job of soldiering.[6]

Charteris maintained that the British soldiers arrived in Palestine as pro-

Zionists, as a result of what they had seen of the Jewish tragedy in Europe. Being non-political, they were not prejudiced and had few preconceived ideas. However, on arrival, they encountered hostility from people whom they saw as 'super intelligent', very unlike the 'natives' whom the British controlled in their territories elsewhere. The soldiers' frustration grew when they were constantly accused by the Jews of being wrong, unjust, inefficient, dishonest and self-interested. But, as Charteris emphasised, the greatest impact on the soldier was made by Jewish terrorism. The soldier spent most of his time engaged in activities which were directly or indirectly connected with terrorism. The insurgents were very hard to find and any retaliatory actions inevitably affected innocent people who vented their anger on the troops. The net result was friction, irritation and frustration. Charteris concluded that it was not altogether surprising that sometimes soldiers took matters into their own hands.[7]

When the members of the United Nations Special Committee on Palestine (UNSCOP) visited Jerusalem in the summer of 1947, they found the British community in Palestine in a state of siege. Wives and children had been evacuated and soldiers and policemen were 'locked up' in 'Bevingrads', enclaves where personnel were bivouacked behind barbed wire.[8] The departure of the families added to the growing sense of isolation, but more influential on army morale was its constant exposure to the terrorist danger.

Insurgents' activity in sensitive spots, such as in and around Jerusalem, was marked during the last two years of the Mandate by the mining of roads and railways. As a result, heavy restrictions were imposed upon the movement of all military vehicles. Intelligence officers, serving at the Southern District HQ, wrote that the effect of all 'this terrorist activity' on the morale of the troops in the sub-district was natural. British policy was criticised as being far too lenient. Troops were in favour of some more definite guidelines which would enable them to walk or travel on the roads at night. Units reported lack of freedom.[9] In another intelligence summary, the army complained again about the deterioration of attitudes towards the Jewish population. On the other hand, the cordial relations which existed with the Arab population improved as the Jewish terrorist activities continued.[10]

The growing anti-Jewish feeling in Palestine became marked in Britain itself. A British officer, who had returned from a visit to the United Kingdom at the beginning of 1947, wrote an interesting report which confirmed increasing anti-semitism amongst the rank and file of the Army in Palestine. The officer, whose name was not mentioned in the report, wrote: 'It is not uncommon when it is known that one comes from Palestine to be asked 'When are you going to polish off the Yids?' or some such question. This anti-semitism is growing. It is easy to understand. There is an increasing number of people who know someone else who has had a relative killed or injured in Palestine'.[11] He mentioned the kidnapping of British officers and soldiers 'with its melodramatic atmosphere' as having a deep effect on the British 'and of course the latest outrage at the King David Hotel'. The officer, speaking of a strong school of thought in favour of withdrawal from Palestine, went on to write that 'the people of England are tired, and they do not feel prepared for a row even in distant Palestine'. He expressed the feeling that the English 'disapprove most heartily of British soldiers losing their lives and feel that the answer would be to clear out and leave the Jews and Arabs to settle the matter in their own way'.

The author summed up: 'The general feeling is one of rising anti-semitism and a feeling that the Jews, by their actions, have forfeited any claim to our consideration. The ordinary people do not distinguish in their mind between the Irgun and the Hagana, nor between the terrorists and the Jews as a whole.'[12] Low morale, as a result of the insurgents' campaign, resentment and hatred towards the Jews and psychological fatigue, reached their peak after the hanging of the British soldiers (see Chapter 4) by the Irgun. The horror expressed by the British, both in the Middle East and at home, was unprecedented in its scale and signalled that the moment had come to prepare for an eventual withdrawal.

## THE REACTION OF PARLIAMENT

The terrorist campaign of the Irgun was aimed not only at undermining the Mandate infrastructure in Palestine and winning hearts within the local Jewish Community, but also at having a direct influence on British public opinion in order to influence decision-makers in London. During 1946 and especially 1947, when the insurgents' activities reached their climax, the resentment of the British people at the continuation of the occupation in Palestine took the form of criticism in the press and a parliamentary outcry. Imperial strategic interests in the Middle East had been overshadowed by the killing of British soldiers in Palestine. The public debate, led by the Opposition, was determined by the number of casualties suffered by the Army and the police at the hands of the terrorists. The Irgun fully exploited this weakness. Parliament devoted several sessions to the situation in Palestine. One of them took place on 7 July 1946, when anti and pro-Zionist MPs, who jointly condemned Jewish terrorism, expressed the view that, if the Government was not able to maintain law and order, it should order its troops to quit the country.

Richard Crossman, a supporter of the Zionist cause and a regular visitor

# שלמה בן יוסף

## איש עכו – בן האלמוות

ראשון בדורנו קידש ממעלות הגרדום את שאיפת החופש העברית –

מאיר את הדרך בפני גבורי ישראל הנותנים את נפשם למען חיי האומה וחרותה.

**הארגון הצבאי הלאומי**
בארץ־ישראל

ל' סיון תש"ז

*A mourning notice informing the public of the hanging of S Ben-Joseph.*

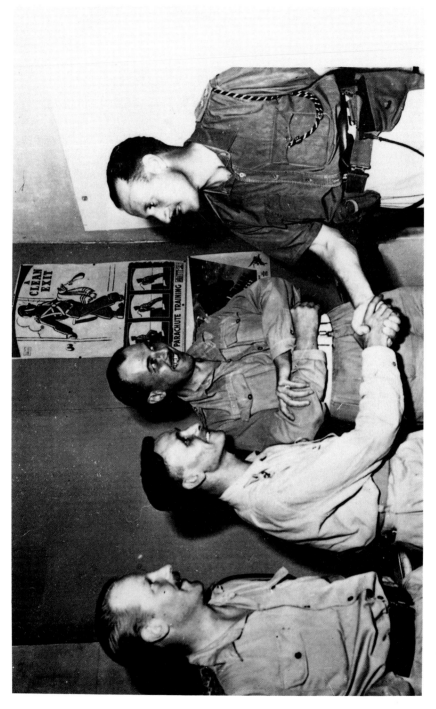

*Kidnapped British officers are greeted by their colleagues after their release by the Irgun.*

The walls of the Acre fort after the break-in by the Irgun of 4 May 1947.

# אזהרה!

חייל עברי, שנפל בשבי האויב, "נידון" ע"י "בית-דין" של צבא הכבוש הבריטי למלקות.

אנו מזהירים את ממשלת הדכוי מפני הוצאה לפועל של עונש משפיל זה.

אם הוא יוצא אל הפועל, יוטל אותו עונש על קציני הצבא הבריטי. כל אחד מהם יהיה עלול ללקות 18 מלקות.

הארגון הצבאי הלאומי
בארץ-ישראל

כסלו תש"ז

# WARNING!

A Hebrew soldier, taken prisoner by the enemy, was sentenced by an illegal British Military "Court" to the humiliating punishment of flogging.

We warn the occupation Government not to carry out this punishment, which is contrary to the laws of soldiers honour. If it is put into effect — every officer of the British occupation army in Eretz-Israel will be liable to be punished in the same way: to get 18 whips.

HAIRGUN HAZVAI HALEUMI (N. M. O.)
b'Eretz-Israel

*The Irgun warn of reprisals after a member is flogged.*

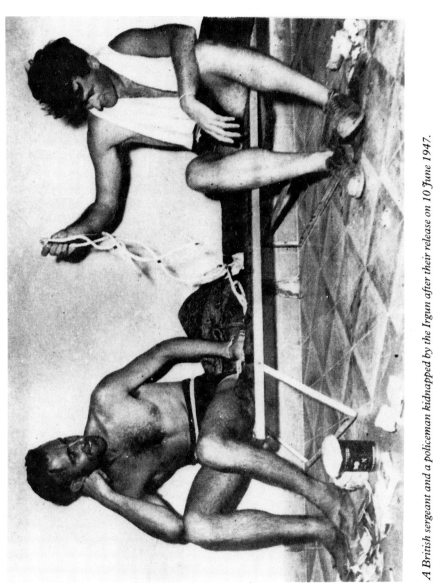

*A British sergeant and a policeman kidnapped by the Irgun after their release on 10 June 1947.*

*The hanged sergeants, Marvin Paice and Clifford Martin, on the day their bodies were discovered by the British Army in a forest near the Jewish town of Netanya.*

*A grim display – the ropes with which the sergeants were hanged.*

*British soldiers leaving the High Commissioners Palace in Jerusalem.*

*The Red Berets leave Haifa.*

to Palestine, said in that debate that the Hagana leaders with whom he had spoken believed that they had learned the lesson of the Arab Revolt, which after three years of violence had resulted, in their opinion, in complete appeasement of Arab claims. Crossman believed that: 'We, in this country, underestimate the fanaticism, the ferocity and I might say, the totalitarianism of Jewish nationalism in Palestine'. He went on to say what the Irgun would have liked the British politicians to think: 'It is impossible to crush a resistance movement which has the passive toleration of the mass of the population. A resistance movement can only be destroyed if it is hated by those whom it relies on for succour or refuge.' He pointed out that if the passive part of the population 'who do not go in for violence, is sufficiently active to succour and give refuge to the active minority of the community, no government, however ruthless, can smash that resistance movement or disarm it'.

This view, according to Crossman, had been given to the Government by military experts in Cairo and Palestine. He echoed the dilemma of the British decision-makers in confronting the Palestine question: 'We are not Nazis', he told the House, 'and we are not prepared to take the step of liquidating the Jewish Community, which would be necessary in order to crush the resistance movement.' Oliver Stanley MP stated that he was convinced that the terrorist action in Palestine involved more than just the Irgun and the Stern group. In the debate he claimed that to 'an outsider such as I am, merely reading newspaper reports ... it would appear that the incidents which have taken place seem on a much bigger scale, involving more men and a higher degree of planning ...'. He expressed the belief that the two extremist groups had a very close connection with the Hagana and called on the government to produce evidence against the latter.

Conservative as well as Labour politicians were united in their condemnation of the Irgun and their deep suspicion of the Hagana. Justifying Operation *Agatha*, which included the arrest of some Jewish Agency leaders, they reminded the House that the Hagana had been responsible for the 'Night of the Bridges' regarded by one of the speakers (D L Lipson, MP for Cheltenham) as an 'act of sabotage, contrary to the law of the land'.[13] Many politicians reserved strong words for the Jewish Agency and accused its members of protecting those who had committed 'those crimes'. Referring to the wave of terrorism in Palestine, one of them (Mr Price MP) said that 'the Zionist movement has been adopting the tactics of their persecutors, the Nazis', and that the 'life of very moderate Jews in Palestine is now being made extremely difficult, if not intolerable ...'.

The House of Commons had many pro-Zionist members from both parties who condemned the Irgun's campaign of violence but equally criticised British policy in Palestine, especially towards the moderate leadership. Michael Foot MP (Plymouth, Devon) for example, argued that if he were a Jew and lived in Palestine, he would be a member of the Hagana and would regard Operation *Agatha* as an action 'which has been taken against the Jewish Agency and against the whole of the Jewish community'.

However, the House, throughout the various debates on the subjects, differed on the best possible ways to fight the terrorism of the Irgun and the Stern in order to isolate them from the rest of the population. Thomas Reid MP (Swindon) voiced the general feeling of the British public by saying that the 'people of this country are disgusted with the acts of terrorism which have been going on in Palestine'. He therefore justified the 'Agatha' operation in which some Jewish leaders had been arrested for alleged co-operation with the Underground. He added that illegal violence should be put down, 'unless the Government was to abdicate and hand over Palestine to chaos'.

In his reply, Prime Minister Attlee, rejected the charge that the counter-guerrilla measures taken by the government amounted to a declaration of war. 'We have had a long series of outrages, a long series of terrorist and illegal actions'. The Prime Minister admitted that, being reluctant to act against the Jewish leadership, his government had been forced by events. Attlee made a distinction between 'isolated actions and extremists' and activities on a 'very very large scale', such as the cutting off of several railways and the blowing up of a whole series of bridges, which he considered as part of military planning. He blamed the Jewish Agency for its responsibility for the connection between the Hagana and the Irgun, about which his government had evidence, and emphasised again that the arrests of Jewish leaders was a policy 'which has been forced upon us'. He concluded that ordinary police action and persuasion had not stopped terrorism, which had increased yet further. Attlee reiterated his Government's commitment not to yield to any kind of violence when it considered its response to the findings of the Anglo-American Committee. He also referred to the delay of a political settlement of the conflict and stressed that this did not justify 'wrecking trains, destroying bridges, shooting soldiers or kidnapping officers'.[14]

By general demand, the House held another debate on the crisis in Palestine on 31 July 1946. The session took place under the shadow of the tragedy of the King David Hotel in Jerusalem and most of the speakers, shocked by the outrage, added their voice to the growing belief that the armed forces should reconsider their tactics. However, they stopped short of demanding an early retreat from the country. They almost unanimously denounced the Community as a whole. The Lord President of the Council, Herbert Morrison, partially attributed the success of the attack to 'the refusal of the Jewish population in Palestine to co-operate with the forces of law and order' and its 'resistance of the most determined kind against searches for terrorists'. Others rightly pointed out that the Yishuv had shifted its position towards the dissidents since the time it roundly condemned the assassination of Lord Moyne in 1944. Unfortunately, said Stanley, the position had changed since then. He could not but regret that 'a policy of violence, which before was followed merely by a small dissident minority, should have received the approval of a body such as the Jewish Agency, which represents so very much of the whole Jewish community in Palestine'. But Stanley admitted that the re-establishment of authority and the suppression of violence, however successful, did not in themselves provide any permanent solution to the problem. In the debate, members of parliament tended to concentrate more on what they regarded as the collaboration between the Jewish establishment and the terrorists.

That attitude reflected the view that the British, although disturbed by the growing waves of violence against them, were more concerned, even at that stage, about the future relationship with the leadership of the Yishuv. Parliament did not delude itself that the terrorist campaign would come to an end, but its debates about the situation throughout 1946 showed that its members were convinced that the worst of it could be controlled. Interestingly, even after the suspected complicity of the Hagana in the King David affair, the British argued that the imprisonment of the Jewish Agency's leaders would deprive the British of their main source of intelligence information on the terrorist activities of the Irgun. Crossman was the one who reminded the House that since the founding of the Irgun and its break with the Hagana in 1938, the Hagana had co-operated with the British and more than 1000 Irgun members had been handed over to the British police authorities. He also disclosed that, in the past, the Hagana had exposed an Irgun attempt to shoot rockets at the King David Hotel, and he maintained that, without Jewish assistance, it would be very difficult to defeat terrorism in Palestine.

However, there were several politicians who saw no other solution to the problem but by a decision to withdraw from the country. One of them was Kenneth Lindsay (representing Combined English Universities) who expressed the general feeling of 'the man in the street'. 'It is not only the Irgun or these terrorists organisations', he said after his first visit to the country, 'it is almost every boy and girl. We are dealing with the whole population'. Referring to the Jewish determination to fight, he said: 'I had the definite feeling that the time had come when my countrymen ought not to stay in the country and be shot at.'

The parliamentary debates were held under the watchful eyes of the Irgun. Begin, listening obsessively in his Tel Aviv underground flat to BBC radio, as was his custom, concluded that the war of 'mini attrition' that the Irgun had waged against the authorities had produced results in London.

Such were the comments made by S N Evans MP (Wednesbury), when he described how events in Palestine had become the 'talk of the town' in London. 'For the first time in my experience, ordinary decent working men are talking in their pubs and clubs, at the barber's and at work, about the lot to which our lads are being subjected in Palestine at this moment'. Some speakers, such as Colonel George Wigg (MP for Dudley) put the blame on the civil administration. 'The soldier is not called in to carry out a policing function with the aid of tanks and similar weapons until the civil authority has failed to discharge its duty'. He went on to say that 'the Government as a whole bear responsibility...' and 'it is a frightful thing to ask the soldier to do a job that the civil administration has failed to do without giving him adequate means for carrying it out'.

A stronger portrayal of Jewish terrorism as being conducted by a group of desperate people manifested itself in a speech made by Major Beamish who called the insurgents 'villainous', 'stupid', and 'unbalanced people'. But he added: 'If anyone is responsible for the death of Jews, Arabs and Englishmen in Palestine, it is those who have fomented the desperation of these terrorists, and encouraged their extreme nationalist ambitions, without any hope of their being fulfilled'. He was also referring to General Barker's alleged anti-semitic remarks after the King David explosion, (which became one of the central issues of the debate) and called for his removal from Palestine.[15]

Parliament also devoted 1 August 1946 to the crisis in Palestine, but as the need for a political settlement was more urgent, attention was concentrated mainly on the American involvement in the problem and its call to admit 100,000 Jews to Palestine. Yet the debate was held under the shadow of the increasingly violent activities in the country against the armed forces and reflected British frustration at their inability to root out terrorism. Winston Churchill, as Leader of the Opposition, referred to the underground groups' activities as 'the dark and the deadly crimes which have been committed by the fanatical extremists'. He repeated other calls to punish the terrorists 'with the full severity of the law'.[16] His party colleagues criticised the way in which the Government was dealing with terror in Palestine. They said that the objective of disarming the Irgun had not been properly thought out and therefore had not been achieved.[17] The debate emphasised yet again how desperate the authorities had grown in that they were pinning all their hope for restoring law and order in Palestine on the moderate Jews. MPs attacked the government for punishing, not the culprits, but the victims, such as the Jewish Agency, the Trade Union Federation and the settlements, which all belonged to the socialist section of the Jewish Community in Palestine. Indeed, the government was more troubled by the alleged co-operation of the Jewish Agency with the insurgents, than by their terrorism which it could not, in any case, combat.

The situation was reflected in a speech made by George Hall, Secretary of State for the Colonies, when he summed up the debate in the Commons on 1 August 1946. Hall made a distinction between the Jewish Agency as a whole and members of its executive who 'supported' terrorism. This was despite the fact that the debate was held against the background of the King David bombing which had taken place a few days earlier. 'For a time, the Jewish Agency co-operated with the government, as the Mandate required and in certain spheres it has continued to do so, but in other directions it has abused its privileged position, and become the instrument of an extreme nationalism,' he said. Hall went on to imply that any success by the British Government in defeating terrorism lay in the hands of the leadership of the Yishuv. He praised them for handing over a list of suspects, after the assassination of Lord Moyne, 300 of whom were traced and arrested. However, he expressed concern that in the aftermath of the King David explosion such assistance was not given, either by the Hagana or the Jewish Agency. The Colonial Secretary concluded his speech by expressing the hope that both communities in Palestine would accept the Anglo-American Plan as a basis for discussion for the sake of international security and peace in the region.[18]

Another debate, on 31 January 1947, found Parliament more than ever inclined to regard evacuation as the best possible option. The general consensus was that British policy of 'half repression and half conciliation' had bolstered the Irgun and weakened the moderates. The pro-Zionists believed that the position of the average Jew in Palestine was difficult since he found himself 'between the devil and the deep blue sea'. In Crossman's opinion, for instance, the authorities had placed him in an unbearable situation. He asked how the Jew was to co-operate with the British authorities 'when terrorism is as great a power in Palestine as the British Government today?' Barnett Janner, who held a similar view, argued that combating terrorism was essential, but insisted that military action alone would not solve the problem. Janner said in this debate that Britain's political stance had encouraged the Irgun. 'If immigration into Palestine was available to more displaced Jews from Europe, terrorism would fail as a policy and cease almost at once'. Another pro-Zionist, Sidney Silverman, also said that young Jewish men and women had opted for terrorism because of the 'utter failure of the Government to show them hope'.

Arthur Creech-Jones, answering allegations by MPs that terrorists had not been brought to justice, gave the House some figures related to the year 1946. During that period, he said that '22 Jews were sentenced to death (although their sentences were commuted to long terms of imprisonment, up to a maximum of 20 years). There have been 83 Jewish terrorists who have been convicted by military courts for carrying or discharging fire arms, all have been sentenced to long term imprisonment. Twenty six have been killed and 28 wounded during action with the police and military.'

However, Creech-Jones admitted that the British could not completely eradicate terrorism in any community, 'unless you get the co-operation and goodwill of the people'.[19] These debates exposed British weakness in not having good enough intelligence or sufficiently effective tactics to uproot the violence by the insurgents, as they had promised in Parliament. At the same time, by failing politically to 'reward' the Community, they missed the chance of being assisted by it. Instead, they caused anger within the Jewish Agency by asking it broadly to collaborate with the 'Saison'. As a result, the leadership, rejected the British call for co-operation by refusing to 'turn the 600,000 Jews in Palestine into informers'. The sense of deadlock and helplessness was reflected in all the Parliamentary debates and significantly affected Army and police morale.

## THE RESPONSE OF THE PRESS

Much of the terrorist campaign of the Irgun was directed at the British media. Begin himself recognised the importance of that factor in the various meetings of the High Command. He told his district commanders on 15 October 1944 that British public opinion was greatly influenced by the Irgun's early activities. For him the press coverage was an indicator not only of the repercussion of the revolt in London, but also of the morale of the British armed forces in Palestine itself. Begin also used British newspapers to raise the morale of his own men. He expressed great satisfaction when *The Times* wrote that Jewish terrorism could drive Palestine into anarchy and when *The New Statesman and the Nation* called for an immediate withdrawal from the country. Begin maintained that such commentaries and editorials were the best proof that the armed struggle had borne fruit even in its early stages.[20]

Most of the media throughout Britain did not make much distinction between the Irgun and the Stern Group. After the establishment of the Hebrew United Resistance Movement, the press included even the Hagana and the Palmach in the category of terrorism. Only a few bothered to dwell on the differences between the four groups. All of them unanimously condemned the violence in strong words and most of them went as far as comparing the methods of the 'Jewish Gangsters' to those of the Nazis.

This comparison was favoured not only by the national newspapers but also by the regional ones. 'The Jewish paramilitary organisations had for me a striking resemblance to the type of person and organisation I met in Nazi Germany', wrote a correspondent for the *Western Evening Herald* from Jerusalem.[21] The *Liverpool Post* reiterated such words by writing that 'there can be no peace in Palestine so long as extremists, whether Jew or Arab, are allowed to adopt the Nazi technique of trying to get their own ends by unscrupulous use of physical force'.[22] *The Observer*, after the assassination of Lord Moyne, wrote that the Stern Gang was a 'product of Jewish Fascism'.[23] *The Times* also resorted to such an equation by stating after the hanging of the two sergeants that 'the bestialities practised by the Nazis themselves could go no further'.[24] Indeed, in the aftermath of that event it was not difficult to find such a comparative tendency in other newspapers. The daily and weekly publications, while taking into account the Jewish sufferings at the hands of the Germans during the war, warned the Yishuv that the deeds of a violent minority would cost the Jews international sympathy. *The Scotsman* commented in November 1944 on the alarming growth of lawlessness in Palestine and called on Jewish communities throughout the world to co-operate with the authorities in stamping out terrorism. It demanded the outlawing of those who indulged in the violence 'at the time when the Jews had hoped to win sympathy and assistance in achieving their post-war aims'.[25]

*The Yorkshire Post*, which regularly printed updated news from Palestine, also delivered warnings to the Jews and wrote that, as much as it supported the Jewish cause, Britain loved 'fair play' and was determined to 'protect the lives of her soldiers and innocent civilians ...'. The paper added that 'the sooner the terrorists and their supporters understand it, the sooner will it be possible for British sympathy with Jewish aspirations in Palestine to take a practical shape'.[26] Even regional publications in Dorset and Bournemouth took up the issue: 'The gangster methods of ... are depriving the Jewish people of some of the sympathy which their great sufferings under the Nazi occupation earned them ...'.[27]

In 1946 and 1947 the criticism was no longer confined to the dissidents only and directed against the Yishuv as a whole. During the two previous years the British media predicted that this might have happened. *The Observer* called on the Jews to work 'courageously and wholeheartedly' with the police and military. 'Refusal to give in information which will uphold the law is in effect refusal to be a citizen'.[28] *The Times* voiced the fear in mid-1945 that the Yishuv would follow the terrorists. 'The real danger would come', it wrote, 'should some event bring into the arena the bulk of the Jewish population, which contains a large number of armed and trained men and women. Should this occur the police force would be too small.'[29] The same newspaper accused the Yishuv less than two years later of collaborating with the insurgents: 'Jews protecting men who they know have been paying extortion money to terrorists, and in other cases they have resorted to violence to the extent of kidnapping or using corporal punishment'.[30] The over-emotional *Sunday Express* blamed the Jewish population for not collaborating with the authorities and concluded that 'He that is not with us, is against us'. The newspaper extended its attacks to the wider Jewish community: 'The murder campaign is fomented, financed and armed by Jews in other lands'.[31]

In their coverage of the violent developments in Palestine, most of the British media highlighted the Arabs as a factor which would be affected by the campaign of the Jewish terrorists. 'If this evil is not rooted out', warned a Scottish newspaper, the Arab reaction against the Jewish population will bring misery to the whole of Palestine ...'.[32] *The Times* wrote that the violence in Palestine was a 'fan to flame the smouldering resentment of the Arabs who campaign already that they are victimised by terrorism and now threaten in their turn to resort to force'.[33] *The Spectator* criticised the recommendation of the Anglo-American Committee because they did not address Jewish terrorism. 'They may', according to the weekly 'do much to exacerbate the Arabs, who of late have been showing themselves better citizens of Palestine than the Jews.'[34] The British newspapers accused the Jewish Underground groups not only of murdering soldiers in the streets of Palestine, but also of creating anti-semitism within the security forces in the country and Britain itself. *The Spectator*, for example, called on the British Government to stick to the White Paper, regain Arab goodwill and save world Jewry from the 'anti-semitism to which the extravagance of Zionist claims must lead'.[35] *The Evening Standard* published a cartoon featuring two insurgents who were ambushing a British soldier. 'What? he is not an anti-Semitic?' said one terrorist to another in the caption, 'we will soon alter that.'[36] Many other publications blamed the Yishuv for not being grateful enough for the efforts made by London to secure a future for them in Palestine.

*The Economist*, however, put the blame on the Government's shoulders, especially in the aftermath of the *Exodus* refugee boat which was forced to leave Palestine and return to France and Germany in July 1946. *The Economist* described the consequences of the 'Exodus' episode not only as a disaster for Britain's relations with the Jews in Palestine, but also as a catastrophe for Britain's moral reputation throughout the world. 'The decision to send the 'Exodus' Jews to Hamburg, to disembark them there by force, to put them in places which retain the physical lay-out and accessories of Nazi concentration camps, and to hold them there under administration partially German, was an act of which nobody can yet measure the consequences. It has not only produced an unprecedented hostility and resentment towards Britain among Zionists everywhere; it has also convinced most Germans that Britain is at last learning the truth of what Hitler said about the Jews, and it has thus wiped out at a stroke whatever has so far been achieved in 're-educating' Germany away from the Nazi creed; last but not least, it has given a great psychological impetus to anti-Semitism in this country.'

*The Economist* went on to touch a very sensitive subject in its commentary in which it judged anti-Semitism in the British civil service to be one of the roots of trouble in Palestine. 'That anti-Jewish sentiment – of a mild brand, it is true, but real enough – flourishes today, though without public expression, in high official circles in Britain is a proposition that only hypocrisy or blind-eye complacency will deny. Its main source is to be found among those who have been concerned in civil or military administration in the Middle East; this background accounts for its strength in the Colonial Office and the War Office. Its existence in the Foreign Office is due to a somewhat different cause: to the fact the Foreign Office conducts diplomatic relations with a number of Arab States, and is continually informed by its mission in their capital how disastrously these relations will be affected by any concessions to the Jews whereas friendly relations with Zion form no part of foreign policy.'[37]

Although British readers were constantly subjected to daily accounts of events in Palestine, it was Oliver Stanley, the Colonial Secretary who complained in Parliament that the public was not aware of the scale of the Jewish violence in the country. He said that officers and men of the Security Service had been murdered in cold blood, innocent passers-by killed and Government buildings destroyed by explosives and fire. *The Birmingham Post* took up the issue the following day and commented on Oliver Stanley's words by stating that 'there are known to be two groups of terrorists, one political and the other merely criminal. Arms have been acquired either by theft from, or by purchase from misguided soldiers.'[38]

No matter which party was in power in Westminster, both were bombarded by endless press attacks on their policies in Palestine. Just as Oliver Stanley had been attacked, so did Creech-Jones, the Colonial Secretary in Attlee's government, come under fire in the remaining years of the Mandate. *The Sunday Express*, in a typical editorial titled 'Rule or Quit', wrote that 'British prestige is being dragged in the mud and British lives are being sacrificed to no purpose. Our soldiers go about their duty in an atmosphere which is bad for their morale. Their comrades are murdered in cold blood and they cannot understand why nothing is being done about it'. The newspaper accused Creech-Jones of being the wrong person to act as a Colonial Secretary since 'he does not like strong action by soldiers' which stood contrary to his pacifist belief 'to return the fire of the enemy'. And the *Express* concluded: 'we have no interest in Palestine except to maintain law and order. If we can not do that we should quit ... In the meantime ... Hang the murderers. Be strong. Visit crime with stern, relentless justice. And above all, no more surrender.'[39]

The British tabloids were more outspoken against the Yishuv and their own Government than the other newspapers. *The Daily Mail*, under the title 'Must Our Boys Die?', also urged an early withdrawal not least because of the inevitable conflict between the two communities. 'Some people are trying to push Britain into the middle of the Jew–Arab war which may break out in Palestine. This country, in fact, is to be the real victim of the United Nations partition policy, which can not be imposed without the use of force.'[40] *The Spectator* complained about the huge cost of maintaining law and order in Palestine in 1944–45 only – £4,600,000 against £550,000 on health and £770,000 on education – which was 'some indication of the deplorable conditions that prevail ...'.[41]

*The New Statesman and Nation*, which Begin liked to quote in his clandestine meetings with his subordinates, complimented the IZL by admitting that the insurgents had the upper hand in Palestine. 'The field was left free for a savage and ruinous war between the tiny and extremely efficient Irgun and the vast but fumbling forces of the British Army.'[42] The same magazine carried an article by the Labour politician Richard Crossman: 'For two years Mr Bevin has played for time, in the hope that something would turn up which would justify the retention of Southern Palestine as a British military base and enable him simultaneously to defeat the Jewish demands for statehood. Nothing has turned up; and we are now left with the choice of either clearing out, bag and baggage, or creating a Jewish State'.[43]

*The Sunday Express*, after the explosion at Goldsmith House, summed up the general sense of outrage which engulfed the streets of London. This time the newspaper, while calling for an urgent retreat, demanded revenge under the title 'It's time we get out': 'What is our plain duty? Not merely to mourn and lament the victims but to pledge ourselves to avenge them by the execution of all who can justly be convicted of being responsible for their death. In the last year 73 Britons were killed and what happened? Not a single one of them has gone to the gallows. On one pretext or another the death sentences have been remitted. It is time this sentimental nonsense was ended. You can not calm a snarling tiger patting it with kid gloves ... The old Jewish law was 'an eye for an eye'. It is time Old Testament justice was applied to those who are making a charnel house of the land of the Old Testament. Unlike the Germans, we can not meet terror with counter-terror. But we can apply justice with force and resolution and we should do it without delay.'[44]

The only paper which consistently tried to air the motives of the Jewish insurgents, while still condemning their deeds, was the *Manchester Guardian*. The liberal daily took a different view even after the assassination of Lord Moyne in Cairo by the Stern Group. Its editorial asserted that it would be unjust to condemn a nation for the acts of a few individuals, 'but it would be unwise to ignore the fever of which this is a symptom'. Then it wrote about the way in which policy in Palestine had been carried out by the Government and concluded that 'a few of the younger youth have lost faith in political action'. *The Guardian* called for the hunting down of those responsible for the murders, but at the same time demanded the continuation of Jewish immigration and the foundation of a Jewish Commonwealth.[45]

The newspaper could be singled out also in the aftermath of the King David outrage. *The Guardian* tried to explain the reason for the joining of the mainstream Hagana with the IZL and FFI in one united paramilitary organisation. 'Hitler made them desperate', it wrote, '... slowly but surely their leaders gave in – some willingly, some reluctantly and some fearfully to the wishes of the rank and file'.[46] However, even the most pro-Zionist publication in Britain could not match the anti-British rhetoric of the American press. As an example of the way events in Palestine were treated by the media in the United States, it is worth examining the attitude of one such newspaper to the King David explosion. *The New York Post*, in its editorial, stressed that in Palestine terrorism became a symbol of despair. But the editor chose to attack the British: 'In Jerusalem Fascist-minded Arab leaders are permitted to return from Germany and from exile, but survivors of Hitler's gas-chambers are still in barbed-wire camps in Germany ...'. And the paper went on: 'There is no *habeas corpus* in Palestine. Any policeman and British soldier can arrest you on mere suspicion ... If you give shelter to your own mother knowing she is an illegal immigrant, you are liable to eight years' imprisonment. Is there any wonder that in their rage and despair, betrayed and embittered, men strike out blindly?'[47]

The hanging of the two sergeants on 30 July 1947 gave the signal for an unprecedented attack on the Irgun and the Jewish community at large. Comparisons with the Nazis were widespread and accusations were not free of anti-semitic overtones, but the public was urged to stop the anti-Jewish riots which broke out all over Britain. The British press also took the opportunity to settle accounts with the Americans ('American women whose dollars helped to buy the rope' was one of them).[48]

However, all the newspapers were united in demanding an immediate withdrawal from the 'death trap' of 'thankless Palestine'. When, after the *Exodus* episode, the British finally made the decision to quit, the press, the public and Parliament greeted it with overwhelming approval and a general sense of relief. In the psychological struggle to drive British public opinion into despair and helplessness, the Irgun certainly won the day.

# Epilogue

It is an irony that Menachem Begin, the commander of the Irgun's revolt, was the first Israeli Prime Minister to have made peace with an Arab country. Equally ironic is the fact that at the time of the Madrid–Middle East peace conference in 1991, Israel was led by Yitzhak Shamir, one of the FFI's leaders. Both events were followed by unprecedented political and territorial concessions that contradicted the previous beliefs of the Right Wing in the country.

The Oslo accord of September 1993 in which Israel and the PLO signed a historic agreement, took place when the Israeli Labour Party was in office. Its support of the new process invited sharp opposition from the Likud Party which was led, until recently, by Irgun veterans. The same old argument that characterised the ideological polarisation during the British Mandate period repeated itself with a vengeance. The modern day versions of the Irgun (with the Revisionists) on the one hand, and the Hagana (with the Socialists) on the other, were engaged yet again in a bitter confrontation. This reached a climax after Palestinian autonomy was established in Gaza and Jericho and following terrorist attacks carried out by Muslim fundamentalists against Israelis.

While the Oslo process turned out to be a minefield for both sides, one of its outcomes did become more successful. This was the peace treaty that Israel signed with Jordan. The support for this agreement in Israel was so overwhelming that even former Irgun members voted in its favour in Parliament. That move eradicated once and for all the Irgun's historic territorial claim to both sides of the river Jordan, which had been its main ideological platform for many years.

The Likud's defeat in the 1992 elections not only paved the way for a Palestinian autonomy in Gaza and a possible Palestinian state, it also brought about the subsequent resignation of Shamir as Premier and thus heralded the demise of the old guard in the country. Shamir, and Begin before him, were probably the last European-born pre-1948 dominant figures to have led modern Israel. They cleared the way for a new generation of politicians who had already proved to be more pragmatic and open-minded in their attitudes towards several aspects of the conflict in the Middle East.

However, the recent public debate between Right and Left could only echo the domestic tension that had existed in the Yishuv during the 1940s. If at that time the Jewish Community had escaped a civil war, one cannot be sure that in the event of further territorial concessions on the West Bank, Israel would be so lucky again.

Sadly, today far more than during the Mandate era, terrorism could determine once again the future of the region. The strong opposition of the Muslim Fundamentalists to the peace process and their declared aim to destroy Israel, could deliver a deadly blow to all the countries involved. This kind of religious–political suicidal violence is more vicious and much more indiscriminate than the campaign once waged by the Irgun against the British. For this and other reasons one cannot compare the Hamas and the Islamic Jihad organisations to the Irgun and the Stern group.

Yet, the official Yishuv leadership has done a lot to restrain the activities of its own 'dissidents'. The mainstream Palestinian leadership, on the other hand, is doing its utmost to appease its opponents and even to co-operate with them. Indeed the three Jewish organisations did just that when they joined forces against the British and established the united Hebrew Resistance Movement. It lasted, however, a mere few months as the ideological gaps were far too wide.

The inability and unwillingness of the PLO to impose its will on the Muslim extremists can cost its leadership dearly. Cracking down on them might increase their popularity. So far, the fundamentalists have been careful not to challenge the authority of the official leadership led by PLO Chairman Yasser Arafat. While building up support in the street, they concentrate on terrorist operations with the immediate aim of accelerating the pace of the Israeli withdrawal from the West Bank and sowing demoralisation within the Israeli public. Such violence could well serve the interests of the more moderate Palestinians, but Israel might run out of patience and adopt a tougher line. Unlike Britain in the 1940s, Israel has nowhere to go and it could change its policy towards the conflict even under the present government.

The likely collapse of the peace process could, therefore, shatter the dream of the Palestinians to have a state of their own. It might well bring about another military confrontation in the region by the year 2000.

# Appendix 1

*Proclamation of Revolt by the Irgun Zvai Leumi*
(Issued by Menachem Begin, 1 February 1944)

### TO THE JEWISH NATION IN ZION

We are now entering the final stage of this World War. At present each and every people is engaged in evaluating its national position. Which are its victories and which are its defeats? What course shall it embark upon in order to achieve its objectives and fulfil its destiny? Who are its friends and who are its enemies? Who is a genuine ally and who is a traitor? And, who will participate in the decisive battle?

Similarly, the people of Israel is obliged to examine its course, to survey the past and arrive at conclusions concerning its future. For, the last few years have been the most horrible in our history; the coming ones – the most crucial in our history.

Let us look at the facts:

1. In 1939 all the political movements in Israel proclaimed that our nation would stand alongside England, France and Poland in their Holy War against the Hitlerite German aggression.
2. Germany proclaimed this World War a 'Jewish War' and that the people of Israel are its Enemy Number One. Nevertheless, the British Government has continuously and stubbornly rejected all proposals to establish a Jewish fighting Force to engage the German armies in direct combat.
3. A truce has been declared between the government and the Jews in the Land of Israel. The Jewish community has offered its unqualified assistance to the Allied Nations in their ways against the Hitlerite tyranny.
4. Over 25,000 young men and women volunteers have joined the British Army in the hope that England would establish a National Jewish Army.

5. In 1941 the Arabs of Iraq exploited Britain's desperate position and with German assistance, attacked her armies; the Arabs of Syria supported Hitler's agents; the Egyptian fifth column exercised tremendous influence there; the Arabs of the Land of Israel awaited the coming of Rommel, the redeemer, while their leader, the Mufti, dispatched orders from Berlin.
6. Jewry stood the test, remaining loyal during the crucial period of 1940–1. The expertise and industrial know-how of the Jews in the Land of Israel has served the entire Middle East arena. Sons of Israel risked and sacrificed their lives in Syria, Egypt and Iraq.
7. Germany began to exterminate the European Jewry. Poland was transformed into a slaughter house; German, Austrian, Dutch and Belgian Jewries have been destroyed; Lithuanian, Latvian and Estonian Jewries lie in their own blood; the remnant of Polish Jewry is in danger of liquidation; Bulgarian Jews are on the verge of deportation; Hungarian Jewry is fearful of its fate. Sword and famine, epidemic and poison are annihilating our European brethren. Throughout all the communities of the Diaspora – blood!
8. Our brethren enjoy no refuge. All countries have barred their doors to them. Even those who escaped from Poland, Rumania, and the Baltic countries to Russian Asia are dying of starvation, cold and epidemics. Yet no one will help them – because they are Jews!
9. In response to the horrible slaughter in Europe, the Allied Nations have merely issued a verbal declaration, worth no more than the paper on which it was written.
10. The British Government has announced that rescue activities are not possible since they 'would interfere with the achievement of victory'. Yet, not satisfied with this malicious, satanic declaration alone, she personally authored the bloody chapters in the saga of Jewish immigration to the Land of Israel: Patria, Mauritius, Struma.
11. The government responsible for the White Paper has now attacked the Jewish population in the Land of Israel. Its agents have carried out lawless murders in the cities and villages. Its judges have invented lies and have sought to defame our people and sully its honour throughout the world.
12. The White Paper remains in force, implemented despite Jewish loyalty and Arab treachery; despite the mass mobilisation of Jews into the British Army; despite the armistice and the calm prevailing in the Land of Israel; despite the mass slaughter of Jews in Europe. And despite the fact that even now, following the rout of Hitlerism, Jews have no future among the hate-ridden, anti-Semitic nations of Europe.

The facts are both simple and horrible. During the four war years, we have lost millions of the best of our people; other millions face annihilation. Yet the Land of Israel remains sealed because it is ruled by a British regime which enforces the White Paper and aims at destroying our people's last hope.

## SONS OF ISRAEL, JEWISH YOUTH!

We are now entering the final stage of the war. Our people's destiny shall be determined at this historic juncture. The British regime has violated the armistice agreement which was declared at the outset of the war. The rules of the Land have disregarded loyalty, concessions and sacrifice. Instead they continue to work towards their goal – the eradication of Zionist efforts to achieve statehood.

Four years have passed. The hopes we had harboured since 1939 have been dashed. We have not been accorded international status; a Jewish Army has not been established; the gates of the Land of Israel have not been opened. The British regime has continued its shameful betrayal of the Jewish Nation and there is no moral basis for its continued presence in the Land of Israel.

Let us fearlessly draw the proper conclusions. There can no longer be an armistice between the Jewish Nation and its youth and a British administration in the Land of Israel which has been delivering our brethren to Hitler. Our nation is at war with this regime and it is a fight to the finish. This war will exact many and heavy sacrifices but we shall enter into it in a conviction that we have remained loyal to our slaughtered brethren, that we fight in their name, and remain true to their final testament.

This, then, is our demand!

## IMMEDIATE TRANSFER OF POWER IN THE LAND OF ISRAEL TO A PROVISIONAL JEWISH GOVERNMENT.

Immediately after its establishment, the Jewish government of the Land of Israel, the only legal representative of the Jewish Nation, shall undertake the following:

A. Establish a National Jewish Army.
B. Negotiate with all authorised bodies to organise the mass evacuation of European Jewry to the Land of Israel.
C. Negotiate with the Russian Government for the evacuation of Jewish refugees from Poland and other countries.

D. Create conditions for the absorption of our sons returning to their homeland.
E. Effect an alliance with the Allied governments aimed at intensifying the war efforts against Germany.
F. Propose – on behalf of the sovereign state of the Land of Israel, on the basis of the Atlantic Charter, and in recognition of the community of interests – a mutual assistance pact with Great Britain, the United States of America, the new French government and any other free nation who recognises the sovereignty and international rights of the Jewish State. An honourable peace and good neighbourliness shall be offered to all the neighbours of the independent Jewish State.
G. Implant the sanctity of the Torah into the life of emancipated nation in its homeland.
H. Guarantee all citizens of the State employment and social justice.
I. Proclaim the extra-territorial status of all places sacred to Christians and Moslems.
J. Grant full equality to the Arab population.

JEWS!

The only way to save our nation, insure our survival and preserve our honour is to establish a Jewish government and implement this programme. We shall follow this course for there is none other. We shall fight. Every Jew in the homeland will fight.

The God of Israel, Lord of Hosts, shall be at our side. There is no retreat. Freedom – or death! Erect an iron wall around your fighting youth! Do not abandon them, for the traitor shall be cursed and the coward held in contempt!

And you shall be called to raise the banner of this citizen's war. You will be called upon:

A. To refuse to pay taxes to the oppressive regime.
B. To demonstrate in the city streets day and night, demanding the establishment of a Jewish government in The Land.
C. To refuse to obey any order issued by the foreign ruler; You shall violate these orders declaring, 'I shall only obey a Jewish government'.
D. Workers shall be called upon to proclaim a general strike in all public and private enterprises. Be prepared for hunger and tribulation, but under no circumstances break the strike, for it is a holy endeavour.
E. Student youth shall be called upon to boycott the schools and devote all their time and energy to this war.

JEWS!

This fighting youth will not be deterred by the prospect of sacrifices and suffering, blood and pain. It will not surrender, nor will it rest until it has succeeded in renewing our days as of yore until it guarantees our people a homeland, freedom, honour, sustenance, and true justice. And if, indeed, you lend them every assistance, very soon, in our time, you shall behold the return of people to Zion and the restoration of Israel. May God grant that this comes to pass.

# Appendix 2

Some IZL Anti-British Operations in Palestine

### 1944

**12 February** Bombing of the immigration offices in Tel Aviv, Jerusalem and Haifa. No casualties.
**27 February** Bombing of the Inland Revenue Offices in Tel Aviv, Jerusalem and Haifa. No casualties.
**23 March** Bombing of the CID centres in Jerusalem, Jaffa and Haifa. Four Britons killed.
**17 May** Attack on the government-run broadcasting station in Ramallah and a failed attempt to make a broadcast from there.
**14 July** Bombing the Land Registry office in Jerusalem. Two Arab guards killed.
**22 August** Attacks on two police stations in the Jaffa area. Weapons taken. Many injuries on both sides. Arrests made.
**27 September** Attacks on four police fortresses in Katra, Bet Dagan, Qalqiliya and Haifa. Two failed. One British death, mutual injuries and arrests.

### 1945

**11 October** Raid on a military camp in Rehovot. Many weapons taken.
**1 November** Abortive attempt to blow up the oil refineries in Haifa. Attack on Lydda railway station.
**22 November** Raid on a military camp in Rishon-Lezion. Weapons taken.
**27 December** Destruction of CID headquarters in Jerusalem in collaboration with the Stern group.

## 1946

**12 January** Train robbery near Hadera. Entire military payroll taken.

**19 January** Abortive attempt to break into the central prison in Jerusalem. One casualty on each side.

**25 February** Attacks on military airfields at Lydda and Qastina. 23 aircraft destroyed. Two insurgents killed. FFI attacked a third airfield.

**6 March** Massive attack on the big military camp of Sarafend. Weapons taken but later abandoned. One insurgent killed, two captured.

**23 April** Attack on Ramat Gan police station and its armoury. A relative success; weapons stolen but three Irgunists killed and one captured.

**1 July** Kidnapping of five British officers in Tel Aviv. Released in a deal with the authorities.

**1 July** 54 detainees escaped the detention centre in Eritrea.

**22 July** King David Hotel bombing. 91 killed, 45 injured, mostly civilian. The British retaliated with Operation *Shark*.

**8 September** Bombing of the oil pipeline in Haifa port.

**9 September** Seven railways in Palestine sabotaged.

**15 September** Robbery of the Ottoman Bank in Jaffa.

**20 September** Destruction of Haifa railway station.

**30 October** Attack on the Jerusalem railway station. Partially destroyed.

**31 October** Bombing of the British Embassy in Rome.

**20 November** Blowing up of the income tax offices in Jerusalem.

**30 November** Attack on a police station inside the security zone in Jerusalem.

**29 December** Irgun flogging of British officers in retaliation for beating of Irgun prisoners.

## 1947

**1 March** Bombing of Goldsmith House Officers' Club in Jerusalem. 17 British officers and soldiers killed, 27 wounded. Martial law imposed.

**12 March** Attack on the Shneler military camp in Jerusalem.

**15 March** Bombing of the Officers' club in Hadera.

**16 March** Haifa–Kirkuk oil pipeline cut.

**18 April** Destruction of a military camp near Netanya.

**4 May** Break-in at Acre fortress. Seven Irgun casualties. 31 prisoners freed.

**1 July** British military train mined in Germany.

**23 July** Attack on British naval headquarters in Haifa.

**30 July** Two British sergeants hanged by Irgun 'kangaroo' court.

**2 August** Attack on the RAF club inside the security zone of Jerusalem.
**14 August** British troop train in Austria derailed.
**29 September** Destruction of the Haifa police headquarters.

## 1948

**19 March** Bombing of the British Officers' Club in Vienna.

# Appendix 3

*Interview with Irgun Commander M Begin*
(taken by the author in January 1992)

*Q:* Can one say that only one definite factor was responsible for the British withdrawal from Palestine? Could it be that it was as a result of combined factors? The British themselves give us contradictory explanations. However, would it not be historically more accurate to argue that the British left Palestine as part of the disintegration process of their Empire which was highlighted by a severe domestic economic crisis and constant friction with America over their Middle Eastern policy?

*A:* After the Second World War – in which Britain took a very heroic stand – the country, as a result of its war effort, became very weak. International factors influenced it as well, since after the war the decisive factor in the West was America. But, even after taking all this into account, I have no doubt – and many British admitted it whole-heartedly – that without the warfare carried out by the Underground, British rule would not have left Eretz-Israel and the state of Israel would not have been established. Please remember what Dr Abba Hillel Silver said: 'The Irgun will go down in history as a factor without which the state of Israel would not have come into being'.

*Q:* What in your opinion was 'the last straw which broke the British camel's back' as far as the Irgun's armed struggle was concerned? Was it the hanging of the two sergeants? Was there any specific event at all which finally convinced them to remove their forces? Or maybe an accumulated weakness which finally reached its breaking-point?

*A:* The activities of the Underground in general prompted them to decide that they had to leave Eretz-Israel; specifically we should single out the break-in at Acre fortress which has been described by a British newspaper as 'the biggest prison break-in in history'. Of course, all the operations of the

IZL, FFI and the Hagana motivated the British, mostly because of their broken prestige, to leave our country.

*Q:* Some British say, that if they had wanted, they could have destroyed the Irgun within a few days, but this would have been at the cost of many innocent lives, which was something they could not afford. You are familiar with the argument that if the British had behaved in Palestine in the way in which the French behaved in Algeria, then the Hebrew resistance would have finished 'in no time'. What is your opinion of such an assessment?

*A:* False claims. The British High Commissioner said that they could destroy the Underground only by adopting Nazi-like methods. And that, he added, we cannot do. The truth is that they took many repressive measures; arrests, exile to Kenya and Eritrea and hanging of fighters. All these did not prevent the liberation of the land, because of the devotion and the heroic activities of the Hebrew Underground.

*Q:* Was not the FFI a terrorist group which only hampered the Irgun's war effort instead of helping it?

*A:* My answer to this question is negative.

*Q:* To what extent did the various Hebrew committees in the United States act without the approval of the Irgun?

*A:* The activity of Hillel Kook and his friends was most important in creating a sympathetic public opinion to the liberation war of the Underground organisations in the country.

*Q:* Was the Irgun influenced by guerrilla groups in other countries militarily and ideologically?

*A:* We learned from the history of our own people and ourselves.

*Q:* Would it be fair to claim that three of the Irgun's most important operations were not successful and were even controversial? The break-in at Acre fortress, however brilliant, ended up with many casualties; the King David bombing was counter-productive; and the hanging of the two sergeants was overshadowed by the mining of the bodies

*A:* These assumptions are unfounded. On the Acre break-in I have written already. At the King David we have proved that we had issued three warnings for the evacuation of the hotel. The hanging retaliation of the two sergeants was a cruel deed, but without it dozens of others of our fighters would have been hanged, if not more. General Barker said 'I will hang a hundred Jews and there would be tranquillity in the country.' He did not witness it and our activities did not allow him that.

*Q:* How many members did the Irgun have at its peak?

*A:* We resumed our warfare with 338 members. But during the war of liberation our numbers grew and reached many thousands, because the younger generation was attracted to us and wanted to participate in the liberation war.

*Q:* In many countries, the leaders of anti-colonialist armed struggle earned the trust and recognition of their people and led their countries into independence. In Israel, the Left, which in the past collaborated with the foreign rulers, translated their strength into political dominance for nearly three decades. How do you explain that the commander of the Irgun became prime minister of Israel only after 29 years of national independence?

*A:* Only one day after the establishment of Israel we announced that we would accept the decision of the majority, as it would be decided in democratic elections. Indeed, it was a relatively prolonged period. But eventually we also won the trust of the people and set up a government in Israel which is running the affairs of the country.

# Selected Bibliography

## PRIMARY SOURCES

*Archival Sources:*
British Library Newspaper Library, London.
Central Zionist Archives, Jerusalem.
Hagana Archive, Tel Aviv.
Imperial War Museum, London.
Israel State Archives, Jerusalem.
Jabotinsky Archives Tel Aviv.
Labour Movement Archives, Berl House, Kfar Saba.
Lehi (FFI) Museum, Tel Aviv.
Oral Documentation Institute, The Hebrew University, Jerusalem.
Public Record Office, London:
   Papers of the British Cabinet Office.
   Papers of the War Office.
   Papers of the Colonial Office.
   Papers of the Foreign Office.
   Wiener Library, London.

*Manuscript Collections:*
Begin, Menachem, *In the Underground*, writings and documents, Jabotinsky Archives, Tel Aviv.
Cunningham, General, Sir Alan. Private Papers, St. Antony's College, Oxford.
MacMillan, General, Sir Gordon. Private Papers, Imperial War Museum, London.

*Published Collections:*
*Hansard* (London Parliament Reports).
*Psychological Warfare and Propaganda: Irgun Documentation*, E Tavin and Y Alexander (eds), Wilmington, 1982.
*Irgun Zvai Leumi. Collection of Archival Sources and Documents. April 1937–April 1941.* The Jabotinsky Institute, Tel Aviv (1990).
*Jewish Terrorist Index*, published by Palestine Police, London, 1946.
*LEHI* – 2 Vols. Writings on the FFI, The Committee for the Publication of LEHI Writings, Tel-Aviv.

LEHI Revealed: Minutes of the First Conference of FFI. (March 1949), Bar Ilan University, Ramat Gan, (1985).
The Protocols of the IZL Command: 23 July 1944–9 November 1944. Jabotinsky Archives.
'The Attack on the British Officers' Club in Jerusalem on 1st March 1947'. Seven Eye-Witnesses, Jabotinsky Institute, Tel Aviv.
Terrorist Methods with Mines and Booby Traps. Headquarters, Chief Engineer, Palestine and Transjordan. December 1994.

*Interviews by the author:*
Amrami, Yoel, July 1987.
Beely, Harold, September 1983.
Eldad, Israel, February 1984.
El'azar, Ya'akov, May 1991.
Horne, Edward, July 1990.
Kahn, Marek, April 1985.
Katz, Samuel, August 1986.
Kook, Hillel, April 1985.
Lankin, Eliyahu, May 1986.
Livni, Eitan, May 1986.
Meridor Ya'akov, February 1986.
Morton, Jeffrey, June 1988.
Niv, David, August 1986, May 1987.
Shmuelevitz Mati, May 1986.
Tavin, Eli, May 1986.
Kadishai, Yehiel, May 1986.

*Newspapers & Magazines*
*Davar* (Heb).
*Edinburgh Evening Despatch.*
*Evening Standard.*
*Ha'areta* (Heb).
*Hamashkif* (Heb).
*Herut* (Heb).
*Irgun Press.*
*Jewish Agency Telegraph.*
*The New Statesman and the Nation.*
*The Birmingham Post.*
*The Daily Mail.*
*The Dundee Courier.*
*The Jewish Chronicle.*
*The Liverpool Post.*
*The Manchester Guardian.*
*The News Chronicle.*
*The New York Post.*

*The Observer.*
*The Oxford Mail.*
*The Palestine Post.*
*The Spectator.*
*The Sunday Express.*
*The Times.*
*The Western Evening Herald.*
*The Yorkshire Post.*

## SECONDARY SOURCES

Alon, Yigal, *Shield of David: The Story of Israel's Armed Forces*, Bloch, New York (1970).
Amichal-Yevin, Ada, *In Purple. The Life of Abraham Stern*. Hadar, Tel-Aviv (1986). (Heb).
Avner, *Memories of an Assassin*, Antony Blond, London (1959). (Heb).
Banai, Yaakov, *Anonymous Soldiers*, Hug Yedidim, Tel-Aviv (1958). (Heb).
Bar Zohar, Michael, *Ben-Gurion*, Weidenfeld, London (1978).
Bauer, Yehuda, *From Diplomacy to Resistance*, Athenaeum, New York (1973).
Begin, Menachem, *The Revolt*, W H Allen, London (1951).
Bell, J Bowyer, *Terror out of Zion*, Academy Press, Dublin (1977).
Bell, J Bowyer, *Assassin*, St. Martin's Press, New York (1979).
Ben-Ami, Yitzhak, *The Altalena*, New York (1981) (In Stencil).
Ben-Ami, Yitzhak, *Years of Wrath. Days of Glory. Memories from the Irgun*, Shengold, New York (1983).
Ben Gurion, David, *The War of Independence Diary*, G Rivlin and E Oren (eds), Ma'archot, Tel-Aviv (1986) (3 Vols., Heb.).
Bentwich, Norman and Helen, *Mandate Memories (1918–1948)*, Schocken, New York (1965).
Bethell, Nicholas, *The Palestinian Triangle*, Deutsch, London (1979).
Bishuti, Bassam, *The Role of the Zionist Terror in the Creation of Israel*, Palestine Research Centre, Beirut (1969).
Bowden, Tom, *The Breakdown of Public Security: the Case of Northern Ireland 1916–1921 and Palestine 1936–1939*, Sage, London (1977).
Brenner, Lenni, *Zionism in the Age of the Dictators*, Croom Helm, London (1983).
Brenner, Lenni, *The Iron Wall: Zionist Revisionism from Jabotinsky to Shamir*, Zed Books, London (1984).
Brenner, Uri, *Altalena*, Ma'arachot, Tel Aviv (1978) (Heb.).
Bullock, Alan, *Ernest Bevin. Foreign Secretary*, Heineman, London (1983).
Burridge, Trevor, *Attlee. A Political Biography*, Cape, London (1985).
Burton, Antony, *Urban Terrorism: Theory, Practice and Response*, Leo Cooper, London (1975).
Caspi, D, Diskin, A, Gutmann, E (eds) *The Roots of Begin's Success*, Croom Helm, London (1984).
Charters, David, *The British Army and Jewish Insurgency in Palestine 1945–1947*,

Macmillan Press & King's College, London.
Clarke, Thurston, *By Blood and Fire*, Hutchinson, London (1980).
Clutterbuck, Richard, *Protest and the Urban Guerrilla*, Cassell, London (1971).
Clutterbuck, Richard, *Guerrillas and Terrorism*, Faber, London (1977).
Cohen, Geula, *Woman of Violence: Memories of a Young Terrorist, 1943–1948*, Hart-Davis, London (1966).
Cohen, Michael, *Palestine: Retreat from the Mandate*, Holmes & Meier, New York (1978).
Cohen, Michael, *Palestine and the Great Powers (1945–1948)*, Princeton (1982).
Cohen, Michael, *Truman and Israel*, University of California Press, Los Angeles (1990).
Crossman, Richard, *Palestine Mission*, Harper, London (1947).
Cross, Colin, *The Fall of the British Empire (1918–1968)*, Hodder & Stoughton, London (1968).
Dalton, Hugh, *High Tide and After (Memories 1945–1960)*, Muler, London (1962).
Dotan, Shmuel, *The Struggle for Eretz-Israel*, Ministry of Defence, Tel Aviv (1981), (Heb).
Elam, Yigal, *Hagana–The Zionist Way to Power*, Zmora, Tel Aviv (1979), (Heb).
Elath, Eliyahu, *The Struggle for Statehood*, Am Oved, Tel Aviv (1982), (3 Vols. Heb).
Eldad, Yisrael, *The Jewish Revolution*, Shengold, New York (1971), (Heb).
Eliav, Binyamin (ed), *The Jewish National Home from the Balfour Declaration to Independence*, Keter, Jerusalem (1976), (Heb).
Eliav, Ya'akov, *Wanted*, Ma'ariv, Tel Aviv (1983), (Heb).
Elidan, Shin, *We Kidnapped British Officers*, Hadar, Tel Aviv (1975), (Heb).
Eshel, Arie, *The Cheated Hangman*, Zmora, Tel Aviv (1991), (Heb).
Ettinger, Shalom, *Zionism, the Arab Problem and the British Mandate*, Karni, Tel Aviv (1987), (Heb).
Faran, Roy, *Winged Dagger*, Collins, London (1948).
Frank, Gerald, *The Deed*, Simon & Schuster, New York (1954).
Gani, Pesach, *The IZL*, Jabotinsky Institute, Tel Aviv (1983), (Heb).
Ganin, Zvi, *Truman, American Jewry, and Israel 1945–1948*, Holmes & Meier, New York (1979).
Garcia-Granados, Jorge, *The Birth of Israel: The Drama as I Saw It*, Alfred Knopf, New York (1948).
Gearty, Conor, *Terror*, Faber & Faber, London (1991).
Gervasi, Frank, *The Life and Times of Menachem Begin: Rebel to Statesman*, Putnam & Sons, New York (1979).
Gilbert, Martin, *Exile and Return: The Emergence of Jewish Statehood*, Weidenfeld and Nicholson, London (1978).
Gitlin, Yitzhak, *The Acre Break-In*, Hadar, Tel Aviv (1962), (Heb).
Golan, Shimon, *Allegiance in the Struggle*, Yad Tavenkin, Tel Aviv (1988), (Heb).
Golani, Yardena, *The Myth of Deir Yassin*, Hadar, Tel Aviv (1976), (Heb).
Goldstein, Ya'acov, Shavit Ya'akov, *Without Compromises. The Agreement between Ben Gurion and V Jabotinsky and Its Failure 1934–1935*, Yariv, Tel Aviv (1979), (Heb).

Gurion, Yitzhak, *The Lawyers of Freedom Fighters*, Jabotinsky Institute, Tel Aviv (1978), (Heb).
Haber, Eitan, *Menachem Begin: The Legend and the Man*, Pelacorte Press, New York (1978).
Hafner, Eli, *Seven Entered the Orchard. Memories of Irgun Soldiers*, Ministry of Defence, Tel Aviv (1980), (Heb).
Hamilton, Nigel, *Monty, The Field-Marshal 1944–1976*, Hamish Hamilton, London (1986).
Haron, Miriam Joyce, *Palestine and The Anglo-American Connection 1945–1950*, Peter Lang, New York (1986).
Harris, Kenneth, *Attlee*, Weidenfeld & Nicholson, London (1984).
Haviv, Kana'an, *Gallows in Netanya*, Hadar, Tel Aviv (1976), (Heb).
Haviv, Kana'an, *Through the Eyes of a Palestinian Policeman. The Birth of the Palestinian Resistance*, Massada, Tel Aviv (1980), (Heb).
Hecht, Ben, *A Child of a Century*, Signet, New York (1954).
Heller, Josef (ed), *The Struggle for the Jewish State. Zionist Politics. 1936–1948*, Shazer, Jerusalem (1984), (Heb).
Hirschler, Gertrude and Eckman, Lester, *Menachem Begin*, Shengold, New York (1979).
Hofman, Bruce, *The Failure of British Military Strategy Within Palestine 1939–1947*, Bar Ilan University Press, Ramat Gan (1983).
Horgin, Ya'akov, *The Attack on Ramat-Gan Police*, Hadar, Tel Aviv (1975), (Heb).
Horne, Edward, *A Job Well Done. A History of the Palestine Police Force 1920–1948*, Palestine Police, Essex (1982).
Horvitz, Jacob, *The Struggle for Jerusalem*, Norton, New York (1950).
Ilan, Amitzur, *America, Britain and Palestine: The Origin and Development of America's Intervention in Britain's Palestine Policy 1938–1947*, Ben Zvi, Jerusalem (1979), (Heb).
Jabotinsky, Vladimir (Ze'ev), *The Jewish War Front*, Allen & Unwin, London (1940).
Jenkins, Roy, *Truman*, Collins, London (1986).
Joice, Miriam, *Anglo-American Relations and the Question of Palestine 1945–1947*, Fordham University, New York (1979).
Katz, Doris, *The Lady Was a Terrorist*, Shiloni, New York (1953).
Katz, Samuel, *Days of Fire*, Karni, Tel Aviv (1966), (Heb).
Kaufman, Menachem, *Non-Zionists in America and the Struggle for Jewish Statehood. 1939–1948*, Sifriya Zionit, Jerusalem (1984), (Heb).
Kimche, Jon, *Seven Fallen Pillars: the Middle East, 1915–1950*, Secker and Warburg, London (1950).
Kimche, Jon and David, *Both Sides of the Hill*, Secker and Warburg, London (1960).
Kitson, Frank, *Gangs and Countergangs*, Barrie & Rockliff, London (1978).
Koestler, Arthur, *Thieves in the Night*, Ahiasaf, Tel Aviv (1944).
Koestler, Arthur, *Promise and Fulfilment: Palestine 1971–1949*, Macmillan, London (1949).
Lankin, Doris, *The Lady Was a Terrorist*, Theta, Cape Town (1983).

Lankin, Eliyahu, *The Story of the Commander of Altalena*, Hadar, Tel Aviv (1967), (Heb).
Lapin, Brian, *End of Empire*, Granada, London (1984).
Laqueur, Walter, *The History of Zionism*, Weidenfeld & Nicholson, London (1972).
Laqueur, Walter, *Terrorism*, Weidenfeld & Nicholson, London (1977).
Lazar, Haim, *Acre Fortress*, Shelach, Tel Aviv (1953), (Heb).
Lev Ami, Shlomo, *By Struggle and by Revolt*, Ma'archot, Tel Aviv (1978), (Heb).
Livni, Eitan, *I.Z.L. Operations and Underground (Memories)*, Edanim, Jerusalem (1987), (Heb).
Louis, Wm. Roger, *The British Empire in the Middle East. Arab Nationalism, the United States and Postwar Imperialism*, Clarendon Press, Oxford (1984).
Louis, Roger and Stooky, Robert (eds), *The End of the Palestine Mandate*, Tauris, London (1986).
Luttvak, Edward and Horwitz, Dan, *The Israeli Army*, Allen Lane, London (1975).
Mardor, Meir, *Secret Mission: Episodes in the History of the Hagana*, Ma'arachot, Tel Aviv (1958), (Heb).
Marlowe, John, *The Seat of Pilate: An Account of the Palestine Mandate*, Cresset, London (1959).
Marlowe, John, *Rebellion in Palestine*, Cresset, London (1946).
Melitz, Arye, *The Attack on the Money Train*, Hadar, Tel Aviv (1975), (Heb).
Meridor, Ya'akov, *Long is the Road to Freedom*, Ahiasaf, Tel Aviv (1950), (Heb).
Milshtein, Uri, *With Blood and Fire Judaea*, Levine Epstein, Tel Aviv (1974), (Heb).
Monroe, Elizabeth, *Britain's Moment in the Middle East, 1914–1956*, Chatto & Windus, London (1963).
Morton, Geoffery, *Just a Job*, Hodder & Stoughton, London (1957).
Moss, Robert, *The Collapse of Democracy*, Temple Smith, London (1975).
Nakdimon, Shlomo, *Altalena*, Edanim, Jerusalem (1978), (Heb).
Naor, Mordechai, *The Black Sabbath*, Kibbutz Meuhad, Tel Aviv (1981), (Heb).
Nedava, Joseph, *The Book of Martyrs*, Hadar, Tel Aviv (1952), (Heb).
Nedava, Joseph, *Who Expelled the British from the Land of Israel*, Amuta, Tel Aviv (1988), (Heb).
Netanyahu, Benjamin, (ed), *Terrorism – How the West Can Win*, Ma'ariv, Tel Aviv (1987), (Heb).
Niv, David, *The Irgun Zvai Leumi*, Klauzner, Tel Aviv (1965–1976), (Heb).
Ofek, Uriel, *The Night of the Bridges*, Kibbutz Meuhad, Tel Aviv (1980), (Heb).
Ovendale, Ritchie, *Britain, the United States and the End of the Palestine Mandate 1942–1948*, The Boydell Press, London (1989).
Pappe, Ilan, *Britain and the Arab-Israeli Conflict 1948–1951*, St Antony's-Macmillan, Oxford (1988).
Pedazur, Elazar, *The History of the Irgun Zvai Leumi*, Shilton Betar, Tel Aviv (1959), (Heb).
Porat, Yehoshua, *Arab Jewish Politics and British Politics in Palestine. 1930–1945*. Ben Zvi, Jerusalem (1985), (Heb).
Ram, Meir, *With the Fighting Family*, Nehushtan, Jerusalem (1977), (Heb).
Ratner, Yohanan, *My Life and Myself*, Schocken, Tel Aviv (1978), (Heb).

Robbins, Baruch, *The Legacy*, Jabotinsky Institute, Tel Aviv (1980).
Samuel, Edwin, *A Lifetime in Jerusalem: The Memories of the Second Viscount Samuel*, Israel Universities Press, Jerusalem (1970).
Schatzberger, Hilda, *Resistance and Tradition in Mandatory Palestine*, Bar Ilan University, Ramat Gan (1958), (Heb).
Shavit, Ya'acov, *The Hunting Season*, Hadar, Tel Aviv (1976).
Shavit, Ya'acov, *Revisionism in Zionism*, Yariv, Tel Aviv (1978), (Heb).
Shavit, Ya'akov, (ed), *'Self-estraint' or 'Reaction' 1936–1939*, Bar Ilan University, Ramat Gan (1983), (Heb).
Shavit, Ya'akov, (ed), *Struggle, Revolt, Resistance*, Shazar, Jerusalem (1987), (Heb).
Shavit, Ya'acov, *Jabotinsky and the Revisionist Movement 1925–1948*, Frank Cass, London (1988).
Shlaim, Avi, *Collusion across the Jordan*, Clarendon Press, Oxford (1988).
Silver, Eric, *Begin. A Biography*, Weidenfeld & Nicholson, London (1984).
Slutsky, Yehuda (ed), *History of the Hagana*, (8 Vols), Ma'arachot, Tel Aviv (1964–1972), (Heb).
Shmuelevistz, Matityahu, *In Red Days*, Ministry of Defence, Tel Aviv (1949), (Heb).
Sofer, Sasson, *Begin. An Anatomy of Leadership*, Basil Blackwell, Oxford (1988).
Sykes, Christopher, *Crossroads to Israel*, Collins, London (1965).
Tavin, Eli, *The Second Front. The IZL in Europe, 1946–1948*, Ron, Tel Aviv (1973), (Heb).
Teveth, Shabtai, *Ben Gurion*, Houghton Mifflin, Boston (1987).
Trevor, Daphna, *Under the White Paper*, Kraus, Munich (1980).
Vinitsky, Joseph, *'251'*, Yedidim, Tel Aviv (1951), (Heb).
Wasserstein, Bernard, *Britain and the Jews of Europe 1935–1945*, Oxford University Press, Oxford (1979).
Weizmann, Chaim, *Trial and Error*, Hamish Hamilton, London (1949).
Wilkinson, Paul, *Political Terrorism*, Macmillan, London (1974).
William, Perl, *The Fourth War Front: From the Holocaust to the Promised Land*, Crown, New York (1979).
Wilson, Harold, *The Chariots of Israel*, Weidenfeld, London (1981).
Wilson, R D, *Cordon and Search*, Gale and Polden, Aldershot (1949).
Wyman, David, *The Abandonment of the Jews: America and the Holocaust 1941–1948*, Pantheon Books, New York (1984).
Yelin-Mor, Nathan, *Lehi. Fighters for the Freedom of Israel*, Shikmona, Tel Aviv (1974) (Heb).
Zaar, Isaac, *Rescue and Liberation*, Bloch, New York (1954).
Zeckaria, Reuven, *Days and Nights in Latrun. A Prison Diary*, Hadar, Tel Aviv (1978), (Heb).

*Selected Articles*
Bauer, Yehuda, 'The Irgun was not Israel's enemy'. *Yediot Aharonot* Daily. 20 August 1971, (Heb).

Begin, Menachem, 'What is the truth about the King David', *Hayom*, 22 July 1966, (Heb).

Begin, Menachem, 'Why the Irgun fought the British' (On the Deir Yassin Affair), *The Times*, 14 April 1971.

Cavendish, Antony, 'Inside intelligence'. *Granta*, London, Summer 1988.

Charters, David, 'Special operations in counter-insurgency: The Farran Case, Palestine 1947', *Journal of the Royal United Services Institute for Defence Studies*, Vol 81, London, August 1952.

Cohen, Gabriel, 'Harold MacMichael and the Question of the Future of Palestine'. *The New Middle-East*, Jerusalem, 1975.

Cust, Archer, 'Recent impressions of the Middle East', *United Empire Journal of the Royal Empire Society*, London, November–December 1949.

Heller, Joseph, 'Avraham Stern (1907–1942): Myth and Reality', *The Jerusalem Quarterly*, Winter 1989.

Heller, Joseph, 'The Stern Gang. Fifty years after. Avraham Stern reappraised', *The Jewish Quarterly*, London, Winter 1990–91.

Meletsky, Menachem, 'The British airplanes were grounded at dawn', *In the Land of Israel*, Tel Aviv, March–April 1988, (Heb).

Milshtein, Uri, '40 Years after the Black Sabbath', *Monitin*, Tel Aviv, June 1987, (Heb).

Niv, David, 'IZL, FFI, PLO'. *Kivunim*, Tel Aviv, August 1985, (Heb).

Pa'il, Meir, 'The struggle and revolt against Britain', *Forum on the Jewish People, Zionism and Israel*, Tel Aviv, Spring 1988, (Heb).

Ray, Alan, 'Anniversary of a murder', *New Statesman and the Nation*, London, 17 July 1972.

Shamir, Yitzhak, 'The IZL and FFI expelled the British, and Thus Israel was established', *Ha'aretz*, Tel Aviv, 14 July 1988, (Heb).

Silver, Eric, 'In Jerusalem: On the uncovering of unwelcome truths; New Accounts of Deir Yassin, *The Guardian*, London, 9 April 1983.

Tavin, Eli, 'The Attack on the British Embassy in Rome', *Ha'uma*, Tel Aviv, June 1971, (Heb).

Wasserstein, Bernard, 'New light on the murder of Lord Moyne', *Zmanim*, Tel Aviv, July 1982, (Heb).

Zadka, Saul, 'Was one of the hanged sergeants a Jew?', *Ha'aretz*, Tel Aviv, 8 July 1987, (Heb).

Zipori, Mordechai, 'The Acre break-in', *Bamahane*, Tel Aviv, August 1969.

# Notes

## INTRODUCTION

1. Interview with Livni.
2. Livni, Eitan; interview and *IZL Operations and Underground (Memories)*, Edanim, Jerusalem,(1987), (Heb.), p122.
3. A year later, at the Labour conference in Bournemouth on 12 June 1946, Bevin responded unfavourably to President Truman's call to let 100,000 European Jewish refugees enter Palestine. He explained this was because of 'an additional expense of £200m pounds'.
4. Niv, David, *The Irgun Zvai Leumi*, Klauzner, Tel Aviv (1965–1976), (Heb.), Vol. 5, p61.
5. At the end of 1946 the Commander of the Armed Forces told the Anglo-American Committee that the Hagana had 80,000 members, the Irgun 5000, out of which 1000 were combat fighters, and the Stern Group 200.
6. FO 371 / 61770, E 2427, 14 March 1947.
7. FO 371 / 61900.
8. Nedava, Joseph, *Who Expelled the British from the Land of Israel*, Amuta, Tel Aviv (1988).
9. *Hansard*, 31 January 1947.
10. Ben Hecht, the pro-Irgun Jewish American writer, indicated in an article that he wrote in 1961 (Hecht, Ben, *Perfidy*, J Messner, New York (1961), p41) that Churchill told Billy Rose, the personal secretary of Bernard Baruch, his close American friend, that the Irgun prompted the British evacuation. 'They gave us so many troubles that we had to deploy 80,000 soldiers in Palestine in order to cope with the situation. This increased our financial cost . . .'.
11. *Hansard*, 25 February 1947.
12. *Hansard*, 12 August 1947.
13. Hamilton, Nigel, *Monty, the Field-Marshal 1944–1976*, Hamish Hamilton, London, (1986), p695.
14. Memorandum, 'Tour of Africa', November/December 1947, annex 206, Montgomery Papers.
15. Fearing the possibility that the Arab port of Jaffa would fall into the hands of the Jews before 15 May 1948, the date set for the final British withdrawal from Palestine, he cabled to General Crocker's Middle East headquarters that 'the

more armed members of the IZL and Stern Gang that you can kill, the better'. (Montgomery Papers, 29 April 1948).
16   Marlowe, John, *The Seat of Pilate*, Cresset Press, London (1959), pp227–8.
17   Bentwich, Norman and Helen, *Mandate Memories 1918–1948*, Schocken, New York (1965).
18   Granados, Jorge Garcia, *The Birth of Israel. The Drama as I saw It*, Alfred & Knopf, New York (1948), pp124, 273, 46.
19   Louis, Wm. Roger and Robert Stooky (eds), *The End of the Palestine Mandate*, Tauris, London (1986), p19.
20   Hansard, 25 February 1947.
21   Begin to Sneh at their meeting held on 9 October 1944. Hagana Archive, 5/25/206.

# BACKGROUND

1   They emphasised the fact that the national Palestinian leaders, notably the Mufti of Jerusalem, had sympathised with Hitler and visited him in Berlin.
2   Irgun's revolt pamphlet, August 1944, Jabotinsky Archives, Tel Aviv.
3   Bauer, Yehuda, *From Diplomacy to Resistance*, Athenaeum, New York (1973), p156.
4   Ben Gurion, David, *Memories*, Am Oved, Tel-Aviv (1974), p304.
5   Begin, Menachem, *The Revolt*, W H Allen, London (1951), p87.
6   *Op. Cit.*, Niv, Vol. 2, p146.
7   Begin Menachem, *In the Underground*, Jabotinsky Institute, Tel Aviv, (1953), p58.
8   Horewitz, Ya'acov, *The Struggle for Palestine*, New York, Norton (1950), p133.
9   Shavit, Ya'acov, *Revisionism in Zionism*, Tel Aviv, Yariv (1978), p88.
10  Elam Yigal, *Hagana – the Zionist Way to Power*, Tel Aviv, Zmora (1979), p257.
11  Milchtein Uri, *With Blood and Fire, Judea*, Tel Aviv, Ma'archot (1972), p48
12  Yelin Mor, Nathan, *LEHI*, Tel Aviv, Shikmona (1974), p308.
13  Jabotinsky, Ze'ev, *The Jewish War Front*, London, Allen & Unwin (1940), p89.
14  *Op. Cit.*, Bauer, p119.
15  *The Palmach Book*, Am Oved, Tel Aviv (1952), p435.
16  Slutsky, Yehuda (ed), *History of the Hagana*, Ma'archot, Tel Aviv (1964–72), (Heb.), p609.
17  *Freedom*, 1946. Vol. 34.
18  Dotan, Shmuel, *The Struggle for Eretz Israel*, MOD, Tel-Aviv (1978), p355.
19  Irgun's pamphlet, June 1946. Jabotinsky Archives.
20  *Op. Cit.*, Begin, *The Revolt*, 49.
21  *Freedom*, 1946, Vol. 27.
22  *Op. Cit.*, Niv, Vol.IV, p251.
23  Amitzur, Ilan, *America, Britain and Palestine*, Jerusalem, Ben Zvi (1979), p198.
24  Bell, J Bowyer, *Terror Out of Zion*, The Academy Press, Dublin (1977), p109.
25  To Lord Gort, FO 921/211 – 25 October 1944.

26 Samuel, Edwin, *A lifetime in Jerusalem*, Vallentine Mitchell, London (1970), p241.

## THE REVOLT

1. *Op. Cit.*, Niv, Vol. II, p82.
2. Interview with David Niv.
3. Interview with Ya'acov Meridor.
4. Bell, J Bowyer, *Terror Out Of Zion*, The Academy Press, Dublin (1977), p107.
5. Samuel Katz, one of the Irgun's High Command members, wrote in his memories *Days of Fire* that Meridor and his colleagues 'became increasingly restless'. He thought that it was probably with a sense of relief that Meridor agreed to hand over his post to Begin.
6. *Op. Cit.*, Shavit, p64.
7. Gervas, Frank, *The Life and Time of Menachem Begin*, Putnam's, New York (1979), p149.
8. *Op. Cit.*, Begin, *The Revolt*, p43.
9. At the time of the Irgun revolt the Rumanian Jewry was in danger of liquidation and the destruction of the Jews in Hungary had not yet take place.
10. *Op. Cit.*, Shavit, p64.
11. *Op. Cit.*, Gervas, p152.
12. *Op. Cit.*, Yelin Mor, p175.
13. Interview with Lev Ami.
14. Gani Pesach, *The IZL*, Jabotinsky Institute, Tel Aviv (1983), p44.
15. Interview with David Niv.
16. Tavin, Eli, *The Second Front*, Ron, Tel Aviv (1973), p30.
17. Hirschler, Gertrude and Lester Eckman, *Menachem Begin*, Shengold, New York (1979), p75.
18. Interview with Meridor.
19. Haber Eitan, *Menachem Begin*, Pelacorte Press, New York (1978), p107.
20. *Op. Cit.*, Gervas, p152.
21. Interview with Levi.
22. Interview with Lankin.
23. *Op. Cit.*, Begin, *The Revolt*, p45.
24. Interview with Lankin.
25. *Ibid.*
26. *Op. Cit.*, Begin, *The Revolt*, p43.
27. Interview with Lankin.
28. *Op. Cit.*, Yelin Mor, p175.
29. *Op. Cit.*, Bauer, p137. The battle of the Bulge was in December 1944.
30. Interview with Lankin.
31. Interview with Katz.
32. *Op. Cit.*, Lev Ami, p201.
33. *Op. Cit.*, Begin, p44.

34 *Op. Cit.*, Bell, p107.
35 Niv, III, p136.
36 IZL High Command protocols, meeting held on 23 July 1944, Jabotinsky Archives.
37 *Op. Cit.*, Begin, *The Revolt*, p51.
38 Bethel, Nicholas, *The Palestinian Triangle*, Deutsch, London (1979), p155.
39 Minutes from the meeting held on 15 October 1944.
40 Minutes of Sneh-Begin meeting, 9 October 1944, Hagana Archives, Tel Aviv.
41 *Ibid.*
42 Minutes of Galili's briefing to Palmach senior members on the subject of the 'dissidents', held on 23 October 1944. The text of that speech was made known only in June 1949.
43 *Op. Cit.*, Begin, *The Revolt*, p48.
44 Interview with Meridor.
45 *Ibid.*
46 Koestler Arthur, *Promise and Fulfilment*, Macmillan, London (1949), p93.
47 Interview with Niv.
48 Interview with Meridor.
49 Irgun pamphlet, 27 February 1944, Jabotinksy Archives.
50 Irgun pamphlet, 24 February 1944, Jabotinsky Archives.
51 Irgun pamphlet, 24 March 1944, Jabotinsky Archives.
52 'Davar', 28 February 1944.
53 'Confronting domestic obstacles', from the Palmach organ, vol. 23, October 1944.
54 Slotsky, III, p267.
55 *Op. Cit.*, Koestler, p84.
56 *Op. Cit.*, Mor, p79.
57 *The Front*, March 1944.
58 *Op. Cit.*, Bell, p176.
59 *Op. Cit.*, Haber, p66.
60 *Op. Cit.*, Bell, p114.
61 Pedhatzur, Elazar, *The History of the Irgun Zvai Leumi*, Shilton Betar, Tel Aviv (1959), p109.
62 Interview with Meridor.
63 Dotan, Shmuel, *The Struggle for Eretz Israel*, Ministry of Defence, Tel Aviv (1981), p244.
64 WO 208 – From Palestine to Secretary of Colonies.
65 FO 371/40126, 5052 – 27 July 1944.
66 *Op. Cit.*, Tavin, p43.
67 *Op. Cit.*, Bell, p111.
68 Interview with David Niv.
69 Minutes from meeting of the Irgun High Command with district officers, Jabotinsky Archives, Tel Aviv.
70 Minutes from the Irgun High Command meeting, Jabotinsky Archives.
71 *Ibid.*

72 *Op. Cit.*, Bethel, p174.
73 FO 371/40127, 5063.
74 *Op. Cit.*, Bell, p123.
75 Wilkinson Paul, *Political Terrorism*, Macmillan, London (1974), p91.
76 WO 208 – from O.A.G. in Palestine to the S. of Colonies.
77 WO 208.
78 IZL High Command Protocols, meeting held on 23 July 1944.
79 IZL High Command Protocols, 30 September 1944.
80 *Ibid.*
81 Minutes of a meeting held on 15 October 1944 between the IZL High Command and its district commanders.

## THE IRGUN AND THE JEWISH COMMUNITY

1 Interview with Ben-Ami.
2 He was referring to the publication in February 1939 of a document by the British Government to restrict Jewish immigration into Palestine and to confiscate weapons from Jewish organisations.
3 Golan, Shimon, *Alliance in Struggle*, Yad Tavenkin, Tel-Aviv (1988) p20.
4 From Sneh's report on his meeting with Begin, written the day after their conversation on 9 October 1944. Hagana Central Archives, Tel Aviv.
5 Begin spoke with great enthusiasm about the role of the Americans, so much so that Sneh suspected him of having some connections with them.
6 Report from the same meeting.
7 Report on the meeting between Jewish Agency leaders and Irgun commanders on 30 October 1944, Jabotinsky Archives.
8 *Ibid.*
9 'The Internal Danger is Increasing', a document written by Begin after the Hagana–Irgun meeting on 31 October 1944, Jabotinsky Archives.
10 *Op. Cit.*, Slutzky, v.III, p536.
11 United Labour Archives, F 13,2;5 November 1944.
12 E Lankin, S Levy, Y Meridor and many others were deported to detention camps in Eastern Africa.
13 One of them was Y Segal who died during interrogation.
14 WO 45376 – a letter from Weizmann to the War Cabinet, 8 December 1944.
15 CID report on Weizmann's visit to Palestine, 12 December 1944.
16 One of those who were abducted without being handed over to the CID was E Tavin, head of the Irgun's intelligence unit. He was kept by Hagana members in a Kibbutz under severe conditions and was not released for six months until the end of the *saison*.
17 Interview with Paglin by Nathan Cohen, Verbal Documentation Archives, Jerusalem. Paglin himself was appointed by Prime Minister Menachem Begin as his adviser for terrorism in 1977. He died in a road accident in 1982.
18 Interview with Meridor.

19  *Op. Cit.*, Yelin Mor, pp237, 243.
20  Eldad, Yisrael, *The Jewish Revolution*, Shengold, New York (1971), p160, and interview with author.
21  Interview with Meridor.
22  *Op. Cit.*, Lev, pp191, 200.
23  Interview with Lankin.
24  *Hansard*, 13 November 1945.
25  *Ibid.*
26  Jewish Agency Protocols, 18 November 1945, Zionist Archive, Jerusalem.
27  Irgun's leaflet No. 147, 18 November 1945, Jabotinsky Archives.
28  Begin, In the Underground collection II, Jabotinsky Archives, pp17–18.
29  F 22/29, 39, 1 December 1945, Berl House Archives, Tzofit, Israel.
30  In Rishpon and Sidna Ali.
31  *Op. Cit.*, Niv, v.IV, pp179–180.
32  Yelin Mor, in his memoirs, gave a detailed account of his preliminary conversation with Begin.
33  *Op. Cit.*, Begin, *The Revolt*, p260.
34  On 7 August, for example, the insurgents robbed a bank in Tel Aviv. A week after that they 'confiscated' explosives from a Jewish company and on 8 October the Stern Group stole money at the gold stock exchange in Jaffa.
35  F 5/3/5, 15 October 1945, the Kibbutz Archive.
36  *Op. Cit.*, Begin, *The Revolt*, p264.
37  WO 261/562.
38  *Ibid.*
39  WO 169/23022 - Intelligence Newsletter No. 17.
40  WO 261/562.
41  Of the kidnapped officers, one escaped, two were released for fear of discovery and three were freed after the mitigation was proclaimed.
42  WO 261/562.
43  *Op. Cit.*, Mor, p357.
44  *Op. Cit.*, Begin, p311.
45  Irgun broadcasting No. 36 & 37, Jabotinsky Archives.
46  Begin's documents, *In the Underground* collection, II, pp236–8.
47  Irgun broacasting No. 43

# TACTICS, METHODS & OPERATIONS

1  A Paglin, the operations commander in chief, claimed that in 1946 the Irgun could have used more than 1000 people for military operations and since 1946, almost 4000 fighters. But that assessment is exaggerated not least because there was an acute shortage of weapons that most of the members could have used (From an interview he gave on 27 November 1970 to the Documentation Institute in Jerusalem).
2  Charters David, Special Operations in Counter-Insurgency: The Farran Case,

Palestine 1947 (Journal of RUSI, Vol LXXXI, August 1952).
3   Interview with Livni.
4   Interview with Lankin.
5   Which included not only English and French, but also Russian, Romanian, Bulgarian, Hungarian and even Greek.
6   Apart from two informers who were employed by the British and whose activities led to the disruption of some operations and the arrest of a few members.
7   The robberies of the IZL and FFI encouraged ordinary criminals to attack banks 'on behalf' of the Underground.
8   Begin tried in vain to convince Yitzhak Shamir of the Stern Group that its members should carry firearms with them day and night. He told him in April 1944 that pistols did not stand a chance against the superiority of the British army. Shamir explained that after the killing of the unarmed Stern, his followers had decided not to fall into the hands of their would-be captors alive.
9   Cunningham Papers, B 1.F 3 MEC, 21 November 1946.
10  *Op. Cit.*, Wilson, p79.
11  WO 261 / 644.
12  WO 261 / 647.
13  The Acre fortress was surrounded on three sides by sea and its fourth side presented the most formidable defence system in the Middle East; 'a castle built by the Crusaders with the strength of the Great Pyramid, defended by a ditch ...'. Napoleon's forces, after aborted bloody assaults, were driven out or captured and instantly beheaded. Eventually he was reluctantly forced to abandon the siege and return to Egypt. (V Cronin, *Napoleon*, pp196–8).
14  After the hanging Begin ordered the setting up of a field court martial for any of the troops who might fall into the Irgun's hands.
15  Mordechai Zipori, one of the Irgun commanders, said that 90 per cent of the Jewish Underground prisoners were held there.
16  *Op. Cit.*, Begin, *The Revolt*, p275.
17  WO 261/662, based on secret report by the airborne divisions, 5 May 1947.
18  *Ibid.*
19  Interview with Niv.
20  WO 261/662.
21  Livni said that 30 Irgunists and 11 Sternists were selected by him after a prolonged argument.
22  Minutes of security conference, 9 May 1947.4/2/31/, Cunningham Papers.
23  *Op. Cit.*, Begin, *The Revolt*, pp278, 280.
24  Irgun's broadcasting ('The Voice of Fighting Zion'), 7 May 1947.
25  *Palestine Post*, 6 May 1947.
26  Irgun's broadcasting, 7 May 1947.
27  The plight of Wise, the third defendant, was highlighted by his young age (18) and the fact that he was a holocaust survivor from Hungary where he lost his family.
28  Irgun's broadcasting, 16 June 1947.
29  *Op. Cit.*, Slutzky, v. III-B, p925.

30 Meinertzhagen R M, p143.
31 Cunningham to Colonial Office, 15 November 1947, Cunningham Papers, 75156/151a CO 733/477.
32 *The Times*, 1 August 1947.
33 Alan Ray, who headed the intelligence unit, to which the two soldiers belonged, wrote an article 25 years after the double execution in which he disclosed that he passed the grievances of his subordinates to the highest possible level. The response to the plea to release the three Irgunists was negative. *The New Statesman*, 17 July 1972.
34 *Op. Cit.*, Begin, *The Revolt*, p290.
35 *United Empire Journal*, November/December 1949.
36 David Dahari was the last Irgun member who supplied the sergeants with food and attended the subsequent hanging. He was asked 40 years later, after exposing himself for the first time, if he was sorry for those who were hanged. His reply was: 'There was no choice; the credibility of the Irgun was at stake'. (*Ma'ariv Daily*, 8 October 1987).
37 CZA S 25/5601.
38 Irgun broadcast, 6 August 1947.
39 *Op. Cit.*, Lev, p374. But in an interview with the author in January 1992 he acknowledged that it was a grave mistake on the Irgun's part which wanted to camouflage the way the soldiers were killed before being put on the trees.
40 Eshel, Arie, *The Cheated Hangman*, Zmora, Tel Aviv (1991), pp184, 190.
41 Irgun broadcast, 30 July 1947.
42 Even the former British prime minister, a strong supporter of Israel, failed to establish the facts about the double hanging. In his book he stated wrongly about the bodies that 'when they were cut down, the bombs went off, killing a Captain of the Royal Engineers'. (Wilson, Harold, *The Chariot of Israel*, Weidenfeld, London (1969).
43 Macatee to Marshal, July 1947. BB Pal/5-2247. BZ181.
44 An Irgun message, 28 July 1947, Jabotinsky Archives.
45 Irgun broadcast, 30 July 1947.
46 Cunningham to Creech-Jones, 8 October 1947, Cunningham Papers B2, f 2 MEC.
47 Marshall to Robert Lovet (his under-secretary), 25 November 1947, State Department Papers, 867n.01/11-2547, B 6761.
48 *Op. Cit.*, Louis, p464.
49 Cunningham Papers, 11/2 Telegram, MILPAL to MIDEAST, 1 August 1947.
50 Alan Ray blamed not only Begin for the hanging, but also Foreign Secretary Bevin. In his opinion Begin wanted to escalate the struggle against the British and to win more sympathy with the Jewish youth. But he added that Bevin in effect sacrificed the two sergeants, because he wanted to create world revulsion not only at the Irgun, but also at Jewish ambitions for statehood. For that reason he refused to spare the life of the three Irgunists, paving the way for the IZL to retaliate in kind.
51 Creech-Jones to Elizabeth Monroe, 23 October 1961, Creech-Jones papers.

## THE KING DAVID AFFAIR

1. WO 261/562 – HQ British Troops in Palestine and Trans-Jordan – G Branch.
2. Irgun's announcement, Jabotinsky Archives, 24 July 1946.
3. Begin, *The Revolt*, p221.
4. The statement, related to Chief Secretary Shaw, became one of the most famous declarations in the country and it always met with British denial.
5. The agent's name was Yanai.
6. Interview with Horne. See also *A Job Well Done*, p309.
7. WO 261/567, Report of D Branch of British Troops in Palestine, p4.
8. WO 261/567-fortnightly intelligence report, 21 July–4 August 1946.
9. *Op. Cit.*, Slutsky, III, p898.
10. WO 261/567-Intelligence Newsletter.
11. *Op. Cit.*, Cohen, p91.
12. Cab. 128/6, 224, 23 July 1946.
13. *Ibid.*
14. Cab. 128/6, 232, 30 July 1946.
15. *Ibid.*
16. Cohen, *Retreat from the Mandate*, New York, Holms & Meier (1978), p85.
17. WO 216/194. Montgomery in a letter to Dempsey, 24 June 1946.
18. Cab. 128/6, X/105646.
19. Cab. 128/6, 253.
20. *Ibid*, p154.
21. Telegram 4689, Inverchapel to FO 22 July 1946, F O 371/52543.
22. Telegram 7262, FO to Inverchapel, 23 July 1946, F O 371/52543.
23. Truman's statement, 23 July 1946, Foreign Relations of the United States, Diplomatic Papers.
24. Ganin, Zvi, *Truman, American Jewry, and Israel 1945–1948*, Holmes & Meier, New York (1979), p123.
25. *Op. Cit.*, E Horne, p305.
26. Cab. 128/6, X/105616.
27. WO 261/646, 6th Airborne Division.
28. WO 261/656.
29. WO 261/562, 'G' Branch Report.
30. *Op. Cit.*, Horne, p306.
31. *Ibid.*
32. *Op. Cit.*, Katz, p98.
33. WO 261/562 – 028995.
34. *Op. Cit.*, Begin, p227.
35. *Ibid.*
36. *Op. Cit.*, Katz, p98.
37. WO 261/646.
38. WO 261/646, 29170.
39. *Op. Cit.*, Begin, p228.
40. *Ibid*, p129.

41  Interview with Katz.
42  WO 261/562 – 028995.
43  *Op. Cit.*, Horne, p306.
44  Except one warning shot at a curfew breaker, which killed a British soldier on the first day of the operation.

## PROPAGANDA AND PSYCHOLOGICAL WARFARE

1  Interview with Tavin.
2  Irgun document, Jobotinsky archives.
3  Ibid.
4  Burton Antony, *Urban Terrorism*, Leo Cooper, London (1975), p160.
5  *Op. Cit.*, Tavin, p16.
6  Minutes of the meeting, 15 October 1944, Irgun document, Jabotinsky Archives.
7  The Governer, Ronald Storrs, was regarded by the Jewish leadership as a 'friend of Zionism'.
8  Minutes of the meeting, 15 October 1944, Irgun's document, Jabotinsky Archives.
9  Minutes of meeting, November 1944, Jabotinsky Archives.
10  Interview with Katz.
11  Kitson Frank, *Gangs and Countergangs* Barrie & Rockliff, London (1978), p55.
12  Interview with Katz.
13  Interview with Kahan.
14  Interview with Gold.
15  'To the British Soldier', Irgun pamphlet, Jabotinsky Archives.
16  *Ibid.*
17  Irgun document, 14 November 1945, Jabotinsky Archives.
18  *Op. Cit.*, Bauer, p167.
19  Irgun document, 29 June 1946, Jabotinsky archives.
20  'Not Terrorism', Irgun document, Jabotinsky Archives.
21  'From the Soldiers of the Underground to the Soldiers of the Occupation Army' – Irgun document.
22  'The Right and the Duty to Rise against Oppression', a declaration by A Moscovitch (private collection).
23  'Why Did I Join the Battle', by I Ganzweich (private collection).
24  Irgun document, Jabotinsky Archives.
25  Declaration by Binder, Irgun document, Jabotinsky Archives.
26  *Ibid.*
27  Barker made his statement on 22 July 1946 and later, in the face of international outcry, he was forced to leave Palestine.
28  Declaration by Luster, Irgun document, Jabotinsky Archives.
29  How the British treat prisoners of war', Irgun document, Jabotinsky Archives.

30 Statement by Feinstein, Irgun document, Jabotinsky Archives.
31 'The lesson of Ireland', document, Jabotinsky Archives.
32 In total, Gruner was 105 days under sentence of death until his execution.
33 'Gruner in court', Irgun document, Jabotinsky archives.
34 Wilson R D, *Cordon and Search*, Gale & Polden, Aldershot (1949), p120.
35 Irgun broadcast, 2 February 1949, Jabotinsky Archives.
36 In recent years relatives of hanged insurgents accused the Irgun of abandoning their loved ones by not ordering them to sign a plea for clemency in order to save their lives.
37 'We shall give the Labour Government a chance to keep its words'. Irgun document, Jabotinsky Archives.
38 The Committee member with whom Begin met was Dr Garcia Granados of Guatemala.
39 Begin claimed that the Irgun's intelligence unit got hold of the statement and publicised it.
40 The Irgun angrily rejected the Hagana's claims and its Command Member Samuel Katz wrote in his memoirs that the attack in Acre was described by British military experts as a 'masterpiece'.
41 They included R Brisco, a former Irish MP; Colonel Paterson, a former commander of the 'Jewish Legions' and some Revisionist leaders from Palestine.
42 Interview with Bergson.
43 *Ibid.*
44 *Op. Cit.*, Niv vol. IV, p130.
45 *Op. Cit.*, Ilan, p62.
46 One of them was 'How well did you sleep last night when a whole people is being led to its death'?
47 *New York Post*, 22 November 1943.
48 Interview with Bergson.
49 Interview with Niv.
50 Correspondence with Ben Ami. See also Niv Vol.III, 112.
51 The American Revisionists, as a result of these divisions, broke away from the Committee, refused to co-operate with its members and established a body of their own, which eventually faded away.
52 Truman to Bergson, 6 May 1943, SVP+1. See also Cohen Michael, *Truman and Israel*, University of California Press, Los Angeles (1990), p41.
53 Interview with Bergson.
54 Among them was 'Hadassa', the famous women's organisation which expressed its misgivings in its organ 'headlines'.
55 Ben Ami, Yitzhak, *Years of Wrath. Days of Glory*, Shengold, New York (1983), p296.
56 Document of the American League for Free Palestine, Wiener Library.
57 The group was headed by Senator G Gilet and consisted of judges and academics.
58 One of them, in a speech during the Labour Party conference on 12 June 1946, referred to the American wish to see 100,000 European Jews emigrating to

Palestine because 'they did not want them in New York'.
59   Whose new play 'A Jewish Fairy Tale' was staged in New York and was partially devoted to the assassination of Lord Moyne.
60   Irgun leaflet, Jabotinsky Archives.
61   Books and films written by Ben Hecht were boycotted in Britain until 1953.
62   Interview with Katz.
63   Interview with Meridor.
64   *Op. Cit.*, Ben Ami, p46.
65   *Op. Cit.*, Katz, p117.
66   Interview with Lankin.
67   *Op. Cit.*, Katz, p118.
68   F O 371/52 537.
69   Interview with Katz.
70   Correspondence with Ben Ami.
71   *Ibid.*
72   *Op. Cit.*, Katz, p117.
73   Interview with Bergson.
74   The agreement is documented in the Jabotinsky Archive.
75   *Ibid.*
76   Interview with Lankin
77   F O 371/31380 E 6663.
78   *Op. Cit.*, Ilan, p114.

## THE BRITISH VIEW

1   WO 208/1705.
2   WO PIC, Paper No. 35.
3   *Ibid.*
4   WO 208/1705.
5   C P Quilliam, Brigadier, Head of Office – WO 208.
6   Biltmore Plan – called after Biltmore Hotel in New York where on 3 May 1942 Weizmann and Ben Gurion initiated a conference at the centre of which was the idea of creating a Jewish 'Commonwealth' in Palestine. This would have stopped short of complete independence, but it would have given the Jewish Agency the authority to control immigration and build settlements in the country. The programme was adopted by the Zionist executive in Palestine, but failed to convince other sections within the Yishuv.
7   WO 208, Brigadier Quilliam.
8   FO 371/40126,5052 – Harold Macmichael to the Secretary of State for the Colonies, 28 July 1944.
9   Horne, Edward, *A Job Well Done*, Palestine Police, Essex (1982), p283.
10  Among them was Begin himself, disguised as a rabbi.
11  WO 208, DDMI, 14 August 1944.
12  *Ibid.*

13 Moyne was in office at the time of the sinking of *Struma*, a small steamship with 769 Rumanian refugees on board which the British did not allow into Palestine. On 23 February 1942 the ship sank in the Black Sea, leaving only one survivor. Not only the IZL and the FFI, even moderate elements within the Yishuv leadership, regarded him as an anti-Zionist politician who refused to become involved in the effort to save Hungarian Jewry from the Nazis. He was alleged by them to have said: 'What would I do with a million Jews?'. However these accusations were not substantiated and his murder, apart from ending Churchill's sympathy for the Jews, helped to shelve some favourable decisions towards the Zionist aspirations which were to be taken by the British Cabinet.
14 *Hansard*, Vol. 404, Col. 2242, 17 November 1944.
15 *Op. Cit.*, Begin, p145.
16 WO 208/1706, Lord Gort, 21 November 1944.
17 *Ibid.*
18 WO 208/1706, Killearn to FO, 18 November 1946.
19 CO 733/457, 751,5/151G1.
20 WO 208/1706, WO to C-in-C M E, 18 November 1944.
21 *Ibid.*
22 WO 169/23021, 1 April 1946, Intelligence Newsletter No. 5.
23 *Ibid.*
24 Cab. C M 60(46).251.
25 WO 261/562, July–September 1946.
26 WO 261/656.
27 WO 261/656, 6th Airborne Intelligence Report.
28 WO 261/562.
29 WO 261/646, VCA 29170, Intelligence Summary No. 8, 24 June 1946.
30 WO 261/562.
31 *Ibid.*
32 WO 261/656, 6th Airborne Division Intelligence Report

## BRITISH MEASURES AGAINST TERRORISM

1 Hofman, Bruce, *The Failure of British Military Strategy within Palestine 1939–1947*, Bar-Ilan University Press, Ramat-Gan (1983).
2 WO 208/1706. 8 November 1944.
3 FO 141/1001.
4 PREM (Prime Minister's Office's Papers) 4/52/5. Gort to Secretary of Colonies. 21 November 1944.
5 WO 208/1706. 12 November 1944.
6 Cab. 127/270 , 17 November 1944.
7 CO 733/466/75988/6, 15 November 1944.
8 Cab. 65/48, 24 November 1944.
9 FO 921/154, 27 November 1944.
10 WO 208/1706.

11  *Ibid.*
12  WO 216/76.
13  WO 216/194, 22 November 1945.
14  *Ibid.*
15  From an undated document, written by Begin, found at the Jabotinsky Archives.
16  'Jewish Detainees in Eritrea'. Record of a meeting, held on 20 December 1945 in the presence of the High Commissioner, the Command in Chief, the Chief Secretary and the General Officer Commanding. Cunningham Papers.
17  Interview with Meridor.
18  Later, in mid-1948, the British had difficulties as to the timing and the means of transferring the detainees back to Palestine which was about to become Israel. The authorities were looking for the best way to return them without upsetting the Arabs. MOD documents, 10 June 1948, minutes from the Chief of Staff Committee (COSC), 28 June 1948.
19  Interview with Eldad.
20  CO 733/466.
21  Defence Committee, Cunningham Papers, V/4.
22  Cab. 128/5, 20 June 1946.
23  WO 216/194.
24  Cunningham Papers, Telegram 3117.
25  Cab. 128/6.
26  WO 32/10260, 33rd meeting of the Defence Committee.
27  *Ibid.*
28  Cunningham Papers, I/3, 21 November 1946.
29  WO 216/194, in a telegram to the WO on 21 November 1946.
30  Cunningham Papers, I/3.
31  *Ibid.*
32  Cunningham I/3, 29 November 1946.
33  *Ibid.*, IV/2, 29 November 1946.
34  WO 32/10260, 31 December 1946.
35  Cab. 128/9, p39 (47).
36  WO 216/194.
37  FO 371/61762 E, 20 January 1947.
38  WO 216/660.
39  WO 216/666 – Memorandum on measures necessary to maintain law and order in Palestine, 23 March 1947.
40  *Ibid.*
41  The youth Alexander Rubovitch, was murdered at the hands of a special unit which was carrying out a 'shoot to kill' policy. The unit was headed by Rom Faran who fled the country after the incident. The FFI, to which the youngster belonged, sent a letter bomb to Faran's residence in England which instantly killed his brother on opening it.
42  His name was Shlomo Ben-Yossef. He fired shots at an Arab bus in the Galil district in retaliation for an Arab attack on Jewish civilians. It was an individual

action and was not approved by his commanders.
43 WO 216/666 – Telegram from C-in-C ME to WO.
44 *Op. Cit.*, Begin, *The Revolt*, p318.
45 *Herut,* December 1946.
46 *Hansard,* 29 December 1947.
47 *Ha'aretz,*17 April 1947.
48 *Op. Cit.*, Begin, *The Revolt*, p356.
49 Cunningham Papers, IV.
50 Irgun Broadcasting, Jabotinsky Archives.
51 *Op. Cit.*, Wilson, p144.
52 *Op. Cit.*, Niv vol.V, p102.
53 'Imposition of Martial Law'. Draft Report by the Chief of Staff. JPSP Vol I. Reported by the Joint Planning Staff. 25 March 1947.
54 Cunningham to Creech-Jones, 2 February 1947. C.O. 537 / 2299.
55 Cab. 128 / 9.
56 Cunningham Papers – Meeting Air Officer Commanding, Chief Secretary, District Commissioner in Jerusalem, Chief of Staff HQ Palestine and Inspector General of Police.
57 WP 201/660 – Intelligence Summary No 33, 6th Airborne Division.
58 *Ibid.*
59 JA (Jewish Association) Executive minutes, Vol. 44/2, CZA.
60 WO 216 / 660 – Report 34, up to 14 March 1947.
61 *Op. Cit.*, Bell, 198.
62 Chiefs of Staff Committee (COSC) meeting DEFE 4/1, COSC Vol. 3/16.
63 High Commissioner Private Papers. F/2/24.
64 *Ibid.*
65 WO 216/666.
66 Ben Gurion to Attlee, 15 March 1947, BGA.
67 *Ibid.*
68 WO 216/666.
69 COSC . JPSP (Joint Planning Staff Papers), Vol. I – 562.
70 Cab. 128/9.
71 *The Times*, 18 March 1947.
72 COSC Vol. 1/562, 20 March 1947.
73 Cunningham Papers, B2, F2, MEC.
74 'Why they lifted Martial Law' – Irgun Communiqué, March 1947. Jabotinsky Archives.

## MORALE & PUBLIC OPINION IN BRITAIN

1 WO 261/646, Quarterly Report, July–October 1946.
2 WO 261/647.
3 COSC Vol. 1/4, Min 2 – January 1947.
4 DEFE 4

5   In 1972 Charteris became a private secretary to the Queen.
6   From a lecture entitled 'A Year as an Intelligence Officer in Palestine', Zionist Archives, S 25/1997.
7   *Ibid.*
8   Lewis Roger, *The British Empire in the Middle East* Clarendon Press, Oxford (1984), p446.
9   WO 261/644, Intelligence Report, 31 December 1946.
10  WO 261/647.
11  WO 261/526, 'Attitude in England to the Palestine Problem'.
12  *Ibid.*
13  *Hansard*, debate on Palestine, 1 July 1946.
14  *Ibid.*
15  *Hansard*, 31 July 1946.
16  *Hansard*, 1 August 1946.
17  Another MP (Wilkes of Newcastle upon Tyne Central) said during that debate that 'the Irgun represented a Right Wing terrorist and Right wing Party . . .' and had to withdraw the phrase 'right wing' following protests in the Commons.
18  Parliament Hansard.
19  *Ibid.*
20  Minutes from the meeting of High Command, held on 15 October 1944.
21  *Western Evening Herald* (Plymouth), 4 July 1946. He also wrote that Jewish parents were forced to give up their teenage sons for the sake of the campaign of violence. Such an allegation was groundless.
22  *The Liverpool Post*, 12 October 1944.
23  *The Observer*, 12 November 1944.
24  *The Times*, 1 August 1947.
25  *The Scotsman*, 12 October 1944.
26  *The Yorkshire Post*, 31 December 1945.
27  *Dorset Daily Echo* and *Bournemouth Echo*, 2 July 1946.
28  *The Observer*, 12 November 1944.
29  *The Times*, 24 July 1945.
30  *The Times*, 19 February 1947.
31  *Sunday Express*, 2 March 1947.
32  *Dundee Courier*, 12 October 1944.
33  *The Times*, 18 March 1947.
34  *The Spectator*, 3 May 1946.
35  *The Spectator*, 31 August 1945
36  *The Evening Standard*, 23 November 1946.
37  *The Economist*, 18 October 1947.
38  *The Birmingham Post*, 12 October 1946.
39  *Sunday Express*, 2 February 1947.
40  *Daily Mail*, 6 November 1947.
41  *The Spectator*, 3 May 1946.
42  *The New Statesman*, 27 July 1946.
43  *The New Statesman*, 20 September 1947.

44 *The Sunday Express*, 2 March 1947.
45 *Manchester Guardian*, 10 November 1944.
46 *The Manchester Guardian*, 25 July, 1946.
47 *The New York Post*, 23 July 1946.
48 *The Daily Mail*, 1st August 1947.

# Index

Acre Fort 71, 75–77, 81, 110, 146, 156, 158
Africa 1, 16, 23, 37, 48, 121, 133, 146, 147
*Agatha*, Operation 139–41, 149, 151, 153, 173
Algeria 26
Allies 16, 29, 32
Alphang, Dean 116, 121
*Am Lochem* (Fighting Nation) 17, 37
America 3, 5, 7, 8, 11, 19, 25, 32, 48, 49, 56, 83, 86, 90, 91, 93, 95, 113
  Irgun's activities in 113–27, 138
American Labour Movement 116
American League for Free Palestine 122
Andres, General 37
Anglo–American Committee 61, 96, 174
Arab Revolt 85, 100, 150, 162, 172
Arabs 3, 5, 6, 7, 8, 10, 11, 15, 16, 20, 23–25
  Irgun's attitude to 34–36, 39, 48, 49, 56, 62, 68, 70, 77, 87, 94, 96, 99, 100, 111, 131, 132, 136, 144, 156, 170, 176
Arafat, Yasser 185
Arch-Cust, Colonel 81
Atlit 59, 60
Attlee, Clement 4, 6, 7, 56, 90, 93, 165, 174
Axis Powers 22

Baldwin, Congressman 118
Balfour Declaration 18, 21, 56
Barazani, Moshe 110, 157
Barclays Bank 70
Barker, Lieutenant General, Sir Evelyn 109, 112, 112, 140, 141, 149, 152, 166, 176
Basel 63
Bastille 77
BBC 175
Beamish, Major 176
Begin, Menachem 1, 4, 5, 11, 18, 22, 23–25, 26, 27
  revolt proclamation 28–36
  personal background 36, 37
  military campaign 37–46
  relations with Hagana 48–51
  Acre break-in 75–78
  the hanging of the two sergeants 78–85
  as propaganda master 110
  rift with Bergson group 123–27
Begson, Peter 25, 114, 117, 118, 120, 122, 123, 126, 127
Ben-Ami, Y 114, 117, 124
Ben-Eliezer A 114
Ben Gurion, David 4, 17, 392, 47, 49–51, 53, 58, 62, 124, 135, 136, 165
*Ben Hecht*, the boat 122
Berkly, Senator 118
Berlin 23, 29, 39

Bet Dagan 43, 133
Betar 36, 82
Bevin, Ernest 2, 9, 11, 56, 57, 62, 84, 90, 108, 112, 121, 137, 182
*Bevingrad* 7, 72, 149, 159, 171
Biltmore Programme 132
Binden M 109
*The Birmingham Post* 181
Black Saturday 8
Blum, G 118
Bournemouth 62, 179
Brandeis, Louis 121
Brando, Marlon 116
Brighton 84
Britain 5–9, 17, 29–31, 32, 33, 83, 85, 86
  attitude towards Palestine question 6–12
  public opinion 102, 169–71, 178–83
  collaboration with Hagana 113–37
  confrontation with Hagana 137–41
  counter-terrorism 142–49, 156–61
  martial law 161–168
  debates in Parliament 172–78
British Army 16, 19, 21, 25, 57, 103, 182
British Empire 75, 84, 111
Bromfield, Louis 121
Bucharest 39
Budapest 39
Bulge 18
Bulgarian 104
Burma 6

Cairo 131, 134–36, 142, 156, 173, 182
*Cantonment*, Operation 154
Capitol Hill 115, 116
Caranegie Hall 116
Casey, Lord 26
Catling, Colonel 44
*Cautious*, Operation 154
Charteris, Martin 170
Chief of the Imperial Staff 3, 8
Choresh S 114
Christians 26, 116, 117, 127
Citrus House 74

Clayton, Brigadier I 143
Cohen, Dov 76
Committee for Palestine Army 115
Committee for Saving the Jewish People 25, 118, 123
Commonwealth 40
Congress 115–18, 127
Connolly, Senator 118
Conservative Party 7
Churchill, Winston 6, 81, 111, 121, 134, 135, 143, 157, 160, 176
CID 4, 39, 40, 49, 54, 66, 97, 106, 132, 162
Committee X 89
Creech-Jones, Arthur 7, 9, 69, 85, 153, 154, 156, 162, 177, 178
Crocker, General, Sir John 82, 84
Crossman, Richard, MP 172, 177, 182
Cunningham, Lieutenant General, Sir Alan 4, 8, 77, 79, 80, 82, 84, 92, 136, 149, 152–55, 158, 160, 164, 166
Cyprus 63, 122

*The Daily Mail* 182
*The Daily Telegraph* 80
Dalton, Hugh 8
Danish 116
*Davar* 79
Dorset 179
Downing Street 83
Dempsey, Lieutenant General Sir Miels 149, 151
Dunkirk 8

Easter uprising 23
*The Economist*, 45, 180, 181
Egypt 23, 29, 34, 70, 75, 144, 159
Eldad, Yisrael 55
*Elephant*, Operation 160
Elkahi, Mordechai 110
Emergency Committee to Save the Jewish People in Europe 115
Eritrea 133, 146
Europe 51, 69, 115, 127, 132
Evans, S N, MP 176

*The Evening Standard* 180
*Exodus* 10, 180, 183

Feinstein, Meir 110, 157
FFI – see Stern Group
Foot, Michael, MP 173
France, (also French) 26, 62, 79, 104, 180
Frankfurter, Felix 119

Garibaldi 22, 30
General Zionists Party 52
Germany, Germans 4, 10, 16, 29, 32, 47, 50, 71, 105, 106, 109, 113, 116, 118, 120, 132, 178, 183
Galili, Yisrael 16, 35, 36, 58, 62, 63
Ganzweich, I 109
Gaza 97, 184
Gillet, Senator 118
Glasgow 84
GOC 90, 91
*Golda*, Operation 82
Gold, Moshe 105
Goldman, Nahum 117, 126
Goldsmith House 5, 7, 10, 72, 78, 160, 182
Golomb, Eliyahu 50
Gort, Field Marshal Lord 134–36, 142–44
Granados, Garcia 9
Greek 104
Gruner, Dov 75, 110, 157

Hagana 2, 11, 15, 19, 22, 24, 25, 26
  rift with Irgun 35, 36, 39, 44, 48, 50
  and confronting Irgun 52–55
  and co-operating with Irgun 57–62, 67, 68, 70, 74, 79, 81,
  and the King–David bombing 87–99, 103, 108, 113, 123, 133, 137–40, 145, 146, 150, 153, 164, 166, 172, 173, 175, 178, 184
Hadari, O 114
*Hahazit* (The Front) 40
Haifa 35, 43, 61, 63, 68, 70, 74, 76, 88, 119, 133, 137, 148, 159, 163

*Hak* (Combat Unit) 42
Halifax 70
Hall, G 118, 121, 176, 177
Hamburg 180
Hart, William Allen 119
Haviv, Abshalom 79, 110
Hebrew Committee for National Liberation (HCNL) 120, 121–24
Hebrew Provisional Government 108
Hebrew Resistance Movement 2, 11, 56–64, 147–49, 178, 185
Hecht, Ben 115, 116, 122
*Herut* (Freedom) 5, 105, 157
*Hippopotamus*, Operation 160
Histadrut 20, 52, 140
Hitler 18, 23, 30, 34, 38, 48, 50, 107, 181, 183
Hollywood 116
Holocaust 3–5, 8, 29, 32, 48, 110, 115, 119, 120
Horne, Edward 87, 99
House of Commons 6, 7, 11, 80, 158
  debate on terrorism in Palestine 172–178
House of Representatives 119
Hungarian Jewry 26, 117, 120

India 6, 56, 160
Iraq 17, 23, 29, 34
Ireland, Irish 22, 23, 110
Irgun
  debate about contribution to British withdrawal 1–12
  historical background 15–18
  Jewish Community 19–21, 47–64
  relations with Revisionists 21–23
  attitude towards Arabs 23–25, 34–36
  despair 28–30
  internal dispute 30–34
  first military activities 37–46
  military character 70–72
  terrorist operations 68–70, 72–75
  Acre break–in 75–78
  hanging of sergeants 78–85
  King David bombing 86–89
  activities in USA 113–127

# INDEX

martial law 95–99, 161–168
propaganda machine 100 – 127
*Irgunpress* 104
Israel, State of 5–12
Italy, Italians 22, 104

Jabotinsky, Vladimir (ze'ev) 16, 21, 31, 36, 37, 50, 75, 114
Jaffa 23, 38, 68, 70, 73, 96, 157
Japanese 114
Janner, Barnett, MP 177
Jericho 184
Jerusalem 1, 5, 6, 10, 23, 24, 41–45, 62, 68, 69, 73, 74, 83, 97, 99, 101, 111, 122, 131, 139, 147, 152, 156, 159–61, 163, 165, 173, 175, 176
King David 86–95
Jewish Immigration 10, 33, 63,103
Jewish National Fund 92
Jewish refugees 5, 11, 25, 29
Jewish Agency 3, 11, 17, 20, 22, 25, 31, 34, 39, 43–45, 47, 49, 50, 51, 53, 55, 57, 60, 62, 64, 117, 131–35, 138, 139, 145, 150, 153, 163, 165, 166, 178
Jewish Army 23, 31, 114, 120, 131
Jewish Brigade 16, 29, 53,103
Jews 6–8, 10, 20, 26
Jewish State 23, 44
Jewish youth 25, 50
Jordan 21, 122, 184
Kahan, Marek 105
Karta 43
Katz, Samuel 34, 97, 104, 123–25
Kibbutzim 22, 59
Kfar Sirkin 70
King David Hotel 5, 7, 63, 71, 72, 86–99, 109, 111, 112, 122
Kirpitchinkoff D 109
Kitson, Frank 104
Koestler, Arthur 37, 39
Kromiers, Z 98

Labour government 59
Labour Party 5, 7, 43, 56, 57, 112, 184

Lankin, Eliyahu 33, 42, 44, 50, 51, 55, 114, 123, 126
'La Regence' 86
Laski, Harold 121
Latrun 97, 146
League for a Free Nation (ALFP) 25
Lev-Ami (Levy), Shlomo 31, 32, 42
Likud Party ix, 5, 184
Lindsay, Kenneth 175
Lipson, D L, MP 173
Liverpool 84
*The Liverpool Post* 179
Livni, Eitan 1,42,65
*Lobster*, Operation 154
London 1–3, 5, 6, 9, 21, 23, 53, 58, 60, 62, 71, 72, 79, 80, 84, 86, 98, 112, 116, 121, 131, 132, 144, 152, 156, 161
London Conference 8, 10
*Lonesome*, Operation 160
Luster C 109, 110
Lydda 70

Manchester 84

*The Manchester Guardian* 80, 183
Martial Law 4, 7
*Maquis* 22,
Martin, Clifford 79, 82
Mazzini 22
Meir (Meirson), Golda 79, 82, 84, 163
Meridor, Ya'acov 28, 32, 36–38, 40, 123, 147
Middle East 7, 16, 49, 69, 113, 119, 135, 144, 172
Macatee, Robert 83
MacCormack, Doc 121
MacMillan, Lieutenant General, Sir Gordon 166
*Mackerel*, Operation 154
MacMichael, John 17, 41, 42, 74, 84, 133
Marshall, George 84
Mandate, British 6–9, 11, 15, 32, 45, 48, 63, 85, 88, 103, 132, 137, 142, 156, 161

Merlin, Samual 114
Montgomery, Field Marshal, Lord 7, 8, 81, 94, 96, 148, 150–53, 170
Moscovitch, A 108
Morrison–Grady Peace Plan 95
Morrison, Herbert 174
Moyne, Lord 22, 44, 52, 53, 55, 121, 134, 135, 142–46, 174, 177, 179, 182
Mufti of Jerusalem 23, 29 62
Munich 39
Muslims 8, 10, 56, 100, 174

Nablus 23, 70, 71
Nakar, Meir 79
Napoleon 75
Nedava, Joseph 5
Netanya 69, 79–81, 157
New-York 11, 119, 122
*The New York Post* 183
National Committee 39, 47, 57, 79
National Hagana 15
Nazis 18, 25, 28, 29, 34, 61, 67, 80, 82, 106, 107, 112, 115, 117, 118, 120, 173, 178–80
*The New Statesman and the Nation* 45, 103, 137, 178, 181
*Noah,* Operation 154

*The Observer* 179
Oslo agreement 184

Paglin, Amichai 54
Paice, Marvin 79
Palestine 2, 3, 6, 9, 10, 12, 16, 23 – 25, 53
Palestine Foundation Fund 92
Palestine Mobile Police (PMP) 159
Palestine Police Force 87, 99
*The Palestine Post* 78, 87
Palmach 35, 55, 59, 78, 140, 147, 178
Paris 39

*Patria* 119
Pearl Harbor 114, 115
Petach Tikva 133

PLO x, 184, 185
Poland 36
Police Mobile Force 99
Polish Army 29, 37
*Polly,* Operation 159
Price, MP 173
Propaganda 4, 10, 25, 26, 66, 72, 85, 100–127

Qalqilya 43, 133
Qantara 69

RAF 70
Rafaeli, B 114
Rafah 97
Ramallah 41, 72, 132
Ramat–Gan 71, 73, 75, 101, 110, 157
Raziel, David 16, 17, 47, 49
Rehovot 60, 154, 163
Reid, Thomas, MP 174
Revisionists – see Zionist Revisionist Party
Revolutionary Propaganda Unit 101, 104
Rishon LeZion 154
Rogers, Will, Congressman 116, 118
Rome 30, 69
Rommel 23, 29, 37, 48
Roosevelt, President 115, 116, 118, 126
Roosevelt, Eleanor 116
Rosh–Ha'ayin 69
Royal Empire Society 81

*Saison* 1, 22, 52–55, 58, 59, 68, 82, 134, 145, 178
Samuel, Edwin 27
Sarafand 73, 156
*The Scotsman* 179
Shamir, Yitzhak x, 55, 98, 184
*Shark,* Operation 95–97, 99, 149, 151, 153
Shaw, Sir John 87, 94, 149
Shertock (Sharet), Moshe 105, 136
Shmuelewitz, Matityahu 77
Silverman, Sidney, MP 177
Sneh, Moshe 35, 49, 89

Soviet Union 22, 37
*The Spectator* 180
Stanley, Oliver 6, 142, 173, 175, 181
State Department 117, 122
Steal Brothers 38
Stern, Avrham 16, 37, 47
Stern group 11, 17–19, 22, 24, 26, 27, 30, 31, 32, 34, 39–41, 42, 44, 45, 49, 53, 54, 55, 58–64, 68, 69, 73, 77, 89, 93, 97, 101, 103, 122, 132, 133, 136, 137, 142, 144, 146, 155, 157, 160, 179, 182, 184, 185
Sudan 146
Suez Canal 6, 8
*The Sunday Express* 180, 181, 182
Swedish 116
Syria 23, 29, 34
Szynk, Arthur 116

Tavin, Elie 32, 42
Tedder, Lord 8, 91
Tel-Aviv 9, 34, 57, 62, 69, 74, 79, 80, 81, 92, 96, 97, 99, 101, 148, 156, 161, 165, 166, 175
Thomas, Senator 118
*The Times* 45, 80, 102, 178–80
Topet, Senator 118
Toscanini, Arturo 121
Trans-Jordan 44
Truman, Harry 11, 95, 103, 119, 121, 148

United Labour Party 52
United Nations 6, 8, 9, 68, 79, 85, 106
United Nations Special Committee on Palestine (UNSCOP) 7, 9, 10, 78, 85, 112, 171
USA – see America

Voice of Fighting Zion 101, 104
Voks, Frank 116

Wailing Wall 42–44
Wales 9
Wallace, Henry 116
Washington 62, 83, 95, 114–116, 119, 127
War Cabinet 43, 53, 144
War Office 161, 166, 181
War Refugee Board 118–20, 126, 127
Wedgewood, Lord 108
Weizmann, Chaim 39, 53, 89, 135, 144
Wells, Orson 116
West Bank 185
*The Western Evening Herald* 179
White House 11, 127
White Paper 18, 20, 30, 38, 41, 48, 56, 57, 119, 131–35
Wigg, Colonel George, MP 176
Wilkin Constable T 40, 44, 133
Wilson, General Sir Henry Maitland 131
Wise, S Rabbi 117, 118
Wise, Ya'acov 79
Workers Party 57
World Zionist Congress 39

Yagur, Kibbutz 133
Yelin Mor, Nathan 30
Yom Kippur 133
*The Yorkshire Post* 179

Zion 29
Zionism, Zionists 5, 8, 10, 26, 83, 112, 114, 131
Zionist Revisionist Party (ZRP) 16, 17, 20, 21, 22, 23, 31, 82, 101, 114, 117, 184